CAMBRIDGE LIBRARY COLLECTION

Books of enduring scholarly value

History

The books reissued in this series include accounts of historical events and movements by eye-witnesses and contemporaries, as well as landmark studies that assembled significant source materials or developed new historiographical methods. The series includes work in social, political and military history on a wide range of periods and regions, giving modern scholars ready access to influential publications of the past.

The Navy in the Civil War

Alfred Thayer Mahan (1840–1914) was an American naval officer, considered one of the most important naval strategists of the nineteenth century. In 1885 he was appointed Lecturer in Naval History and Tactics at the US Naval War College, and served as President of the institution between 1886 and 1889. His series of books examining the role of sea power in history influenced the rapid growth of international navies in the period before World War I. This book, first published in 1883 and reissued here in its 1898 London edition, examines the role of the navy in the American Civil War of 1861–5. It covers actions in the Gulf of Mexico and along the length of the Mississippi, where the Union's blockade starved the Confederate army of vital resources. Mahan himself had served on the Union side, and interviewed veterans in order to supplement the official naval records.

Cambridge University Press has long been a pioneer in the reissuing of out-of-print titles from its own backlist, producing digital reprints of books that are still sought after by scholars and students but could not be reprinted economically using traditional technology. The Cambridge Library Collection extends this activity to a wider range of books which are still of importance to researchers and professionals, either for the source material they contain, or as landmarks in the history of their academic discipline.

Drawing from the world-renowned collections in the Cambridge University Library, and guided by the advice of experts in each subject area, Cambridge University Press is using state-of-the-art scanning machines in its own Printing House to capture the content of each book selected for inclusion. The files are processed to give a consistently clear, crisp image, and the books finished to the high quality standard for which the Press is recognised around the world. The latest print-on-demand technology ensures that the books will remain available indefinitely, and that orders for single or multiple copies can quickly be supplied.

The Cambridge Library Collection will bring back to life books of enduring scholarly value (including out-of-copyright works originally issued by other publishers) across a wide range of disciplines in the humanities and social sciences and in science and technology.

The Navy in the Civil War

The Gulf and Inland Waters

Alfred Thayer Mahan

Cambridge
University Press

CAMBRIDGE UNIVERSITY PRESS

Cambridge, New York, Melbourne, Madrid, Cape Town, Singapore,
São Paolo, Delhi, Dubai, Tokyo, Mexico City

Published in the United States of America by Cambridge University Press, New York

www.cambridge.org
Information on this title: www.cambridge.org/9781108026222

This edition first published 1898
This digitally printed version 2010

ISBN 978-1-108-02622-2 Paperback

THE GULF AND INLAND WATERS

DAVID GLASCOE FARRAGUT.

THE NAVY IN THE CIVIL WAR

THE GULF AND INLAND WATERS

BY

A. T. MAHAN

CAPTAIN U. S. NAVY

LONDON

SAMPSON LOW, MARSTON, & COMPANY, LTD.

St. Dunstan's House

FETTER LANE, FLEET STREET, E. C.

1898

Printed by the Trow Directory, Printing and Bookbinding Company
New York, U. S. A.

PREFACE.

The narrative in these pages follows chiefly the official reports, and it is believed will not be found to conflict seriously with them. Official reports, however, are liable to errors of statement and especially to the omission of facts, well known to the writer but not always to the reader, the want of which is seriously felt when the attempt is made not only to tell the gross results but to detail the steps that led to them. Such omissions, which are specially frequent in the earlier reports of the Civil War, the author has tried to supply by questions put, principally by letter, to surviving witnesses. A few have neglected to answer, and on those points he has been obliged, with some embarrassment, to depend on his own judgment upon the circumstances of the case; but by far the greater part of the officers addressed, both Union and Confederate, have replied very freely. The number of his correspondents has been too numerous to admit of his thanking them by name, but he begs here to renew to them all the acknowledgments which have already been made to each in person.

A. T. M.

June, 1883.

CONTENTS.

PAGE

List of Maps, ... ix

CHAPTER I.

Preliminary, ... 1

CHAPTER II.

From Cairo to Vicksburg, ... 9

CHAPTER III.

From the Gulf to Vicksburg, ... 52

CHAPTER IV.

The Recoil from Vicksburg, ... 98

CHAPTER V.

The Mississippi Opened, ... 110

CHAPTER VI.

PAGE
MINOR OCCURRENCES IN 1863, ... 175

CHAPTER VII.

TEXAS AND THE RED RIVER, ... 185

CHAPTER VIII.

MOBILE, ... 218

APPENDIX, ... 251

INDEX, ... 255

LIST OF MAPS AND PLANS.

		PAGE
MISSISSIPPI VALLEY—CAIRO TO MEMPHIS, .	*to face*	9
MISSISSIPPI VALLEY—VICKSBURG TO THE GULF, .	"	52
BATTLE OF NEW ORLEANS, ...		74
BATTLE AT VICKSBURG, ...		92
MISSISSIPPI VALLEY—HELENA TO VICKSBURG,	*to face*	115
BATTLE AT GRAND GULF, ...		159
RED RIVER DAM, ...		208
BATTLE OF MOBILE BAY, ...	*to face*	229

THE GULF AND INLAND WATERS.

CHAPTER I.

PRELIMINARY.

THE naval operations described in the following pages extended, on the seaboard, over the Gulf of Mexico from Key West to the mouth of the Rio Grande; and inland over the course of the Mississippi, and its affluents, from Cairo, at the southern extremity of the State of Illinois, to the mouths of the river.

Key West is one of the low coral islands, or keys, which stretch out, in a southwesterly direction, into the Gulf from the southern extremity of the Florida peninsula. It has a good harbor, and was used during, as since, the war as a naval station. From Key West to the mouth of the Rio Grande, the river forming the boundary between Mexico and the State of Texas, the distance in a straight line is about eight hundred and forty miles. The line joining the two points departs but little from an east and west direction, the mouth of the river, in 25° 26′ N., being eighty-three miles north of the island; but the shore line is over sixteen hundred miles, measuring from the southern extremity of Florida. Beginning at that point, the west side of the peninsula runs north-northwest till it reaches the 30th degree of latitude; turning then, the coast follows that parallel approximately till it reaches the delta of the Mississippi. That delta, situated about midway between the east and west ends of the line, projects southward into the Gulf of Mexico as far as parallel 29° N., terminating in a long, narrow arm, through which the river enters the Gulf by three principal branches, or passes. From the delta the shore sweeps gently round, inclining first a little to the north of west, until near the boundary between the States of Louisiana and Texas; then it curves to the southwest until a point is reached about one hundred miles north of the mouth of the Rio Grande, whence it turns abruptly south. Five States, Florida, Alabama, Mississippi, Louisiana, and Texas, in the order named, touch the waters bounded by this long, irregular line; but the shore of two of them, Alabama and Mississippi, taken together, extends over little more than one hundred miles. All five joined at an early date in the secession movement.

The character of the coast, from one end to the other, varies but slightly in appearance. It is everywhere low, and either sandy or marshy. An occasional bluff of moderate height is to be seen. A large proportion of the line is skirted by low sandy islands, sometimes joined by narrow necks to the mainland, forming inland sounds of considerable extent, access to which is generally impracticable for vessels of much draft of water. They, however, as well as numerous bays and the mouths of many small rivers, can be entered by light vessels acquainted with the ground; and during the war small steamers and schooners frequently escaped through them, carrying cargoes of cotton, then of great value. There is but little rise and fall of the tide in the Gulf, from one to two feet, but the height of the water is much affected by the direction of the wind.

The principal ports on or near the Gulf are New Orleans

in Louisiana, Mobile in Alabama, and Galveston in Texas. Tallahassee and Apalachicola, in Florida, also carried on a brisk trade in cotton at the time of the secession. By far the best harbor is Pensacola Bay, in Florida, near the Alabama line. The town was not at that time a place of much commerce, on account of defective communication with the interior; but the depth of water, twenty-two feet, that could be carried over the bar, and the secure spacious anchorage within made it of great value as a naval station. It had been so used prior to the war, and, although falling at first into the hands of the Confederates, was shortly regained by the Union forces, to whom, from its nearness to Mobile and the passes of the Mississippi, as well as from its intrinsic advantages, it was of great importance throughout the contest.

The aim of the National Government in connection with this large expanse of water and its communications was two-fold. First, it was intended to enter the Mississippi River from the sea, and working up its stream in connection with the land forces, to take possession of the well-known positions that gave command of the navigation. Simultaneously with this movement from below, a similar movement downward, with the like object, was to be undertaken in the upper waters. If successful, as they proved to be, the result of these attacks would be to sever the States in rebellion on the east side of the river from those on the west, which, though not the most populous, contributed largely in men, and yet more abundantly in food, to the support of the Confederacy.

The second object of the Government was to enforce a strict blockade over the entire coast, from the Rio Grande to Florida. There were not in the Confederate harbors powerful fleets, or even single vessels of war, which it was necessary to lock up in their own waters. One or two *quasi* men-of-war escaped from them, to run short and, in the main, harmless careers; but the cruise that inflicted the greatest damage on the commerce of the Union was made by a vessel that never entered a Southern port. The blockade was not defensive, but offensive; its purpose was to close every inlet by which the products of the South could find their way to the markets of the world, and to shut out the material, not only of war, but essential to the peaceful life of a people, which the Southern States were ill-qualified by their previous pursuits to produce. Such a blockade could be made technically effectual by ships cruising or anchored outside; but there was a great gain in actual efficiency when the vessels could be placed within the harbors. The latter plan was therefore followed wherever possible and safe; and the larger fortified places were reduced and occupied as rapidly as possible consistent with the attainment of the prime object—the control of the Mississippi Valley.

Before the war the Atlantic and Gulf waters of the United States, with those of the West Indies, Mexico, and Central America, were the cruising ground of one division of vessels, known as the Home Squadron. At the beginning of hostilities this squadron was under the command of Flag-Officer G. J. Pendergrast, who rendered essential and active service during the exciting and confused events which immediately followed the bombardment of Fort Sumter. The command was too extensive to be administered by any one man, when it became from end to end the scene of active war, so it was soon divided into three parts. The West India Squadron, having in its charge United States interests in Mexico and Central America as well as in the islands, remained under the care of Flag-Officer Pendergrast. Flag-Officer Stringham assumed command of the Atlantic Squadron, extending as far south as Cape Florida; and the Gulf, from Caps Florida to the Rio Grande, was assigned to Flag-Officer Wil liam Mervine, who reached his station on the 8th of June, 1861. On the 4th of July the squadron consisted of twenty-one vessels, carrying two hundred and eighty-two guns, and manned by three thousand five hundred men.

Flag-Officer Mervine was relieved in the latter part of September. The blockade was maintained as well as the number and character of the vessels permitted, but no fighting of any consequence took place. A dashing cutting-out expedition from the flag-ship Colorado, under Lieutenant J. H. Russell, assisted by Lieutenants Sproston and Blake, with subordinate officers and seamen, amounting in all to four boats and one hundred men, seized and destroyed an armed schooner lying alongside the wharf of the Pensacola Navy Yard, under the protection of a battery. The service was gallantly carried out; the schooner's crew, after a desperate resistance, were driven on shore, whence, with the guard, they resumed their fire on the assailants. The affair cost the flag-ship three men killed and nine wounded.

Under Mervine's successor, Flag-Officer W. W. McKean, more of interest occurred. The first collision was unfortunate, and, to some extent, humiliating to the service. A squadron consisting of the steam-sloop Richmond, sailing-sloops Vincennes and Preble, and the small side-wheel steamer Water Witch had entered the Mississippi early in the month of October, and were at anchor at the head of the passes. At 3.30 A.M., October 12th, a Confederate ram made its appearance close aboard the Richmond, which, at the time, had a coal schooner alongside. The ram charged the Richmond, forcing a small hole in her side about two feet below the water-line, and tearing the schooner adrift. She dropped astern, lay quietly for a few moments off the port-quarter of the Richmond, and then steamed slowly up the river, receiving broadsides from the Richmond and Preble, and throwing up a rocket. In a few moments three dim lights were seen up the river near the eastern shore. They were shortly made out to be fire-rafts. The squadron slipped their chains, the three larger vessels, by direction of the senior officer, retreating down the Southwest Pass to the sea; but in the attempt to cross, the Richmond and Vincennes grounded on the bar. The fire-rafts drifted harmlessly on to the western bank of the river, and then burned out. When day broke, the enemy's fleet, finding the head of the passes abandoned, followed down the river, and with rifled guns kept up a steady but not very accurate long-range fire upon the stranded ships, not venturing within reach of the Richmond's heavy broadside. About 10 A.M., apparently satisfied with the day's work, they returned up river, and the ships shortly after got afloat and crossed the bar.

The ram which caused this commotion and hasty retreat was a small vessel of three hundred and eighty-four tons, originally a Boston tug-boat called the Enoch Train, which had been sent to New Orleans to help in improving the channel of the Mississippi. When the war broke out she was taken by private parties and turned into a ram on speculation. An arched roof of 5-inch timber was thrown over her deck, and this covered with a layer of old-fashioned railroad iron, from three-fourths to one inch thick, laid lengthways. At the time of this attack she had a cast-iron prow under water, and carried a IX-inch gun, pointing straight ahead through a slot in the roof forward; but as this for some reason could not be used, it was lashed in its place. Her dimensions were: length 128 feet, beam 26 feet, depth 12½ feet. She had twin screws, and at this time one engine was running at high pressure and the other at low, both being in bad order, so that she could only steam six knots; but carrying the current with her she struck the

Richmond with a speed of from nine to ten. Although afterward bought by the Confederate Government, she at this time still belonged to private parties; but as her captain, pilot, and most of the other officers refused to go in her, Lieutenant A. F. Warley, of the Confederate Navy, was ordered to the command by Commodore Hollins. In the collision her prow was wrenched off, her smoke-stack carried away and the condenser of the low-pressure engine gave out, which accounts for her "remaining under the Richmond's quarter," "dropping astern," and "lying quietly abeam of the Preble, apparently hesitating whether to come at her or not." As soon as possible she limped off under her remaining engine.

Although it was known to the officers of the Union fleet that the enemy had a ram up the river, it does not appear that any preparation for defence had been made, or plan of action adopted. Even the commonplace precaution of sending out a picket-boat had not been taken. The attack, therefore, was a surprise, not only in the ordinary sense of the word, but, so far as appears, in finding the officer in command without any formed ideas as to what he would do if she came down. "The whole affair came upon me so suddenly that no time was left for reflection, but called for immediate action." These are his own words. The natural outcome of not having his resources in hand was a hasty retreat before an enemy whose force he now exaggerated and with whom he was not prepared to deal; a move which brought intense mortification to himself and in a measure to the service.

It is a relief to say that the Water Witch, a small vessel of under four hundred tons, with three light guns, commanded by Lieutenant Francis Winslow, held her ground, steaming up beyond the fire-rafts until daylight showed her the larger vessels in retreat.

During the night of November 7th the U. S. frigate Santee, blockading off Galveston, sent into the harbor two boats, under the command of Lieutenant James E. Jouett, with the object of destroying the man-of-war steamer General Rusk. The armed schooner Royal Yacht guarding the channel was passed unseen, but the boats shortly after took the ground and were discovered. Thinking it imprudent to attack the steamer without the advantage of a surprise, Lieutenant Jouett turned upon the schooner, which was carried after a sharp conflict. The loss of the assailants was two killed and seven wounded. The schooner was burnt.

On November 22d and 23d Flag-Officer McKean, with the Niagara and Richmond, made an attack upon Fort McRea on the western side of the entrance to Pensacola Bay; Fort Pickens, on the east side, which remained in the power of the United States, directing its guns upon the fort and the Navy Yard, the latter being out of reach of the ships. The fire of McRea was silenced the first day; but on the second a north-west wind had so lowered the water that the ships could not get near enough to reach the fort. The affair was entirely indecisive, being necessarily conducted at very long range.

From this time on, until the arrival of Flag-Officer David G. Farragut, a guerilla warfare was maintained along the coast, having always the object of making the blockade more effective and the conditions of the war more onerous to the Southern people. Though each little expedition contributed to this end, singly they offer nothing that it is necessary to chronicle here. When Farragut came the squadron was divided. St. Andrew's Bay, sixty miles east of Pensacola, was left in the East Gulf Squadron; all west of that point was Farragut's command, under the name of the Western Gulf Blockading Squadron. Stirring and important events were now at hand, before relating which the course of the war on the Upper Mississippi demands attention.

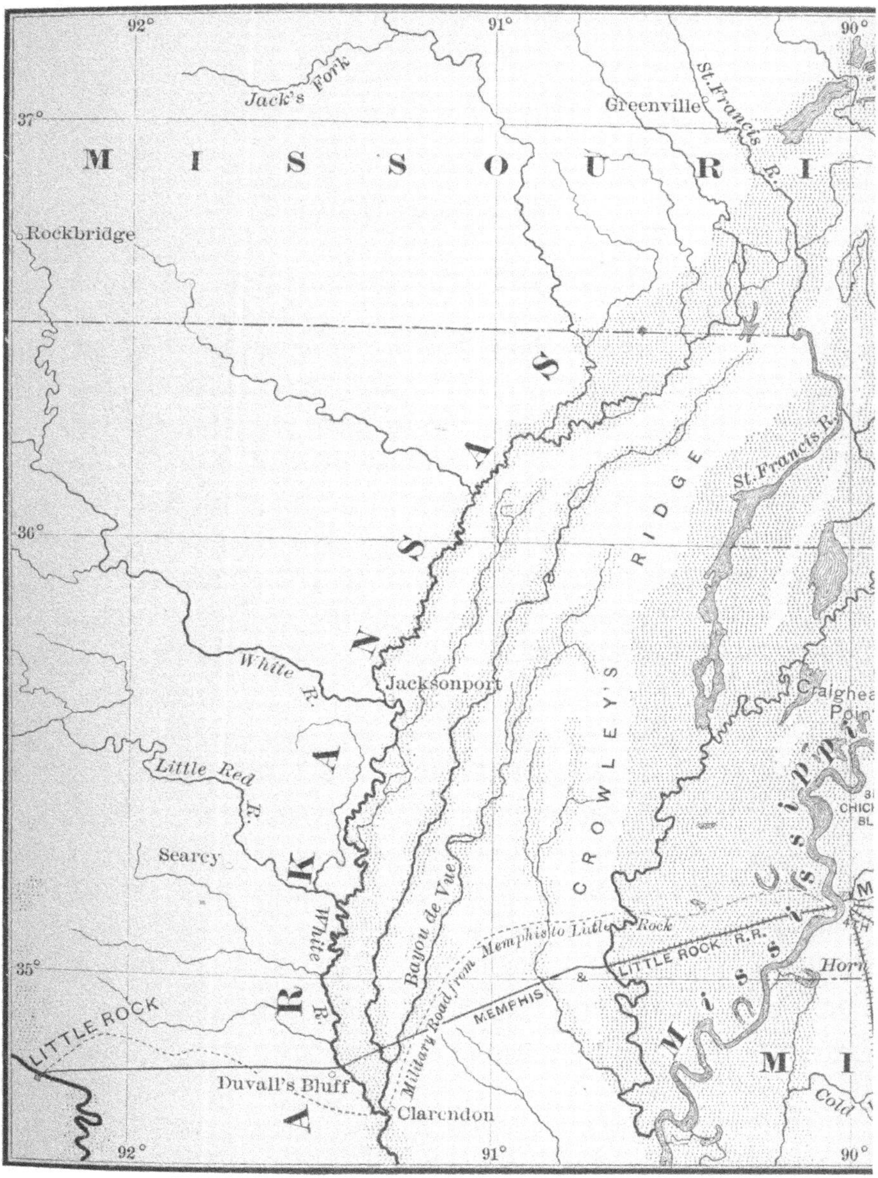

MISSISSIPPI VALLEY—

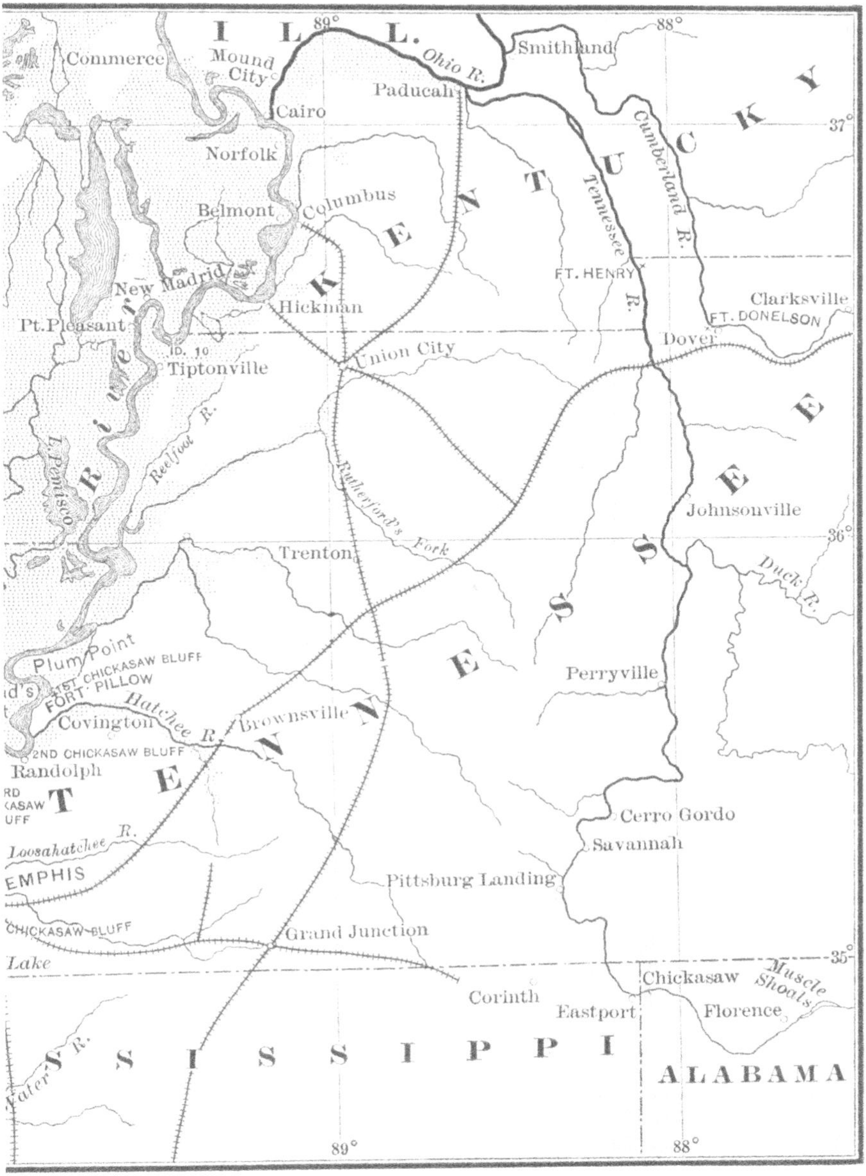

CAIRO TO MEMPHIS.

CHAPTER II.

FROM CAIRO TO VICKSBURG.

AT the 37th parallel of north latitude the Ohio, which drains the northeast portion of the Valley of the Mississippi, enters that river. At the point of junction three powerful States meet. Illinois, here bounded on either side by the great river and its tributary, lies on the north ; on the east it is separated by the Ohio from Kentucky, on the west by the Mississippi from Missouri. Of the three Illinois was devoted to the cause of the Union, but the allegiance of the two others, both slave-holding, was very doubtful at the time of the outbreak of hostilities.

The general course of the Mississippi here being south, while that of the Ohio is southwest, the southern part of Illinois projects like a wedge between the two other States. At the extreme point of the wedge, where the rivers meet, is a low point of land, subject, in its unprotected state, to frequent overflows by the rising of the waters. On this point, protected by dikes or levees, is built the town of Cairo, which from its position became, during the war, the naval arsenal and dépôt of the Union flotilla operating in the Mississippi Valley.

From Cairo to the mouths of the Mississippi is a distance of ten hundred and ninety-seven miles by the stream. So devious, however, is the course of the latter that the two points are only four hundred and eighty miles apart in a due north and south line; for the river, after having inclined to the westward till it has increased its longitude by some two degrees and a half, again bends to the east, reaching the Gulf on the meridian of Cairo. Throughout this long distance the character of the river-bed is practically unchanged. The stream flows through an alluvial region, beginning a few miles above Cairo, which is naturally subject to overflow during floods; but the surrounding country is protected against such calamities by raised embankments, or dikes, known throughout that region as levees.

The river and its tributaries are subject to very great variations of height, which are often sudden and unexpected, but when observed through a series of years present a certain regularity. They depend upon the rains and the melting of the snows in their basins. The greatest average height is attained in the late winter and early spring months; another rise takes place in the early summer; the months of August, September, and October give the lowest water, the rise following them being due to the autumnal rains. It will be seen at times that these rises and falls, especially when sudden, had their bearing upon the operations of both army and navy.

At a few points of the banks high land is encountered. On the right, or western, bank there is but one such, at Helena, in the State of Arkansas, between three and four hundred miles below Cairo. On the left bank such points are more numerous. The first is at Columbus, twenty-one miles down the stream; then follow the bluffs at Hickman, in Kentucky; a low ridge (which also extends to the right bank) below New Madrid, rising from one to fifteen feet above overflow; the four Chickasaw bluffs in Tennessee, on the southernmost of which is the city of Memphis; and finally a rapid succession of similar bluffs extending for two hundred and fifty miles, at short intervals, from Vicksburg, in Mississippi, about six hundred miles below Cairo, to Baton Rouge, in Louisiana. Of these last Vicksburg, Grand Gulf, and Port Hudson became the scenes of important events of the war.

It is easy to see that each of these rare and isolated points afforded a position by the fortification of which the passage of an enemy could be disputed, and the control of the stream maintained, as long as it remained in the hands of the defenders. They were all, except Columbus and Hickman, in territory which, by the act of secession, had become hostile to the Government of the United States; and they all, not excepting even the two last-named, were seized and fortified by the Confederates. It was against this chain of defences that the Union forces were sent forth from either end of the line; and fighting their way, step by step, and post by post, those from the north and those from the south met at length around the defences of Vicksburg. From the time of that meeting the narratives blend until the fall of the fortress; but, prior to that time, it is necessary to tell the story of each separately. The northern expeditions were the first in the field, and to them this chapter is devoted.

The importance of controlling the Mississippi was felt from the first by the United States Government. This importance was not only strategic; it was impossible that the already powerful and fast-growing Northwestern States should see without grave dissatisfaction the outlet of their great highway pass into the hands of a foreign power. Even before the war the necessity to those States of controlling the river was an argument against the possibility of disunion, at least on a line crossing it. From the military point of view, however, not only did the Mississippi divide the Confederacy, but the numerous streams directly or indirectly tributary to it, piercing the country in every direction, afforded a ready means of transport for troops and their supplies in a country of great extent, but otherwise ill-provided with means of carriage. From this consideration it was but a step to see the necessity of an inland navy for operating on and keeping open those waters.

The necessity being recognized, the construction of the required fleet was at the first entrusted to the War Department, the naval officers assigned for that duty reporting to the military officer commanding in the West. The fleet, or flotilla, while under this arrangement, really constituted a division of the army, and its commanding officer was liable to interference, not only at the hands of the commander-in-chief, but of subordinate officers of higher rank than himself.

On May 16, 1861, Commander John Rodgers was directed to report to the War Department for this service. Under his direction there were purchased in Cincinnati three river-steamers, the Tyler, Lexington, and Conestoga. These were altered into gunboats by raising around them perpendicular oak bulwarks, five inches thick and proof against musketry, which were pierced for ports, but bore no iron plating. The boilers were dropped into the hold, and steam-pipes lowered as much as possible. The Tyler mounted six 64-pounders in broadside, and one 32-pounder stern gun; the Lexington, four 64s and two 32s; the Conestoga, two broadside 32s and one light stern gun. After being altered, these vessels were taken down to Cairo, where they arrived August 12th, having been much delayed by the low state of the river; one of them being dragged by the united power of the three over a bar on which was one foot less water than her draught.

On the 7th of August, a contract was made by the War Department with James B. Eads, of St. Louis, by which he undertook to complete seven gunboats, and deliver them at Cairo on the 10th day of October of the same year. These vessels were one hundred and seventy-five feet long and fifty feet beam. The propelling power was one large paddle-wheel, which was placed in an opening prepared for it, midway of the breadth of the vessel and a little forward of the stern, in such wise as to be materially protected by the sides and casemate. This opening, which was eighteen feet wide, extended forward sixty feet from the stern, dividing the after-body into two parts, which were connected abaft the wheel by planking thrown from one side to the other. This after-part was called the fantail. The casemate extended from the curve of the bow to that of the stern, and was carried across the deck both forward and aft, thus forming a square box, whose sides sloped in and up at an angle of forty-five degrees, containing the battery, the machinery, and the paddle-wheel. The casemate was pierced for thirteen guns, three in the forward end ranging directly ahead, four on each broadside, and two stern guns.

As the expectation was to fight generally bows on, the forward end of the casemate carried iron armor two and a half inches thick, backed by twenty-four inches of oak. The rest of the casemate was not protected by armor, except abreast of the boilers and engines, where there were two and a half inches of iron, but without backing. The stern, therefore, was perfectly vulnerable, as were the sides forward and abaft the engines. The latter were high pressure, like those of all Western river-boats, and, though the boilers were dropped into the hold as far as possible, the light draught and easily pierced sides left the vessels exposed in action to the fearful chance of an exploded boiler. Over the casemate forward was a pilot-house of conical shape, built of heavy oak, and plated on the forward side with $2\frac{1}{2}$-inch iron, on the after with 1½-inch. With guns, coal, and stores on board, the casemate deck came nearly down to the water, and the vessels drew from six to seven feet, the peculiar outline giving them no small resemblance to gigantic turtles wallowing slowly along in their native element. Below the water the form was that of a scow, the bottom being flat. Their burden was five hundred and twelve tons.

The armament was determined by the exigencies of the time, such guns as were available being picked up here and there and forwarded to Cairo. The army supplied thirty-five old 42-pounders, which were rifled, and so threw a 70-pound shell. These having lost the metal cut away for grooves, and not being banded, were called upon to endure the increased strain of firing rifled projectiles with actually less strength than had been allowed for the discharge of a round ball of about half the weight. Such make-shifts are characteristic of nations that do not prepare for war, and will doubtless occur again in the experience of our navy; fortunately, in this conflict, the enemy was as ill-provided as ourselves. Several of these guns burst; their crews could be seen eyeing them distrustfully at every fire, and when at last they were replaced by sounder weapons, many were not turned into store, but thrown, with a sigh of relief, into the waters of the Mississippi. The remainder of the armament was made up by the navy with old-fashioned 32-pound and VIII-inch smooth-bore guns, fairly serviceable and reliable weapons. Each of these seven gunboats, when thus ready for service, carried four of the above-described rifles, six 32-pounders of 43 cwt., and three VIII-inch shell-guns; total, thirteen.

The vessels, when received into service, were named after cities standing upon the banks of the rivers which they were to defend—Cairo, Carondelet, Cincinnati, Louisville, Mound

City, Pittsburg, St. Louis. They, with the Benton, formed the backbone of the river fleet throughout the war. Other more pretentious, and apparently more formidable, vessels, were built; but from thorough bad workmanship, or appearing too late on the scene, they bore no proportionate share in the fighting. The eight may be fairly called the ships of the line of battle on the western waters.

The Benton was of the same general type as the others, but was purchased by, not built for, the Government. She was originally a snag-boat, and so constructed with special view to strength. Her size was 1,000 tons, double that of the seven; length, 202 feet; extreme breadth, 72 feet. The forward plating was 3 inches of iron, backed by 30 inches of oak; at the stern, and abreast the engines, there was $2\frac{1}{2}$-inch iron, backed by 12 inches of oak; the rest of the sides of the casemates was covered with $\frac{5}{8}$-inch iron. With guns and stores on board, she drew nine feet. Her first armament was two IX-inch shell-guns, seven rifled 42s, and seven 32-pounders of 43 cwt.; total, sixteen guns. It will be seen, therefore, that she differed from the others simply in being larger and stronger; she was, indeed, the most powerful fighting-machine in the squadron, but her speed was only five knots an hour through the water, and her engines so little commensurate with her weight that Flag-Officer Foote hesitated long to receive her. The slowness was forgiven for her fitness for battle, and she went by the name of the old war-horse.

There was one other vessel of size equal to the Benton, which, being commanded by a son of Commodore Porter, of the war of 1812, got the name Essex. After bearing a creditable part in the battle of Fort Henry, she became separated by the batteries of Vicksburg from the upper squadron, and is less identified with its history. Her armament was three IX-inch, one X-inch, and one 32-pounder.

On the 6th of September Commander Rodgers was relieved by Captain A. H. Foote, whose name is most prominently associated with the equipment and early operations of the Mississippi flotilla. At that time he reported to the Secretary that there were three wooden gunboats in commission, nine ironclads and thirty-eight mortar-boats building. The mortar-boats were rafts or blocks of solid timber, carrying one XIII-inch mortar.

The construction and equipment of the fleet was seriously delayed by the lack of money, and the general confusion incident to the vast extent of military and naval preparations suddenly undertaken by a nation having a very small body of trained officers, and accustomed to raise and expend comparatively insignificant amounts of money. Constant complaints were made by the officers and contractors that lack of money prevented them from carrying on their work. The first of the seven ironclads was launched October 12th and the seven are returned by the Quartermaster's Department as received December 5, 1861. On the 12th of January, 1862, Flag-Officer Foote reported that he expected to have all the gunboats in commission by the 20th, but had only one-third crews for them. The crews were of a heterogeneous description. In November a draft of five hundred were sent from the seaboard, which, though containing a proportion of men-of-war's men, had a yet larger number of coasting and merchant seamen, and of landsmen. In the West two or three hundred steamboat men, with a few sailors from the Lakes, were shipped. In case of need, deficiencies were made up by drafts from regiments in the army. On the 23d of December, 1861, eleven hundred men were ordered from Washington to be thus detailed for the fleet. Many difficulties, however, arose in making the transfer. General Halleck insisted that the officers of the regiments must accompany their men on board, the whole body to be regarded as marines and to owe obedience to no naval officer except the commander of the gunboat. Foote refused this, saying it would be ruinous to discipline; that the second in command, or executive officer, by well-established naval usage, controlled all officers, even though senior in rank to himself; and that there were no quarters for so many more officers, for whom, moreover, he had no use. Later on Foote writes to the Navy Department that not more than fifty men had joined from the army, though many had volunteered; the derangement of companies and regiments being the reason assigned for not sending the others. It does not appear that more than these fifty came at that time. There is no more unsatisfactory method of getting a crew than by drafts from the commands of other men. Human nature is rarely equal to parting with any but the worst; and Foote had so much trouble with a subsequent detachment that he said he would rather go into action half manned than take another draft from the army. In each vessel the commander was the only trained naval officer, and upon him devolved the labor of organizing and drilling this mixed multitude. In charge of and responsible for the whole was the flag-officer, to whom, though under the orders of General Fremont, the latter had given full discretion.

Meanwhile the three wooden gunboats had not been idle during the preparation of the main ironclad fleet. Arriving at Cairo, as has been stated, on the 12th of August, the necessity for action soon arose. During the early months of the war the State of Kentucky had announced her intention of remaining a neutral between the contending parties. Neither of the latter was willing to precipitate her, by an invasion of her soil, into the arms of the other, and for some time the operations of the Confederates were confined to

Tennessee, south of her borders, the United States troops remaining north of the Ohio. On September 4th, however, the Confederates crossed the line and occupied in force the bluffs at Columbus and Hickman, which they proceeded at once to fortify. The military district about Cairo was then under the command of General Grant, who immediately moved up the Ohio, and seized Paducah, at the mouth of the Tennessee River, and Smithland, at the mouth of the Cumberland. These two rivers enter the Ohio ten miles apart, forty and fifty miles above Cairo. Rising in the Cumberland and Alleghany Mountains, their course leads through the heart of Tennessee, to which their waters give easy access through the greater part of the year. Two gunboats accompanied this movement, in which, however, there was no fighting.

On the 10th of September, the Lexington, Commander Stembel, and Conestoga, Lieutenant-Commanding Phelps, went down the Mississippi, covering an advance of troops on the Missouri side. A brisk cannonade followed between the boats and the Confederate artillery, and shots were exchanged with the gunboat Yankee. On the 24th, Captain Foote, by order of General Fremont, moved in the Lexington up the Ohio River to Owensboro. The Conestoga was to have accompanied this movement, but she was up the Cumberland or Tennessee at the time ; arriving later she remained, by order, at Owensboro till the falling of the river compelled her to return, there being on some of the bars less water than she drew. A few days later this active little vessel showed herself again on the Mississippi, near Columbus, endeavoring to reach a Confederate gunboat that lay under the guns of the works ; then again on the Tennessee, which she ascended as far as the Tennessee State Line, reconnoitring Fort Henry, subsequently the scene of Foote's first decisive victory over the enemy. Two days later the Cumberland was entered for the distance of sixty miles. On the 28th of October, accompanied by a transport and some companies of troops, she again ascended the Cumberland, and broke up a Confederate camp, the enemy losing several killed and wounded. The frequent appearances of these vessels, while productive of no material effect beyond the capture or destruction of Confederate property, were of service in keeping alive the attachment to the Union where it existed. The crews of the gunboats also became accustomed to the presence of the enemy, and to the feeling of being under fire.

On the 7th of November a more serious affair took place. The evening before, the gunboats Tyler, Commander Walke, and Lexington, Commander Stembel, convoyed transports containing three thousand troops, under the command of General Grant, down the Mississippi as far as Norfolk, eight miles, where they anchored on the east side of the river. The following day the troops landed at Belmont, which is opposite Columbus and under the guns of that place. The Confederate troops were easily defeated and driven to the river's edge, where they took refuge on their transports. During this time the gunboats engaged the batteries on the Iron Banks, as the part of the bluff above the town is called. The heavy guns of the enemy, from their commanding position, threw easily over the boats, reaching even to and beyond the transports on the opposite shore up stream. Under Commander Walke's direction the transports were moved further up, out of range.

Meanwhile the enemy was pushing reinforcements across the stream below the works, and the Union forces, having accomplished the diversion which was the sole object of the expedition, began to fall back to their transports. It would seem that the troops, yet unaccustomed to war, had been somewhat disordered by their victory, so that the return was not accomplished as rapidly as was desirable, the enemy pressing down upon the transports. At this moment the gunboats, from a favorable position, opened upon them with grape, canister, and five-second shell, silencing them with great slaughter. When the transports were under way the two gunboats followed in the rear, covering the retreat till the enemy ceased to follow.

In this succession of encounters the Tyler lost one man killed and two wounded. The Lexington escaped without loss.

When a few miles up the river on the return, General McClernand, ascertaining that some of the troops had not embarked, directed the gunboats to go back for them, the general himself landing to await their return. This service was performed, some 40 prisoners being taken on board along with the troops.

In his official report of this, the first of his many gallant actions on the rivers, Commander Walke praises warmly the efficiency as well as the zeal of the crews of the gunboats, though as yet so new to their duties.

The flotilla being at this time under the War Department, as has been already stated, its officers, each and all, were liable to orders from any army officer of superior rank to them. Without expressing a decided opinion as to the advisability of this arrangement under the circumstances then existing, it was entirely contrary to the established rule by which, when military and naval forces are acting together, the commander of each branch decides what he can or can not do, and is not under the control of the other, whatever the relative rank. At this time Captain Foote himself had only the rank of colonel, and found, to use his own expression, that "every brigadier could interfere with him." On the 13th of November, 1861, he received the appointment of flag-officer, which gave him the same rank as a major-general, and put him above the orders of any except the commander-in-chief of the department. Still the subordinate naval officers were liable to orders at any time from any general with whom they might be, without the knowledge of the flag-officer. It is creditable to the good feeling and sense of duty of both the army and navy that no serious difficulty arose from this anomalous condition of affairs, which came to an end in July, 1862, when the fleet was transferred to the Navy Department.

After the battle of Belmont nothing of importance occurred in the year 1861. The work on the ironclads was pushed on, and there are traces of the reconnoissances by the gunboats in the rivers. In January, 1862, some tentative movements, having no particular result, were made in the direction of Columbus and up the Tennessee. There was a great desire to get the mortar-boats completed, but they were not ready in time for the opening operations at Fort Henry and Donelson, their armaments not having arrived.

On the 2d of February, Flag-Officer Foote left Cairo for Paducah, arriving the same evening. There were assembled the four armored gunboats, Essex, Commander Wm. D. Porter; Carondelet, Commander Walke; St. Louis, Lieutenant Paulding; and Cincinnati, Commander Stembel; as well as the three wooden gunboats, Conestoga, Lieutenant Phelps; Tyler, Lieutenant Gwin; and Lexington, Lieutenant Shirk. The object of the expedition was to attack, conjointly with the army, Fort Henry on the Tennessee, and, after reducing the fort, to destroy the railroad bridge over the river connecting Bowling Green with Columbus. The flag-officer deplored that scarcity of men prevented his coming with four other boats, but to man those he brought it had been necessary to strip Cairo of all men except a crew for one gunboat.

Only 50 men of the 1,100 promised on December 23d had been received from the army.

Fort Henry was an earthwork with five bastions, situated on the east bank of the Tennessee River, on low ground, but in a position where a slight bend in the stream gave it command of the stretch below for two or three miles. It mounted twenty guns, but of these only twelve bore upon the ascending fleet. These twelve were: one X-inch columbiad, one 60-pounder rifle, two 42- and eight 32-pounders. The plan of attack was simple. The armored gunboats advanced in the first order of steaming, in line abreast, fighting their bow guns, of which eleven were brought into action by the four. The flag-officer purposed by continually advancing, or, if necessary, falling back, to constantly alter the range, thus causing error in the elevation of the enemy's guns, presenting, at the same time, the least vulnerable part, the bow, to his fire. The vessels kept their line by the flag-ship Cincinnati. The other orders were matters of detail, the most important being to fire accurately rather than with undue rapidity. The wooden gunboats formed a second line astern, and to the right of the main division.

Two days previous to the action there were heavy rains which impeded the movements of the troops, caused the rivers to rise, and brought down a quantity of drift-wood and trees. The same flood swept from their moorings a number of torpedoes, planted by the Confederates, which were grappled with and towed ashore by the wooden gunboats.

Half an hour after noon on the 6th, the fleet, having waited in vain for the army, which was detained by the condition of the roads, advanced to the attack. The armored vessels opened fire, the flag-ship beginning, at seventeen hundred yards distance, and continued steaming steadily ahead to within six hundred yards of the fort. As the distance decreased, the fire on both sides increased in rapidity and accuracy. An hour after the action began the 60-pound rifle in the fort burst, and soon after the priming wire of the 10-inch columbiad jammed and broke in the vent, thus spiking the gun, which could not be relieved. The balance of force was, however, at once more than restored, for a shot from the fort pierced the casemate of the Essex over the port bow gun, ranged aft, and killing a master's mate in its flight, passed through the middle boiler. The rush of high-pressure steam scalded almost all in the forward part of the casemate, including her commander and her two pilots in the pilot-house. Many of the victims threw themselves into the water, and the vessel, disabled, drifted down with the current out of action. The contest was vigorously continued by the three remaining boats, and at 1.45 P.M. the Confederate flag was lowered. The commanding officer, General Tilghman, came on board and surrendered the fort and garrison to the fleet; but the greater part of the Confederate forces had been previously withdrawn to Fort Donelson, twelve miles distant, on the Cumberland. Upon the arrival of the army the fort and material captured were turned over to the general commanding.

In this sharp and decisive action the gunboats showed themselves well fitted to contend with most of the guns at that time to be found upon the rivers, provided they could fight bows on. Though repeatedly struck, the flag-ship as often as thirty-one times, the armor proved sufficient to deflect or resist the impact of the projectiles. The disaster, however, that befel the Essex made fearfully apparent a class of accidents to which they were exposed, and from which more than one boat, on either side, on the Western waters subsequently suffered. The fleet lost two killed and nine wounded, besides twenty-eight scalded, many of whom died.

The Essex had also nineteen soldiers on board; nine of whom were scalded, four fatally.

The surrender of the fort was determined by the destruction of its armament. Of the twelve guns, seven, by the commander's report, were disabled when the flag was hauled down. One had burst in discharging, the rest were put out of action by the fire of the fleet. The casualties were few, not exceeding twenty killed and wounded.

Flag-Officer Foote, having turned over his capture to the army, returned the same evening to Cairo with three armored vessels, leaving the Carondelet. At the same time the three wooden gunboats, in obedience to orders issued before the battle, started up river under the command of Lieutenant Phelps, reaching the railroad bridge, twenty-five miles up, after dark. Here the machinery for turning the draw was found to be disabled, while on the other side were to be seen some transport steamers escaping up stream. An hour was required to open the draw, when two of the boats proceeded in chase of the transports, the Tyler, as the slowest, being left to destroy the track as far as possible. Three of the Confederate steamers, loaded with military stores, two of them with explosives, were run ashore and fired. The Union gunboats stopped half a mile below the scene, but even at that distance the force of the explosion shattered glasses, forced open doors, and raised the light upper decks.

The Lexington, having destroyed the trestle-work at the end of the bridge, rejoined the following morning; and the three boats, continuing their raid, arrived the next night at Cerro Gordo, near the Mississippi line. Here was seized a large steamer called the Eastport, which the Confederates were altering into a gunboat. There being at this point large quantities of lumber, the Tyler was left to ship it and guard the prize.

The following day, the 8th, the two boats continued up river, passing through the northern part of the States of Mississippi and Alabama, to Florence, where the Muscle Shoals prevented their farther progress. On the way two more steamers were seized, and three were set on fire by the enemy as they approached Florence. Returning the same night, upon information received that a Confederate camp was established at Savannah, Tennessee, on the bank of the river, a party was landed, which found the enemy gone, but seized or destroyed the camp equipage and stores left behind. The expedition reached Cairo again on the 11th, bringing with it the Eastport and one other of the captured steamers. The Eastport had been intended by the Confederates for a gunboat, and was in process of conversion when captured. Lieutenant Phelps reported her machinery in first-rate order and the boilers dropped into the hold. Her hull had been sheathed with oak planking and the bulkheads, forward, aft, and thwartships, were of oak and of the best workmanship. Her beautiful model, speed, and manageable qualities made her specially desirable for the Union fleet, and she was taken into the service. Two years later she was sunk by torpedoes in the Red River, and, though partially raised, it was found impossible to bring her over the shoals that lay below her. She was there blown up, her former captor and then commander, Lieutenant Phelps, applying the match.

Lieutenant Phelps and his daring companions returned to Cairo just in time to join Foote on his way to Fort Donelson. The attack upon this position, which was much stronger than Fort Henry, was made against the judgment of the flag-officer, who did not consider the fleet as yet properly prepared. At the urgent request of Generals Halleck and Grant, however, he steamed up the Cumberland River with three ironclads and the wooden gunboats, the Carondelet having already, at Grant's desire, moved round to Donelson.

Fort Donelson was on the left bank of the Cumberland, twelve miles southeast of Fort Henry. The main work was on a bluff about a hundred feet high, at a bend commanding the river below. On the slope of the ridge, looking down stream, were two water batteries, with which alone the fleet had to do. The lower and principal one mounted eight 32-pounders and a X-inch columbiad; in the upper there were two 32-pounder carronades and one gun of the size of a X-inch smooth-bore, but rifled with the bore of a 32-pounder and said to throw a shot of one hundred and twenty-eight pounds. Both batteries were excavated in the hillside, and the lower had traverses between the guns to protect them from an enfilading fire, in case the boats should pass their front and attack them from above. At the time of the fight these batteries were thirty-two feet above the level of the river.

General Grant arrived before the works at noon of February 12th. The gunboat Carondelet, Commander Walke, came up about an hour earlier. At 10 A.M. on the 13th, the gunboat, at the general's request, opened fire on the batteries at a distance of a mile and a quarter, sheltering herself partly behind a jutting point of the river, and continued a deliberate cannonade with her bow guns for six hours, after which she withdrew. In this time she had thrown in one hundred and eighty shell, and was twice struck by the enemy, half a dozen of her people being slightly injured by splinters. On the side of the enemy an engineer officer was killed by her fire.

The fleet arrived that evening, and attacked the following day at 3 P.M. There were, besides the Carondelet, the armored gunboats St. Louis, Lieutenant Paulding; Louisville, Commander Dove; and Pittsburg, Lieutenant E. Thompson; and the wooden vessels Conestoga and Tyler, commanded as before. The order of steaming was the same as at Henry, the wooden boats in the rear throwing their shell over the armored vessels. The fleet reserved its fire till within a mile, when it opened and advanced rapidly to within six hundred yards of the works, closing up later to four hundred yards. The fight was obstinately sustained on both sides, and, notwithstanding the commanding position of the batteries, strong hopes were felt on board the fleet of silencing the guns, which the enemy began to desert, when, at 4.30 P.M., the wheel of the flag-ship St. Louis and the tiller of the Louisville were shot away. The two boats, thus rendered unmanageable, drifted down the river; and their consorts, no longer able to maintain the unequal contest, withdrew. The enemy returned at once to their guns, and inflicted much injury on the retiring vessels.

Notwithstanding its failure, the tenacity and fighting qualities of the fleet were more markedly proved in this action than in the victory at Henry. The vessels were struck more frequently (the flag-ship fifty-nine times, and none less than twenty), and though the power of the enemy's guns was about the same in each case, the height and character of the soil at Donelson placed the fleet at a great disadvantage. The fire from above, reaching their sloping armor nearly at right angles, searched every weak point. Upon the Carondelet a rifled gun burst. The pilot-houses were beaten in, and three of the four pilots received mortal wounds. Despite these injuries, and the loss of fifty-four killed and wounded, the fleet was only shaken from its hold by accidents to the steering apparatus, after which their batteries could not be brought to bear.

Among the injured on this occasion was the flag-officer, who was standing by the pilot when the latter was killed. Two splinters struck him in the arm and foot, inflicting wounds apparently slight; but the latter, amid the exposure and anxiety of the succeeding operations, did not heal, and finally compelled him, three months later, to give up the command.

On the 16th the Confederates, after an unsuccessful attempt to cut their way through the investing army, hopeless of a successful resistance, surrendered at discretion to General Grant. The capture of this post left the way open to Nashville, the capital of Tennessee, and the flag-officer was anxious to press on with fresh boats brought up from Cairo; but was prevented by peremptory orders from General Halleck, commanding the Department. As it was, however, Nashville fell on the 25th.

After the fall of Fort Donelson and the successful operations in Missouri, the position at Columbus was no longer tenable. On the 23d Flag-Officer Foote made a reconnoissance in force in that direction, but no signs of the intent to abandon were as yet perceived. On March 1st, Lieutenant Phelps, being sent with a flag of truce, reported the post in process of being evacuated, and on the 4th it was in possession of the Union forces. The Confederates had removed the greater part of their artillery to Island No. 10.

About this time, March 1st, Lieutenant Gwin, commanding the Lexington and Tyler on the Tennessee, hearing that the Confederates were fortifying Pittsburg Landing, proceeded to that point, carrying with him two companies of sharpshooters. The enemy was readily dislodged, and Lieutenant Gwin continued in the neighborhood to watch and frustrate any similar attempts. This was the point chosen a few weeks later for the concentration of the Union army, to which Lieutenant Gwin was again to render invaluable service.

After the fall of Columbus no attempt was made to hold Hickman, but the Confederates fell back upon Island No. 10 and the adjacent banks of the Mississippi to make their next stand for the control of the river. The island, which has its name (if it can be called a name) from its position in the numerical series of islands below Cairo, is just abreast the line dividing Kentucky from Tennessee. The position was singularly strong against attacks from above, and for some time before the evacuation of Columbus the enemy, in anticipation of that event, had been fortifying both the island and the Tennessee and Missouri shores. It will be necessary to describe the natural features and the defences somewhat in detail.

From a point about four miles above Island No. 10 the river flows south three miles, then sweeps round to the west and north, forming a horse-shoe bend of which the two ends are east and west from each other. Where the first horse-shoe ends a second begins; the river continuing to flow north, then west and south to Point Pleasant on the Missouri shore. The two bends taken together form an inverted S (∾). In making this detour, the river, as far as Point Pleasant, a distance of twelve miles, gains but three miles to the south. Island No. 10 lay at the bottom of the first bend, near the left bank. It was about two miles long by one-third that distance wide, and its general direction was nearly east and west. New Madrid, on the Missouri bank, is in the second bend, where the course of the river is changing from west to south. The right bank of the stream is in Missouri, the left bank partly in Kentucky and partly in Tennessee. From Point Pleasant the river runs southeast to Tiptonville, in Tennessee, the extreme point of the ensuing operations.

When Columbus fell the whole of this position was in the hands of the Confederates, who had fortified themselves at New Madrid, and thrown up batteries on the island as well as on the Tennessee shore above it. On the island itself were four batteries mounting twenty-three guns, on the Tennessee shore six batteries mounting thirty-two guns. There was also a floating battery, which, at the beginning of operations, was moored abreast the middle of the island, and is variously reported as carrying nine or ten IX-inch guns. New Madrid, with its works, was taken by General Pope before the arrival of the flotilla.

The position of the enemy, though thus powerful against attack, was one of great isolation. From Hickman a great swamp, which afterward becomes Reelfoot Lake, extends along the left bank of the Mississippi, discharging its waters into the river forty miles below Tiptonville. A mile below Tiptonville begin the great swamps, extending down both sides of the Mississippi for a distance of sixty miles. The enemy therefore had the river in his front, and behind him a swamp, impassable to any great extent for either men or supplies in the then high state of the river. The only way of receiving help, or of escaping, in case the position became untenable, was by way of Tiptonville, to which a good road led. It will be remembered that between New Madrid and Point Pleasant there is a low ridge of land, rising from one to fifteen feet above overflow.

As soon as New Madrid was reduced, General Pope busied himself in establishing a series of batteries at several prominent points along the right bank, as far down as opposite Tiptonville. The river was thus practically closed to the enemy's transports, for their gunboats were unable to drive out the Union gunners. Escape was thus rendered impracticable, and the ultimate reduction of the place assured; but to bring about a speedy favorable result it was necessary for the army to cross the river and come upon the rear of the enemy. The latter, recognizing this fact, began the erection of batteries along the shore from the island down to Tiptonville.

On the 15th of March the fleet arrived in the neighborhood of Island No. 10. There were six ironclads, one of which was the Benton carrying the flag-officer's flag, and ten mortar-boats. The weather was unfavorable for opening the attack, but on the 16th the mortar-boats were placed in position, reaching at extreme range all the batteries, as well on the Tennessee shore as on the island. On the 17th an attack was made by all the gunboats, but at the long range of two thousand yards. The river was high and the current rapid, rendering it very difficult to manage the boats. A serious injury, such as had been received at Henry and at Donelson, would have caused the crippled boat to drift at once into the enemy's arms; and an approach nearer than that mentioned would have exposed the unarmored sides of the vessels, their most vulnerable parts, to the fire of the batteries. The fleet of the flag-officer was thought none too strong to defend the Upper Mississippi Valley against the enemy's gunboats, of whose number and power formidable accounts were continually received; while the fall of No. 10 would necessarily be brought about in time, as that of Fort Pillow afterward was, by the advance of the army through Tennessee. Under these circumstances, it cannot be doubted that Foote was justified in not exposing his vessels to the risks of a closer action; but to a man of his temperament the meagre results of long-range firing must have been peculiarly trying.

The bombardment continued throughout the month. Meanwhile the army under Pope was cutting a canal through the swamps on the Missouri side, by which, when completed on the 4th of April, light transport steamers were able to go from the Mississippi above, to New Madrid below, Island No. 10 without passing under the batteries.

On the night of the 1st of April an armed boat expedition, under the command of Master J. V. Johnson, carrying, besides the boat's crew, fifty soldiers under the command of Colonel Roberts of the Forty-second Illinois Regiment, landed at the upper battery on the Tennessee shore. No resistance was experienced, and, after the guns had been spiked by the troops, the expedition returned without loss to the ships. In a despatch dated March 20th the flag-officer had written: "When the object of running the blockade becomes adequate to the risk I shall not hesitate to do it." With the passage of the transports through the canal, enabling the troops to cross if properly protected, the time had come. The exploit of Colonel Roberts was believed to have disabled one battery, and on the 4th of the month, the floating battery before the island, after a severe cannonade by the gunboats and mortars, cut loose from her moorings and drifted down the river. It is improbable that she was prepared, in her new position, for the events of the night.

At ten o'clock that evening the gunboat Carondelet, Commander Henry Walke, left her anchorage, during a heavy thunder-storm, and successfully ran the batteries, reaching New Madrid at 1 A.M. The orders to execute this daring move were delivered to Captain Walke on the 30th of March. The vessel was immediately prepared. Her decks were covered with extra thicknesses of planking; the chain cables were brought up from below and ranged as an additional protection. Lumber and cord-wood were piled thickly round the boilers, and arrangements made for letting the steam escape through the wheel-houses, to avoid the puffing noise ordinarily issuing from the pipes. The pilot-house, for additional security, was wrapped to a thickness of eighteen inches in the coils of a large hawser. A barge, loaded with bales of hay, was made fast on the port quarter of the vessel, to protect the magazine.

The moon set at ten o'clock, and then too was felt the first breath of a thunder-storm, which had been for some time gathering. The Carondelet swung from her moorings and started down the stream. The guns were run in and ports closed. No light was allowed about the decks. Within the darkened casemate or the pilot-house all her crew, save two, stood in silence, fully armed to repel boarding, should boarding be attempted. The storm burst in full violence as soon as her head was fairly down stream. The flashes of lightning showed her presence to the Confederates who rapidly manned their guns, and whose excited shouts and commands were plainly heard on board as the boat passed close under the batteries. On deck, exposed alike to the storm and to the enemy's fire, were two men ; one, Charles Wilson, a seaman, heaving the lead, standing sometimes knee-deep in the water that boiled over the forecastle ; the other, an officer, Theodore Gilmore, on the upper deck forward, repeating to the pilot the leadsman's muttered " No bottom." The storm spread its sheltering wing over the gallant vessel, baffling the excited efforts of the enemy, before whose eyes she floated like a phantom ship ; now wrapped in impenetrable darkness, now standing forth in the full blaze of the lightning close under their guns. The friendly flashes enabled her pilot, William R. Hoel, who had volunteered from another gunboat to share the fortunes of the night, to keep her in the channel ; once only, in a longer interval between them, did the vessel get a dangerous sheer toward a shoal, but the peril was revealed in time to avoid it. Not till the firing had ceased did the squall abate.

The passage of the Carondelet was not only one of the most daring and dramatic events of the war; it was also the death-blow to the Confederate defence of this position. The concluding events followed in rapid succession. Having passed the island, as related, on the night of the 4th, the Carondelet on the 6th made a reconnoissance down the river as far as Tiptonville, with General Granger on board, exchanging shots with the Confederate batteries, at one of which a landing was made and the guns spiked. That night the Pittsburg also passed the island, and at 6.30 A.M. of the 7th the Carondelet got under way, in concert with Pope's operations, went down the river, followed after an interval by the Pittsburg, and engaged the enemy's batteries, beginning with the lowest. This was silenced in three-quarters of an hour, and the others made little resistance. The Carondelet then signalled her success to the general and returned to cover the crossing of the army, which began at once. The enemy evacuated their works, pushing down toward Tiptonville, but there were actually no means for them to escape, caught between the swamps and the river. Seven thousand men laid down their arms, three of whom were general officers. At ten o'clock that evening the island and garrison surrendered to the navy, just three days to an hour after the Carondelet started on her hazardous voyage. How much of this result was due to the Carondelet and Pittsburg may be measured by Pope's words to the flag-officer: "The lives of thousands of men and the succéss of our operations hang upon your decision; with two gunboats all is safe, with one it is uncertain."

The passage of a vessel before the guns of a fortress under cover of night came to be thought less dangerous in the course of the war. To do full justice to the great gallantry shown by Commander Walke, it should be remembered that this was done by a single vessel three weeks before Farragut passed the forts down the river with a fleet, among the members of which the enemy's fire was distracted and divided; and that when Foote asked the opinion of his subordinate commanders as to the advisability of making the attempt, all, save one, "believed that it would result in the almost certain destruction of the boats, passing six forts under the fire of fifty guns." This was also the opinion of Lieutenant Averett, of the Confederate navy, who commanded the floating battery at the island—a young officer, but of clear and calm judgment. "I do not believe it is impossible," he wrote to Commodore Hollins, "for the enemy to run a part of his gunboats past in the night; but those that I have seen are slow and hard to turn, and it is probable that he would lose some, if not all, in the attempt." Walke alone in the council of captains favored the trial, though the others would doubtless have undertaken it as cheerfully as he did. The daring displayed in this deed, which, to use the flag-officer's words, Walke "so willingly undertook," must be measured by the then prevalent opinion and not in the light of subsequent experience. Subsequent experience, indeed, showed that the danger, if over-estimated, was still sufficiently great.

Justly, then, did it fall to Walke's lot to bear the most conspicuous part in the following events, ending with the surrender. No less praise, however, is due to the flag-officer for the part he bore in this, the closing success of his career. There bore upon him the responsibility of safe-guarding all the Upper Mississippi, with its tributary waters, while at the same time the pressure of public opinion, and the avowed impatience of the army officer with whom he was co-operating, were stinging him to action. He had borne for months the strain of overwork with inadequate tools; his health was impaired, and his whole system disordered from the effects of his unhealed wound. Farragut had not then entered the mouth of the Mississippi, and the result of his enterprise was yet in the unknown future. Reports, now known to be exaggerated, but then accepted, magnified the power of the Confederate fleet in the lower waters. Against these nothing stood, nor was soon likely, as it then seemed, to stand except Foote's ironclads. He was right, then, in his refusal to risk his vessels. He showed judgment and decision in resisting the pressure, amounting almost to a taunt, brought upon him. Then, when it became evident that the transports could be brought through the canal, he took what he believed to be a desperate risk, showing that no lack of power to assume responsibility had deterred him before.

In the years since 1862, Island No. 10, the scene of so much interest and energy, has disappeared. The river, constantly wearing at its upper end, has little by little swept away the whole, and the deep current now runs over the place where the Confederate guns stood, as well as through the channel by which the Carondelet passed. On the other shore a new No. 10 has risen, not standing as the old one, in the stream with a channel on either side, but near a point and surrounded by shoal water. It has perhaps gathered around a steamer, which was sunk by the Confederates to block the passage through a chute then existing across the opposite point.

While Walke was protecting Pope's crossing, two other gunboats were rendering valuable service to another army a hundred miles away, on the Tennessee River. The United States forces at Pittsburg Landing, under General Grant, were attacked by the Confederates in force in the early morning of April 6th. The battle continued with fury all day, the enemy driving the centre of the army back half way from their camps to the river, and at a late hour in the afternoon making a desperate attempt to turn the left, so as to get possession of the landing and transports. Lieutenant Gwin, commanding the Tyler, and senior officer present, sent at 1.30 P.M. to ask permission to open fire. General Hurlburt, commanding on the left, indicated, in reply, the direction of the enemy and of his own forces, saying, at the same time, that without reinforcements he would not be able to maintain his then position for an hour. At 2.50 the Tyler opened fire as indicated, with good effect, silencing their batteries. At 3.50 the Tyler ceased firing to communicate with General Grant, who directed her commander to use his own judgment. At 4 P.M. the Lexington, Lieutenant Shirk, arrived, and the two boats began shelling from a position three-quarters of a mile above the landing, silencing the Confederate batteries in thirty minutes. At 5.30 P.M., the enemy having succeeded in gaining a position on the Union left, an eighth of a mile above the landing and half a mile from the river, both vessels opened fire upon them, in conjunction with the field batteries of the army, and drove them back in confusion.

The army being largely outnumbered during the day, and forced steadily back, the presence and services of the two gunboats, when the most desperate attacks of the enemy were made, were of the utmost value, and most effectual in enabling that part of our line to be held until the arrival of the advance of Buell's army from Nashville, about 5 P.M., allowed the left to be reinforced and restored the fortunes of the day. During the night, by request of General Nelson, the gunboats threw a shell every fifteen minutes into the camp of the enemy.

Considering the insignificant and vulnerable character of these two wooden boats, it may not be amiss to quote the language of the two commanders-in-chief touching their services; the more so as the gallant young officers who directed their movements are both dead, Gwin, later in the war, losing his life in action. General Grant says: "At a late hour in the afternoon a desperate attempt was made to turn our left and get possession of the landing, transports, etc. This point was guarded by the gunboats Tyler and Lexington, Captains Gwin and Shirk, United States Navy, commanding, four 20-pounder Parrotts, and a battery of rifled guns. As there is a deep and impassable ravine for artillery and cavalry, and very difficult for infantry, at this point, no troops were stationed here, except the necessary artillerists and a small infantry force for their support. Just at this moment the advance of Major-General Buell's column (a part of the division under General Nelson) arrived, the two generals named both being present. An advance was immediately made upon the point of attack, and the enemy soon driven back. In this repulse much is due to the presence of the gunboats." In the report in which these words occur it is unfortunately not made clear how much was due to the gunboats before Buell and Nelson arrived.

The Confederate commander, on the other hand, states that, as the result of the attack on the left, the "enemy broke and sought refuge behind a commanding eminence covering the Pittsburg Landing, not more than half a mile distant, under the guns of the gunboats, which opened a fierce and annoying fire with shot and shell of the heaviest description." Among the reasons for not being able to cope with the Union forces next day, he alleges that "during the night the enemy broke the men's rest by a discharge, at measured intervals, of heavy shells thrown from the gunboats;" and further on he speaks of the army as "sheltered by such an auxiliary as their gunboats." The impression among Confederates there present was that the gunboats saved the army by saving the landing and transports, while during the night the shrieking of the VIII-inch shells through the woods, tearing down branches and trees in their flight, and then sharply exploding, was demoralizing to a degree. The nervous strain caused by watching for the repetition, at measured intervals, of a painful sensation is known to most.

General Hurlburt, commanding on the left during the fiercest of the onslaught, and until the arrival of Buell and Nelson, reports: "From my own observation and the statement of prisoners his (Gwin's) fire was most effectual in stopping the advance of the enemy on Sunday afternoon and night."

Island No. 10 fell on the 7th. On the 11th Foote started down the river with the flotilla, anchoring the evening of the 12th fifty miles from New Madrid, just below the Arkansas line. Early the next morning General Pope arrived with 20,000 men. At 8 A.M. five Confederate gunboats came in sight, whereupon the flotilla weighed and advanced to meet them. After exchanging some twenty shots the Confederates retreated, pursued by the fleet to Fort Pillow, thirty miles below, on the first, or upper Chickasaw bluff. The flag-officer continued on with the gunboats to within a mile of the fort, making a leisurely reconnoissance, during which he was unmolested by the enemy. The fleet then turned, receiving a few harmless shots as they withdrew, and tied up to the Tennessee bank, out of range.

The following morning the mortar-boats were placed on the Arkansas side, under the protection of gunboats, firing as soon as secured. The army landed on the Tennessee bank above the fort, and tried to find a way by which the rear of the works could be reached, but in vain. Plans were then arranged by which it was hoped speedily to reduce the place by the combined efforts of army and navy; but these were frustrated by Halleck's withdrawal of all Pope's forces, except 1,500 men under command of a colonel. From this time the attacks on the fort were confined to mortar and long-range firing. Reports of the number and strength of the Confederate gunboats and rams continued to come in, generally much exaggerated; but on the 27th news of Farragut's successful passage of the forts below New Orleans, and appearance before that city, relieved Foote of his most serious apprehensions from below.

On the 23d, Captain Charles H. Davis arrived, to act as second in command to the flag-officer, and on the 9th of May the latter, whose wound, received nearly three months before at Donelson, had become threatening, left Davis in temporary command and went North, hoping to resume his duties with the flotilla at no distant date. It was not, however, so to be. An honorable and distinguished career of forty years afloat ended at Fort Pillow. Called a year later to a yet more important command, he was struck down by the hand of death at the instant of his departure to assume it. His services in the war were thus confined to the Mississippi flotilla. Over the birth and early efforts of that little fleet he had presided; upon his shoulders had fallen the burden of anxiety and unremitting labor which the early days of the war, when all had to be created, everywhere entailed. He was repaid, for under him its early glories were achieved and its reputation established; but the mental strain and the draining wound, so long endured in a sickly climate, hastened his end.

The Confederate gunboats, heretofore acting upon the river at Columbus and Island No. 10, were in the regular naval service under the command of Flag-Officer George N. Hollins, formerly of the United States Navy. At No. 10 the force consisted of the McRae, Polk, Jackson, Calhoun, Ivy, Ponchartrain, Maurepas, and Livingston; the floating battery had also formed part of his command. Hollins had not felt himself able to cope with the heavy Union gunboats. His services had been mainly confined to a vigorous but unsuccessful attack upon the batteries established by Pope on the Missouri shore, between New Madrid and Tiptonville, failing in which the gunboats fell back down the river. They continued, however, to make frequent night trips to Tiptonville with supplies for the army, in doing which Pope's comparatively light batteries did not succeed in injuring them, the river being nearly a mile wide. The danger then coming upon New Orleans caused some of these to be withdrawn, and at the same time a novel force was sent up from that city to take their place and dispute the control of the river with Foote's flotilla.

In the middle of January, General Lovell, commanding the military district in which New Orleans was, had seized, under the directions of the Confederate Secretary of War, fourteen river steamboats. This action was taken at the suggestion of two steamboat captains, Montgomery and Townsend. The intention was to strengthen the vessels with iron casing at the bows, and to use them with their high speed as rams. The weakness of the sterns of the ironclad boats, their slowness and difficulty in handling, were well known to the Confederate authorities. Lovell was directed to allow the utmost latitude to each captain in fitting his own boat, and, as there was no military organization or system, the details of the construction are not now recoverable. The engines, however, were protected with cotton bales and pine bulwarks, and the stems for a length of ten feet shod with iron nearly an inch thick, across which, at intervals of about two feet, were bolted iron straps, extending aft on either bow for a couple of feet so as to keep the planking from starting when the blow was delivered. It being intended that they should close with the enemy as rapidly as possible, but one gun was to be carried; a rule which seems not to have been adhered to. While the force was to be under the general command of the military chief of department, all interference by naval officers was jealously forbidden; and, in fact, by implication, any interference by any one. Lovell seems to have watched the preparations with a certain anxious amusement, remarking at one time, "that fourteen Mississippi pilots and captains will never agree when they begin to talk;" and later, "that he fears too much latitude has been given to the captains." However, by the 15th of April he had despatched eight, under the general command of Captain Montgomery, to the upper river; retaining six at New Orleans, which was then expecting Farragut's attack. These eight were now lying under the guns of Fort Pillow; the whole force being known as the River Defence Fleet.

When Foote left, the ironclads of the squadron were tied up to the banks with their heads down stream, three on the Tennessee, and four on the Arkansas shore, as follows:

Arkansas Shore.

Mound City, COMMANDER A. H. KILTY.
Cincinnati, COMMANDER R. N. STEMBEL.
St. Louis, LIEUTENANT HENRY ERBEN.
Cairo, LIEUTENANT N. C. BRYANT.

Tennessee Shore.

Benton (flag-ship), LIEUTENANT S. L. PHELPS.
Carondelet, COMMANDER HENRY WALKE.
Pittsburg, LIEUTENANT EGBERT THOMPSON.

The place at which they lay on the Tennessee side is called Plum Point; three miles lower down on the Arkansas side is another point called Craighead's. Fort Pillow is just below Craighead's, but on the opposite bank. It was the daily custom for one of the gunboats to tow down a mortar-boat and place it just above Craighead's, remaining near by during the twenty-four hours as guard. The mortar threw its shells across the point into Pillow, and as the fire was harassing to the enemy, the River Defence Fleet, which was now ready for action, determined to make a dash at her. Between 4 and 5 A.M. on the morning of the 10th of May, the day after Foote's departure, the Cincinnati placed Mortar No. 16, Acting-Master Gregory, in the usual position, and then made fast herself to a great drift-pile on the same side, with her head up stream; both ends of her lines being kept on board, to be easily slipped if necessary. The mortar opened her fire at five. At six the eight Confederate rams left their moorings behind the fort and steamed up, the black smoke from their tall smoke-stacks being seen by the fleet above as they moved rapidly up river. At 6.30 they came in sight of the vessels at Plum Point. As soon as they were seen by the Cincinnati she slipped her lines, steamed out into the river, and then rounded to with her head down stream, presenting her bow-guns, and opening at once upon the enemy. The latter approached gallantly but irregularly, the lack of the habit of acting in concert making itself felt, while the fire of the Cincinnati momentarily checked and, to a certain extent, scattered them. The leading vessel, the General Bragg, was much in advance of her consorts. She advanced swiftly along the Arkansas shore, passing close by the mortar-boat and above the Cincinnati; then rounding to she approached the latter at full speed on the starboard quarter, striking a powerful blow in this weak part of the gunboat. The two vessels fell alongside, the Cincinnati firing her broadside as they came together; then the ram swinging clear made down stream, and, although the Confederate commander claims that her tiller ropes alone were out of order, she took no further part in the fray.

Two other Confederates now approached the Cincinnati, the General Price and General Sumter. One of them succeeded in ramming in the same place as the Bragg, and it was at this moment that Commander Stembel, who had gathered his men to board the enemy, was dangerously shot by a rifle-ball through the throat, another officer of the vessel, Master Reynolds, falling at the same time mortally wounded. The other assailant received a shot through her boilers from the Benton, which was now in action; an explosion followed and she drifted down stream. The Cincinnati, aided by a tug and the Pittsburg, then steamed over to the Tennessee shore, where she sank on a bar in eleven feet of water.

As soon as the rams were seen, the flag-ship had made a general signal to get under way, but the morning being calm, the flags did not fly out well. Orders were passed by hail to the Carondelet and Pittsburg, and the former vessel slipped immediately and stood down. The Mound City on the other side did not wait for signals, but, being in advance, started at once, taking the lead with the Carondelet; the Benton following, her speed being less. The Carondelet got up in time to open fire upon the Bragg as she retreated, and to cut the steam-pipe of the other of the two rams which had attacked the Cincinnati after the Bragg's fatal assault.

The fourth Confederate, the General Van Dorn, passed by the Cincinnati and her assailants and met the Mound City. The latter, arriving first of the Union squadron on the Arkansas side of the river, had already opened upon the Sumter and Price, and now upon the Van Dorn also with her bow-guns. The Confederate rounded to and steered to ram amidships, but the Mound City sheered and received a glancing blow in the starboard bow. This disabled her, and to avoid sinking she was run on the Arkansas shore.

Two of the Union gunboats and three rams were now disabled; the latter drifting down with the current under the guns of Fort Pillow. Those remaining were five in number, and only two gunboats, the Benton and Carondelet, were actually engaged, the St. Louis just approaching. The enemy now retired, giving as a reason that the Union gunboats were taking position in water too shoal for the rams to follow.

There can be no denying the dash and spirit with which this attack was made. It was, however, the only service of value performed by this irregular and undisciplined force. At Memphis, a month later, and at New Orleans, the fleet proved incapable of meeting an attack and of mutual support. There were admirable materials in it, but the mistake of withdrawing them from strict military control and organization was fatal. On the other hand, although the gunboats engaged fought gallantly, the flotilla as an organization had little cause for satisfaction in the day's work. Stated baldly, two of the boats had been sunk while only four of the seven had been brought into action. The enemy were severely punished, but the Cincinnati had been unsupported for nearly half an hour, and the vessels came down one by one.

After this affair the Union gunboats while above Pillow availed themselves of shoal spots in the river where the rams could not approach them, while they could use their guns. Whatever the injuries received by the Confederates, they were all ready for action at Memphis a month later. The Cincinnati and Mound City were also speedily repaired and again in service by the end of the month. The mortar-boat bore her share creditably in the fight, levelling her piece as nearly as it could be and keeping up a steady fire. It was all she could do and her commander was promoted.

Shortly after this, a fleet of rams arrived under the command of Colonel Charles Ellet, Jr. Colonel Ellet was by profession a civil engineer, and had, some years before, strongly advocated the steam ram as a weapon of war. His views had then attracted attention, but nothing was done. With the outbreak of the war he had again urged them upon the Government, and on March 27, 1862, was directed by the Secretary of War to buy a number of river steamers on the Mississippi and convert them into rams upon a plan of his own. In accordance with this order he bought,[1] at Pittsburg, three stern-wheel boats, having the average dimensions of 170 feet length, 31 feet beam, and over 5 feet hold; at Cincinnati, three side-wheel boats, of which the largest was 180 feet long by 37 feet beam, and 8 feet hold; and at New Albany, one side-wheel boat of about the same dimensions; in all seven boats, chosen specially with a view to strength and speed. To further strengthen them for their new work, three heavy, solid timber bulkheads, from twelve to sixteen inches thick, were built, running fore and aft from stem to stern, the central one being over the keelson. These bulkheads were braced one against the other, the outer ones against the hull of the boat, and all against the deck and floor timbers, thus making the whole weight of the boat add its momentum to that of the central bulkhead at the moment of collision. The hull was further stayed from side to side by iron rods and screw-bolts. As it would interfere with this plan of strengthening to drop the boilers into the hold, they were left in place; but a bulwark

---

Letter of Colonel Ellet to Lieutenant McGunnegle. United States Navy.

of oak two feet thick was built around them. The pilot-houses were protected against musketry.

It is due to Colonel Ellet to say that these boats were not what he wished, but merely a hasty adaptation, in the short period of six weeks, of such means as were at once available to the end in view. He thought that after striking they might probably go down, but not without sinking the enemy too. When they were ready he was given the command, and the rank of Colonel, with instructions which allowed him to operate within the limits of Captain Davis's command, and in entire independence of that officer; a serious military error which was corrected when the Navy Department took control of the river work.

No further attack was made by the Confederate fleet, and operations were confined to bombardment by the gunboats and constant reply on the part of the forts until June 4th. That night many explosions were heard and fires seen in the fort, and the next morning the fleet moved down, found the works evacuated and took possession. Memphis and its defences became no longer tenable after Beauregard's evacuation of Corinth on the 30th of May.

On June 5th, the fleet with transports moved down the river, anchoring at night two miles above the city. The next morning at dawn the River Defence Fleet was sighted lying at the levee. They soon cast off, and moved into the river, keeping, however, in front of the city in such a way as to embarrass the fire of the Union flotilla.

The Confederate vessels, still under Montgomery's command, were in number eight, mounting from two to four guns each: the Van Dorn, flag steamer; General Price, General Lovell, General Beauregard, General Thompson, General Bragg, General Sumpter, and the Little Rebel.

The Union gunboats were five, viz.: the Benton, Louisville, Carondelet, St. Louis, recently taken charge of by Lieutenant McGunnegle, and Cairo. In addition, there were present and participating in the ensuing action, two of the ram fleet, the Queen of the West and the Monarch, the former commanded by Colonel Ellet in person; the latter by a younger brother, Lieutenant-Colonel A. W. Ellet.

The Confederates formed in double line for their last battle, awaiting the approach of the flotilla. The latter, embarrassed by the enemy being in line with the city, kept under way, but with their heads up stream, dropping slowly with the current. The battle was opened by a shot from the Confederates, and then the flotilla, casting away its scruples about the city, replied with vigor. The Union rams, which were tied up to the bank some distance above, cast off at the first gun and steamed boldly down through the intervals separating the gunboats, the Queen of the West leading, the Monarch about half a mile astern. As they passed, the flotilla, now about three-quarters of a mile from the enemy, turned their heads down the river and followed, keeping up a brisk cannonade; the flag-ship Benton leading. The heights above the city were crowded by the citizens of Memphis, awaiting with eager hope the result of the fight. The ram attack was unexpected, and, by its suddenness and evident determination, produced some wavering in the Confederate line, which had expected to do only with the sluggish and unwieldy gunboats. Into the confusion the Queen dashed, striking the Lovell fairly and sinking her in deep water, where she went down out of sight. The Queen herself was immediately rammed by the Beauregard and disabled; she was then run upon the Arkansas shore opposite the city. Her commander received a pistol shot, which in the end caused his death. The Monarch following, was charged at the same time by the Beauregard and Price; these two boats, however, missed their mark and crashed together, the Beauregard cutting the Price down to the water-line, and tearing off her port wheel. The Price then followed the Queen, and laid herself up on the Arkansas shore. The Monarch successfully rammed her late assailant, the Beauregard, as she was discharging her guns at the Benton, which replied with a shot in the enemy's boiler, blowing her up and fatally scalding many of her people. She went down near shore, being towed there by the Monarch. The Little Rebel in the thickest of the fight got a shot through her steam-chest; whereupon she also made for the limbo on the Arkansas shore, where her officers and crew escaped.

The Confederates had lost four boats, three of them among the heaviest in their fleet. The remaining four sought safety in flight from the now unequal contest, and a running fight followed, which carried the fleet ten miles down the river and resulted in the destruction of the Thompson by the shells of the gunboats and the capture of the Bragg and Sumter. The Van Dorn alone made good her escape, though pursued some distance by the Monarch and Switzerland, another of the ram fleet which joined after the fight was decided. This was the end of the Confederate River Defence Fleet, the six below having perished when New Orleans fell. The Bragg, Price, Sumpter, and Little Rebel were taken into the Union fleet.

The city of Memphis surrendered the same day. The Benton and the flag-officer, with the greater part of the fleet, remained there till June 29th. On the 10th Davis received an urgent message from Halleck to open communication by way of the White River and Jacksonport with General Curtis, who was coming down through Missouri and Arkansas, having for his objective point Helena, on the right bank of the Mississippi. The White River traverses Arkansas from the Missouri border, one hundred and twenty miles west of the Mississippi, and pursuing a southeasterly and southerly course enters the Mississippi two hundred miles below Memphis, one hundred below Helena. A force was despatched, under Commander Kilty, comprising, besides his own ship, the St. Louis, Lieutenant McGunnegle, with the Lexington and Conestoga, wooden gunboats, Lieutenants Shirk and Blodgett. An Indiana regiment under Colonel Fitch accompanied the squadron. On the 17th of June, at St. Charles, eighty-eight miles up, the enemy were discovered in two earthworks, mounting six guns. A brisk engagement followed, the Mound City leading; but when six hundred yards from the works a 42-pound shell entered her casemate, killing three men in its flight and then exploding her steam-drum. Of her entire crew of 175, but 3 officers and 22 men escaped uninjured; 82 died from wounds or scalding, and 43 were either drowned or killed in the water, the enemy, in this instance, having the inhumanity to fire on those who were there struggling for their lives. Unappalled by this sickening catastrophe, the remaining boats pressed on to the attack, the Conestoga taking hold of the crippled vessel to tow her out of action. A few minutes later, at a signal from Colonel Fitch, the gunboats ceased firing, and the troops, advancing, successfully stormed the battery. The commander of the post was Captain Joseph Fry, formerly a lieutenant in the United States Navy, who afterward commanded the filibustering steamer Virginius, and was executed in Cuba, with most of his crew, when captured by the Spaniards in 1874. There being no further works up the stream and but one gunboat of the enemy, the Ponchartrain, this action gave the control of the river to the fleet.

After taking possession of St. Charles, the expedition went on up the river as far as a point called Crooked Point Cut-off, sixty-three miles above St. Charles, and one hundred and fifty-one miles from the mouth of the river. Here it was compelled to turn back by the falling of the water. The hindrance caused by the low state of the rivers led Davis to recommend a force of light-draught boats, armed with howitzers, and protected in their machinery and pilot-houses against musketry, as essential to control the tributaries of the Mississippi during the dry season. This was the germ of the light-draught gunboats, familiarly called "tinclads" from the thinness of their armor, which in the following season were a usual and active adjunct to the operations of the heavier vessels.

On the 29th of June, Flag-Officer Davis, who had received that rank but a week before, went down the river, taking with him the Benton, Carondelet, Louisville, and St. Louis, with six mortar-boats. Two days later, July 1st, in the early morning, Farragut's fleet was sighted, at anchor in the river above Vicksburg. A few hours more and the naval forces from the upper waters and from the mouth of the Mississippi had joined hands.

CHAPTER III.

FROM THE GULF TO VICKSBURG.

THE task of opening the Mississippi from its mouth was entrusted to Captain David G. Farragut, who was appointed to the command of the Western Gulf Blockading Squadron on the 9th of January, 1862. On the 2d of February he sailed from Hampton Roads, in his flag-ship, the Hartford, of twenty-four guns; arriving on the 20th of the same month at Ship Island in Mississippi Sound, which was then, and, until Pensacola was evacuated by the Confederates, continued to be the principal naval station in the West Gulf. Here he met Flag-Officer McKean, the necessary transfers were made, and on the 21st Farragut formally assumed the command of the station which he was to illustrate by many daring deeds, and in which he was to make his brilliant reputation.

With the exception of the vessels already employed on the blockade, the flag-ship was the first to arrive of the force destined to make the move up the river. One by one they came in, and were rapidly assembled at the Southwest Pass, those whose draught permitted entering at once; but the scanty depth of water, at that time found on the bar, made it necessary to lighten the heavier vessels. The Pensacola, while at Ship Island, chartered a schooner, into which she discharged her guns and stores; then taking her in tow went down to the Pass. She arrived there on the 24th of March and made five different attempts to enter when the

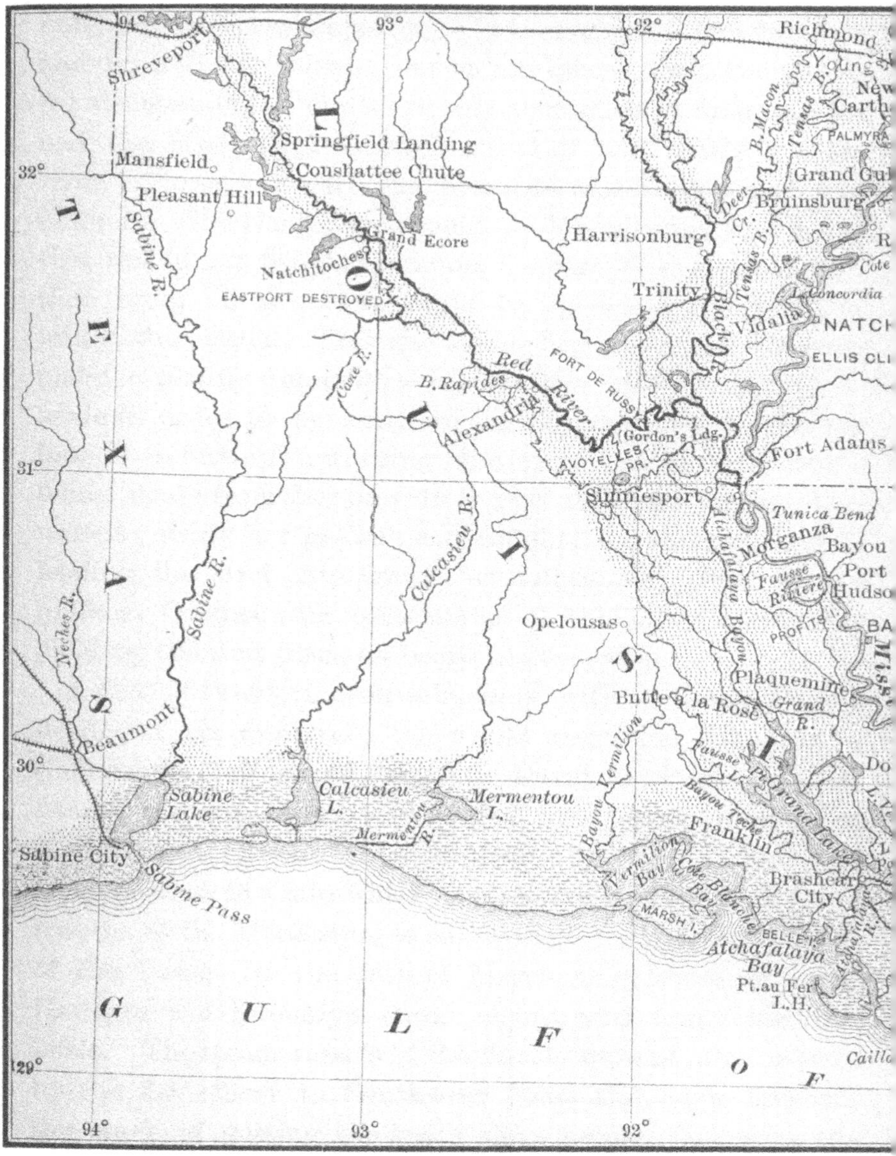

MISSISSIPPI VALLEY—

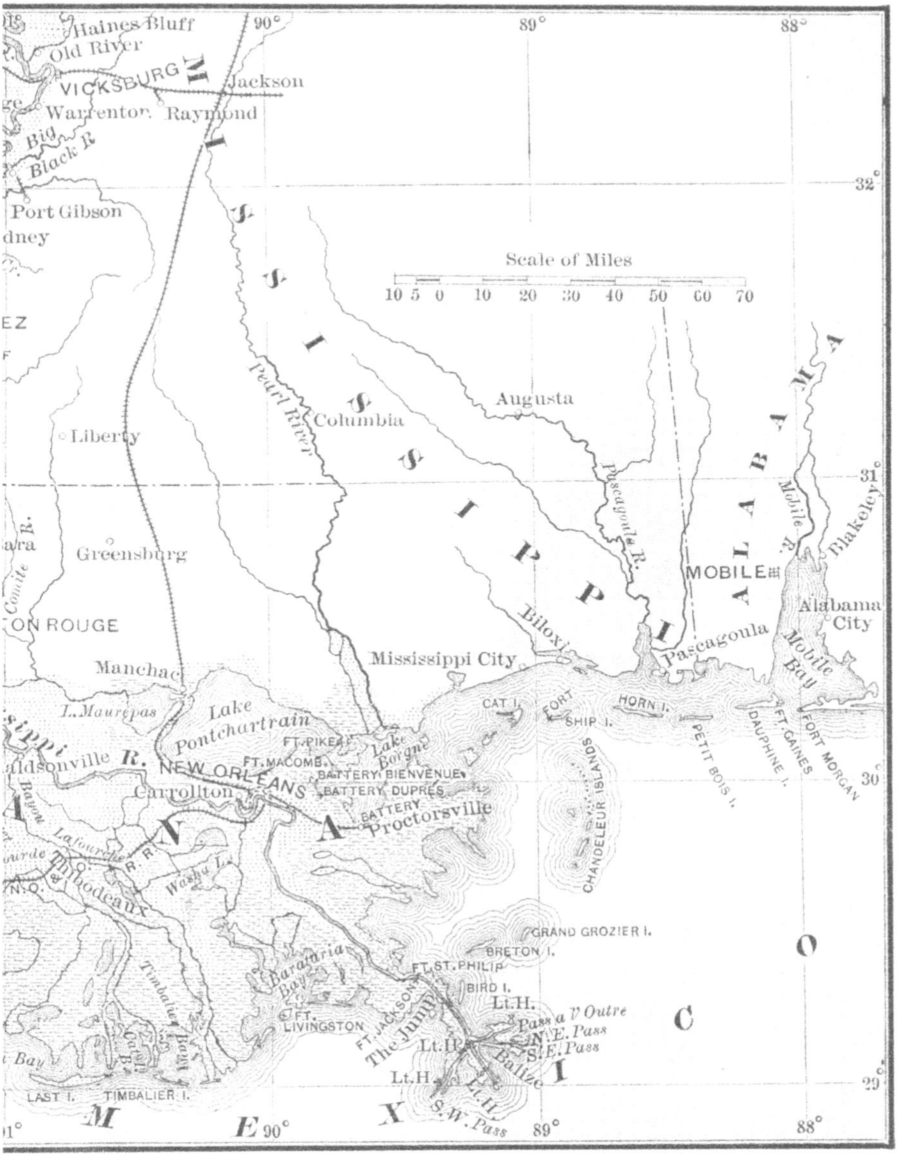

VICKSBURG TO THE GULF.

water seemed favorable. In the first four she grounded, though everything was out of her, and was got off with difficulty, on one occasion parting a hawser which killed two men and injured five others; but on the 7th of April, the powerful steamers of the mortar flotilla succeeded in dragging her and the Mississippi through a foot of mud fairly into the river. These two were the heaviest vessels that had ever entered. The Navy Department at Washington had hopes that the 40-gun frigate Colorado, Captain Theodorus Bailey, then lying off the Pass, might be lightened sufficiently to join in the attack. This was to the flag-officer and her commander plainly impracticable, but the attempt had to be made in order to demonstrate its impossibility. After the loss of a fortnight working she remained outside, drafts being made from her crew to supply vacancies in the other vessels; while her gallant captain obtained the privilege of leading the fleet into action, as a divisional officer, in the gunboat Cayuga, the commander of the latter generously yielding the first place on board his own ship.

A fleet of twenty mortar-schooners, with an accompanying flotilla of six gunboats, the whole under the command of Commander (afterward Admiral) David D. Porter, accompanied the expedition. Being of light draught of water, they entered without serious difficulty by Pass à l'Outre, one of three branches into which the eastern of the three great mouths of the Mississippi is subdivided. Going to the head of the Passes on the 18th of March, they found there the Hartford and Brooklyn, steam sloops, with four screw gunboats. The steam vessels of the flotilla were at once ordered by the flag-officer to Southwest Pass, and, after finishing the work of getting the heavy ships across, they were employed towing up the schooners and protecting the advance of the surveyors of the fleet.

The squadron thus assembled in the river consisted of four screw sloops, one side-wheel steamer, three screw corvettes, and nine screw gunboats, in all seventeen vessels, of all classes, carrying, exclusive of brass howitzers, one hundred and fifty-four guns. Their names and batteries were as follows:

Name.	Tons.	Guns.	Commanding Officer.
Screw Sloops.			
Hartford	1990	24	Flag-Officer David G. Farragut. Fleet-Captain Henry H. Bell. Commander Richard Wainwright.
Pensacola	2158	23	Captain Henry W. Morris.
Brooklyn	2070	22	Captain Thomas T. Craven.
Richmond	1929	24	Commander James Alden.
Side-Wheel.			
Mississippi	1692	17	Commander Melancthon Smith.
Screw Corvettes.			
Oneida	1032	9	Commander S. Phillips Lee.
Varuna	1300	10	Commander Charles S. Boggs.
Iroquois	1016	7	Commander John De Camp.
Screw Gunboats.			
Cayuga	507	2	Lieutenant Napoleon B. Harrison.
Itasca	507	2	Lieutenant C. H. B. Caldwell.
Katahdin	507	2	Lieutenant George H. Preble.
Kennebec	507	2	Lieutenant John H. Russell.
Kineo	507	2	Lieutenant George M. Ransom.
Pinola	507	2	Lieutenant Pierce Crosby.
Sciota	507	2	Lieutenant Edward Donaldson.
Winona	507	2	Lieutenant Edward T. Nichols.
Wissahickon.....	507	2	Lieutenant Albert N. Smith.

About ninety per cent. of the batteries of the eight larger vessels were divided, as is usual, between the two sides of the ship, so that only one half of the guns could be used at any one time, except in the rare event of having an enemy on each side; and even then the number of the crew is based on the expectation of fighting only one broadside. A few guns, however, varying in number in different ships, were mounted on pivots so that they could be fought on either side. In estimating the number of available guns in a fleet of sea-going steamers of that day, it may be roughly said that sixty per cent. could be brought into action on one side. In the Mississippi Squadron sometimes only one-fourth could be used. To professional readers it may seem unnecessary to enter on such familiar and obvious details ; but a military man, in making his estimate, has fallen into the curious blunder of making a fleet fire every gun, bow, stern, and both broadsides, into one fort, a hundred yards square ; a feat which only could be performed by landing a ship in the centre of the works, in which case it could enjoy an all-round fire. The nine gunboats carried one heavy and one light gun, both pivots and capable of being fought on either side. None of this fleet could fire right ahead. All the vessels were built for ships of war, with the exception of the Varuna, which was bought from the merchant service.[1]

The mortar-schooners each carried one XIII-inch mortar. Of the six gunboats attached to this part of the expedition, one, the Owasco, was of the same class as the Cayuga and others. The Clifton, Jackson, and Westfield were large side-wheel ferry boats, of the ordinary double-ended type ; carrying, however, heavy guns. They were powerful as tug-boats and easily managed; whereas the Miami, also a double-ender, but built for the Government, was like most of her kind, hard to steer or manœuvre, especially in a narrow stream and tideway. The sixth was the Harriet Lane, a side-wheel steamer of 600 tons, which had been transferred from the Revenue Service.

---

[1] For particulars of batteries, see Appendix.

The tonnage and batteries of these steamers were:[1]

Name.	Tons.	Guns.	Commanding Officer.
Screw Gunboat.			
Owasco.............	507	2	Lieutenant John Guest.
Paddle-Wheel Steamers.			
Westfield (Double-enders.)	891	6	Commander William B. Renshaw.
Miami (Double-enders.)	730	5	Lieutenant A. Davis Harrell.
Clifton (Double-enders.)	892	7	Lieutenant Charles H. Baldwin.
Jackson (Double-enders.)	777	7	Lieutenant Selim E. Woodworth.
Harriet Lane	619	3	Lieutenant Jonathan M. Wainwright.

When the ships were inside, the flag-officer issued special instructions for their preparation for the river service. They were stripped to the topmasts, and landed all spars and rigging, except those necessary for the topsails, jib, and spanker. Everything forward was brought close in to the bowsprit, so as not to interfere with the forward range of the battery. Where it could be done, guns were especially mounted on the poop and forecastle, and howitzers placed in the tops, with iron bulwarks to protect their crews from musketry. The vessels were ordered to be trimmed by the head, so that if they took the bottom at all it would be forward. In a rapid current, like that of the Mississippi, a vessel which grounded aft would have her bow swept round at once and fall broadside to the stream, if she did not go ashore. To get her pointed right again would be troublesome; and the same consideration led to the order that, in case of accident to the engines involving loss of power to go ahead, no attempt should be made to turn the ship's head down stream. If the wind served she should be handled under sail; but if not, an anchor should be let go, with cable

[1] For detailed account of these batteries, see Appendix.

enough to keep her head up stream while permitting her to drop bodily down. Springs were prepared on each quarter; and, as the ships were to fight in quiet water, at short range, and in the dark, special care was taken so to secure the elevating screws that the guns should not work themselves to too great elevation.

In accordance with these instructions the ships stripped at Pilot Town, sending ashore spars, boats, rigging, and sails; everything that was not at present needed. The chronometers of the fleet were sent on board the Colorado. The larger ships snaked down the rigging, while the gunboats came up their lower rigging, carrying it in and securing it close to the mast. The flag-ship being now at the Head of the Passes remained there, the flag-officer shifting his flag from one small vessel to another as the requirements of the squadron called him to different points. A detachment of lighter vessels, one of the corvettes and a couple of gunboats, occupied an advance station at the "Jump," a bayou entering the river on the west side, eight miles above the Head of the Passes; the enemy's gunboats were thus unable to push their reconnoissances down in sight of the main fleet while the latter were occupied with their preparations. The logs of the squadron show constant bustle and movement, accompanied by frequent accidents, owing to the swift current of the river, which was this year exceptionally high, even for the season. A hospital for the fleet was established in good houses at Pilot Town, but the flag-officer had to complain of the entire insufficiency of medical equipment, as well as a lack of most essentials for carrying on the work. Ammunition of various kinds was very deficient, and the squadron was at one time threatened with failure of fuel, the coal vessels arriving barely in time.

The first and at that time the only serious obstacle to the

upward progress of the fleet was at the Plaquemine Bend, twenty miles from the Head of the Passes, and ninety below New Orleans. At this point the river, which has been running in a southeasterly direction, makes a sharp bend, the last before reaching the sea, runs northeast for a mile and three-quarters, and then resumes its southeast course. Two permanent fortifications existed at this point, one on the left, or north bank of the stream, called Fort St. Philip, the other on the right bank, called Fort Jackson. Jackson is a little below St. Philip, with reference to the direction of the river through the short reach on which they are placed, but having regard to the general southeast course, may be said to be lower down by 800 yards; the width of the river actually separating the faces of the two works. At the time the fleet arrived, the woods on the west bank had been cleared away below Jackson almost to the extreme range of its guns, thus affording no shelter from observation; the east bank was nearly treeless. Extending across the river from below Jackson, and under the guns of both works, was a line of obstructions which will be described further on.

The works of St. Philip consisted of the fort proper, a structure of brick and earth mounting in barbette four VIII-inch columbiads and one 24-pounder; and two water batteries on either side of the main work, the upper mounting sixteen 24-pounders, the lower, one VIII-inch columbiad, one VII-inch rifle, six 42-pounders, nine 32s, and four 24s. There were here, then, forty-two guns commanding the river below the bend, up which the ships must come, as well as the course of the stream in their front. Besides these there were one VIII-inch and one X-inch mortar in the fort; one XIII-inch mortar, whose position does not appear; and a battery of four X-inch sea-coast mortars, situated below and to the northeast of the lower water battery. These last pieces for vertical shell-firing had no influence upon the ensuing contest; the XIII-inch mortar became disabled at the thirteenth fire by its own discharge, and the X-inch, though 142 shell were fired from them, are not so much as mentioned in the reports of the fleet.

Fort Jackson, on the southern bank of the bend, was a pentagonal casemated work, built of brick. In the casemates were fourteen 24-pounder smooth-bore guns, and ten flanking howitzers of the same calibre. Above these, in barbette, were two X-inch and three VIII-inch columbiads, one VII-inch rifle, six 42-pounders, fifteen 32s, and eleven 24s; total in the fort, sixty-two. Just outside of and below the main work, covering the approach to it, was a water battery carrying one X-inch and two VIII-inch columbiads, and two rifled 32-pounders.[1] Of the guns in Jackson, the flanking howitzers and half a dozen of the 24- and 32-pounders could, from their position, have had little or no share in the battle with the fleet.

The number and calibre of the guns have been thus minutely stated because it can scarcely fail to cause surprise that so many of them were so small. Of 109 in the two works, 56 were 24-pounders. The truth is that the Confederacy was very badly off for cannon, and the authorities in Richmond had their minds firmly made up that the great and dangerous attack was to come from above. General Lovell, commanding the department, begged hard for heavy cannon, but to no avail; not only were all available sent north, but constant drafts were made upon the supplies he himself had. New Orleans, the central point which he was called on to defend, was approachable, not only by the Mississippi, but through a dozen bayous which, from Pearl

---

[1] These threw projectiles weighing from sixty to eighty pounds.

River on the east to the Atchafalaya Bayou on the west, gave access to firm ground above Forts St. Philip and Jackson, and even above the city. Works already existing to cover these approaches had to be armed, and new works in some cases erected, constituting, in connection with St. Philip and Jackson, an exterior line intended to block approach from the sea. A second, or interior, line of works extended from the river, about four miles below New Orleans, to the swamps on either hand, and was carried on the east side round to Lake Ponchartrain in rear of the city. These were for defence from a land attack by troops that might have penetrated through any of the water approaches; and a similar line was constructed above the city. The interior works below the city, where they touched the river on the right bank, were known as the McGehee, and on the left bank as the Chalmette line of batteries. The latter was the scene of Jackson's defeat of the English in 1815. All these works needed guns. All could not be supplied; but the necessity of providing as many as possible taxed the general's resources. In March, 1862, when it was determined to abandon Pensacola, he asked for some of the X-inch columbiads that were there, but all that could be spared from the north were sent to Mobile, where the commanding officer refused to give them up. In addition to other calls, Lovell had to spare some guns for the vessels purchased for the navy on Lake Ponchartrain and for the River Defence Fleet.

General Duncan had general charge of all the works of the exterior line, and was of course present at Plaquemine Bend during the attack. Colonel Higgins was in command of both the forts, with headquarters at Jackson, Captain Squires being in immediate command of St. Philip.

Auxiliary to the forts there were four vessels of the Confederate Navy, two belonging to the State of Louisiana, and six of the River Defence Fleet. The latter were commanded by a Captain Stephenson, who entirely refused to obey the orders of Commander Mitchell, the senior naval officer, while professing a willingness to co-operate. The constitution of this force has already been described. There were also above, or near, the forts five unarmed steamers and tugs, only one of which, the tug Mosher, needs to be named.

The naval vessels were the Louisiana, sixteen guns; McRae, seven guns, six light 32-pounders and one IX-inch shell-gun; Jackson, two 32-pounders; and the ram Manassas, now carrying one 32-pounder carronade firing right ahead. Since her exploit at the Head of the Passes in the previous October, the Manassas had been bought by the Confederate Government, docked and repaired. She now had no prow, the iron of the hull only being carried round the stem. Her engines and speed were as poor as before. Lieutenant Warley was still in command. The State vessels were the Governor Moore and General Quitman, the former carrying two rifled 32s, and the latter two smooth-bores of the same calibre; these were sea-going steamers, whose bows were shod with iron like those of the River Defence Fleet and their engines protected with cotton. The Moore was commanded by Beverley Kennon, a trained naval officer, but not then in the Confederate Navy; the Quitman's captain, Grant, was of the same class as the commanders of the River Defence Fleet. The Manassas had some power as a ram, and the Moore, by her admirable handling, showed how much an able man can do with poor instruments, but the only one of the above that might really have endangered the success of the Union fleet was the Louisiana. This was an iron-clad vessel of type resembling the Benton, with armor strong enough to resist two XI-inch shells of the fleet that struck her at short range. Her armament was two VII-inch rifles, three IX-inch and four VIII-inch shell-guns, and seven VI-inch rifles. With this heavy battery she might have been very dangerous, but Farragut's movements had been pushed on with such rapidity that the Confederates had not been able to finish her. At the last moment she was shoved off from the city on Sunday afternoon, four days before the fight, with workmen still on board. When her great centre stern wheel revolved, the water came in through the seams of the planking, flooding the battery deck, but her engines were not powerful enough to manage her, and she had to be towed down by two tugs to a berth just above Fort St. Philip, where she remained without power of movement till after the fight.

When ready, the fleet began moving slowly up the river, under the pilotage of members of the Coast Survey, who, already partly familiar with the ground, were to push their triangulation up to the forts themselves and establish the position of the mortars with mathematical precision; a service they performed with courage and accuracy. The work of the surveyors was carried on under the guns of the forts and exposed to the fire of riflemen lurking in the bushes, who were not wholly, though they were mostly, kept in check by the gunboats patrolling the river. On the 16th the fleet anchored just below the intended position of the mortar-boats on the west bank of the stream. The day following was spent in perfecting the arrangements, and by the morning of the 18th two divisions of mortar-boats were anchored in line ahead, under cover of the wood on the right bank, each one dressed up and down her masts with bushes, which blended indistinguishably with the foliage of the trees. Light lines were run as springs from the inshore bows and quarters; the exact bearing and distance of Fort

Jackson was furnished to each commander, and at 10 A.M. the bombardment began. The van of the fourteen schooners was at this moment 2,950 yards, the rear 3,980 yards from Fort Jackson, to which the mortar attack was confined; an occasional shell only being sent into St. Philip.

The remaining six schooners, called the second division, from the seniority of its commanding officer, were anchored on the opposite side, 3,900 yards below Jackson. Here they were able to see how their shell were falling, an advantage not possessed by those on the other shore; but there were no trees to cover them. An attempt to disguise them was made by covering their hulls with reeds and willows, but was only partly successful; and as the enemy's fire, which began in reply as soon as the mortars opened, had become very rapid and accurate, the gunboats of the main squadron moved up to support those of the flotilla and draw off part of it. Before noon two of the leading schooners in this division were struck by heavy shot and were dropped down 300 yards. The whole flotilla continued firing until 6 P.M., when they ceased by signal. That night the second division was moved across the river and took position with the others.

Until five o'clock the firing was sustained and rapid from both forts. At that time the citadel and out-houses of Jackson were in flames, and the magazine in great danger; so the enemy's fire ceased.

All the mortars opened again on the morning of the 19th and continued until noon, after which the firing was maintained by divisions, two resting while the third worked. Thus, about 168 shell were fired every four hours, or nearly one a minute. At 10 A.M. of the 19th one schooner was struck by a shot, which passed out through her bottom, sinking her. This was the only vessel of the flotilla thus destroyed.

Although Jackson was invisible from the decks of the

mortar-boats and the direction given by sights fixed to the mastheads, the firing was so accurate and annoying as to attract a constant angry return from the fort. To draw off and divide this one of the corvettes and two or three of the gunboats took daily guard duty at the head of the line, from 9 A.M. one day to the same hour the next. The small vessels advancing under cover of the trees on the west bank would emerge suddenly, fire one or two shots drifting in the stream, and then retire; the constant motion rendering the aim of the fort uncertain. Nevertheless some ugly hits were received by different ships.

Every night the enemy sent down fire-rafts, but these, though occasioning annoyance to the fleet, were productive of no serious damage beyond collisions arising from them. They were generally awkwardly started, and the special mistake was made of sending only one at a time, instead of a number, to increase the confusion and embarrassment of the ships. The crews in their boats towed them ashore, or the light steamers ran alongside and put them out with their hose.

Mortar-firing, however good, would not reduce the forts, nor lay New Orleans at the mercy of the fleet. It was necessary to pass above. Neither the flag-officer on the one hand, nor the leaders of the enemy on the other had any serious doubt that the ships could go by if there were no obstructions; but the obstructions were there. As originally laid these had been most formidable. Cypress trees, forty feet long and four to five feet in diameter, were laid longitudinally in the river, about three feet apart to allow a water-way. Suspended from the lower side of these logs by heavy iron staples were two 2½-inch iron cables, stretching from one side of the river to the other. To give the framework of trunks greater rigidity, large timbers, six by four inches, were pinned down on the upper sides. The cables were secured on the left bank to trees; on the right bank, where there were no trees, to great anchors buried in the ground. Between the two ends the raft was held up against the current by twenty-five or thirty 3,000-pound anchors, with sixty fathoms of chain on each. This raft, placed early in the winter, showed signs of giving in February, when the spring-floods came sweeping enormous masses of drift upon it, and by the 10th of March the cables had snapped, leaving about a third of the river open. Colonel Higgins was then directed to restore it. He found it had broken from both sides, and attempted to replace it by sections, but the current, then running four knots an hour, made it impossible to hold so heavy a structure in a depth of one hundred and thirty feet and in a bottom of shifting sand, which gave no sufficient holding ground for the anchors. Seven or eight heavily built schooners, of about two hundred tons, were then seized and placed in a line across the river in the position of the raft. Each schooner lay with two anchors down and sixty fathoms of cable on each; the masts were unstepped and, with the rigging, allowed to drift astern to foul the screws of vessels attempting to pass. Two or three 1-inch chains were stretched across from schooner to schooner, and from them to sections of the old raft remaining near either shore.

Such was the general character of the obstructions before the fleet. The current, and collisions with their own vessels, had somewhat disarranged the apparatus, but it was essentially in this condition when the bombardment began. It was formidable, not on account of its intrinsic strength, but because of the swift current down and the slowness of the ships below, which, together, would prevent them from striking it a blow of sufficient power to break through. If they failed thus to force their way they would be held under the fire of the forts, powerless to advance.

It is believed that, in a discussion about removing the obstructions, Lieutenant Caldwell, commanding the Itasca, volunteered to attempt it with another vessel, and suggested taking out the masts of the two. The Itasca and the Pinola, Lieutenant-Commanding Crosby, were assigned to the duty, and Fleet-Captain Bell given command of both; a rather unnecessary step, considering the age and character of the commanders of the vessels. To handle two vessels in such an enterprise, necessarily undertaken on a dark night, is not easy, and it is a hardship to a commander to be virtually superseded in his own ship at such a time. This was also felt in assigning divisional commanders for the night attack only, when they could not possibly manage more than one ship and simply overshadowed the captain of the vessel.

On the afternoon of the 20th, the Itasca and Pinola each went alongside one of the sloops, where their lower masts were taken out, and, with the rigging, sent ashore. At 10 P.M. Captain Bell went aboard both and addressed the officers and crews about the importance of the duty before them. He remained on board the Pinola and the two vessels then got underway, the Pinola leading. All the mortar-boats now opened together, having at times nine shells in the air at once, to keep down the fire of Jackson in case of discovery, although the two gunboats showed for little, being very deep in the water.

As they drew near the obstructions two rockets were thrown up by the enemy, whose fire opened briskly; but the masts being out, it was not easy to distinguish the vessels from the hulks. The Pinola struck the third from the eastern shore and her men jumped on board. The intention was to explode two charges of powder with a slow match over the chains, and a torpedo by electricity under the bows of the hulk, a petard operator being on board. The charges were placed, and the Pinola cast off. The operator claims that he asked Bell to drop astern by a hawser, but that instead of so doing, he let go and backed the engines. Be this as it may, the ship went rapidly astern, the operator did not or could not reel off rapidly enough, and the wires broke. This hulk therefore remained in place, for the timed fuzes did not act.

The Itasca ran alongside the second hulk from the east shore and threw a grapnel on board, which caught firmly in the rail; but through the strength of the current the rail gave way and the Itasca, taking a sheer to starboard, drifted astern with her head toward the bank. As quickly as possible she turned round, steamed up again and boarded the hulk nearest the east shore on its port, or off-shore side, and this time held on, keeping the engine turning slowly and the helm aport to ease the strain on the grapnel. Captain Caldwell, Acting-Masters Amos Johnson and Edmund Jones, with parties of seamen, jumped on board with powder-cans and fuzes; but, as they were looking for the chains, it was found that they were secured at the bows, by lashing or otherwise, to the hulk's anchor chain, the end of the latter being led in through the hawse-pipe, around the windlass and bitted. When its windings had been followed up and understood, Captain Caldwell was told that the chain could be slipped. He then contemplated firing the hulk, but while the materials for doing so were sought for, the chain was slipped without orders. The vessels went adrift, and, as the Itasca's helm was to port and the engines going ahead, they turned inshore and grounded hard and fast a short distance below, within easy range of both forts.

A boat was at once sent to the Pinola, which was steaming up to try again, and she came to her consort's assistance.

Two lines were successfully run to the Itasca, but she had grounded so hard that both parted, though the second was an 11-inch hawser. The Pinola now drifted so far down, and was so long in returning, that the Itasca thought herself deserted; and the executive officer, Lieutenant George B. Bacon, was despatched to the Hartford for a more powerful vessel. The hour for the moon to rise was also fast approaching and the fate of the Itasca seemed very doubtful.

The Pinola, however, came back, having in her absence broken out a 13-inch hawser, the end of which was passed to the grounded vessel. The third trial was happy and the Pinola dragged the Itasca off, at the same time swinging her head up the river. Lieutenant Caldwell, who was on the bridge, when he saw his ship afloat, instead of returning at once, steadied her head up stream and went ahead fast with the engines. The Itasca moved on, not indeed swiftly, but firmly toward and above the line of hulks, hugging the eastern bank. When well above Caldwell gave the order, "Starboard;" the little vessel whirled quickly round and steered straight for the chains. Carrying the full force of the current with her and going at the top of her own speed, she passed between the third hulk, which the Pinola had grappled, and the fourth. As her stem met the chain she slid bodily up, rising three or four feet from the water, and dragging down the anchors of the hulks on either side; then the chains snapped, the Itasca went through, and the channel of the river was free.

The following morning the hulks were found to be greatly shifted from their previous positions. The second from the east shore remained in place, but the third had dragged down and was now astern of the second, as though hanging to it. The hulk nearest the west shore was also unmoved, but the other three had dragged down and were lying more or less below, apparently in a quartering direction from the first. A broad open space intervened between the two groups. The value of Caldwell's work was well summed up by General M. L. Smith, the Confederate Engineer of the Department: "The forts, in my judgment, were impregnable so long as they were in free and open communication with the city. This communication was not endangered while the obstruction existed. The conclusion, then, is briefly this: While the obstruction existed the city was safe; when it was swept away, as the defences then existed, it was in the enemy's power."

The bombardment continued on the 21st, 22d, and 23d with undiminished vigor, but without noteworthy incident in the fleet. The testimony of the Confederate officers, alike in the forts and afloat, is unanimous as to the singular accuracy of the mortar fire. A large proportion of the shells fell within the walls of Jackson. The damage done to the masonry was not irreparable, but the quarters and citadel, as already stated, were burned down and the magazine endangered. The garrison were compelled to live in the casemates, which were partially flooded from the high state of the river and the cutting of the levee by shells. Much of the bedding and clothing were lost by the fire, thus adding to the privations and discomfort. On the 21st Jackson was in need of extensive repairs almost everywhere, and the officers in command hoped that the Louisiana, which had come down the night before, would be able to keep down the mortar fire, at least in part. When it was found she had no motive power they asked that she should take position below the obstructions on the St. Philip side, where she would be under the guns of the forts, but able to reach the schooners. If she could not be a ship of war, at least let her be a floating battery. Mitchell declined for several reasons. If a mortar-shell fell vertically on the decks of the Louisiana it would go through her bottom and sink her; the mechanics were still busy on board and could not work to advantage under fire; the ports were too small to give elevation to the guns, and so they could not reach the mortars. If this last were correct no other reason was needed; but as the nearest schooner was but 3,000 yards from Jackson, it seems likely he deceived himself, as he certainly did in believing "on credible information" that a rifled gun on the parapet of Jackson, of the same calibre as that of the Louisiana, had not been able to reach. Three schooners had been struck, one at the distance of 4,000 yards, during the first two days of the bombardment, not only by rifled, but by VIII- and X-inch spherical projectiles; and the second division had been compelled to shift its position. Looking only to the Louisiana, the decision of the naval officers was natural enough; but considering that time pressed, that after five days' bombardment the fleet must soon attack, that it was improbable, if New Orleans fell, that the Louisiana's engines could be made efficient and she herself anything but a movable battery, the refusal to make the desired effort looks like caring for a part, at the sacrifice of the whole, of the defence. On the last day Mitchell had repeated warnings that the attack would soon come off, and was again asked to take a position to enfilade the schooners, so that the cannoneers of Jackson might be able to stand to their guns. Mitchell sent back word that he hoped to move in twenty-four hours, and received from Higgins, himself an old seaman and naval officer, the ominous rejoinder: "Tell Captain Mitchell that there will be no to-morrow for New Orleans, unless he immediately takes up the position assigned to him with the Louisiana."[1]

[1] Mitchell's conduct was approved by a Naval Court of Inquiry. Higgins, who was most emphatic in his condemnation, could not appear as a witness, the War

That same day, all arrangements of the fleet being completed, the orders to be ready to attack the following night were issued. Every preparation that had occurred to the minds of the officers as tending to increase the chance of passing uninjured had been made. The chain cables of the sheet anchors had been secured up and down the sides of the vessels, abreast the engines, to resist the impact of projectiles. This was general throughout the squadron, though the Mississippi, on account of her side-wheels, had to place them inside instead of out; and each commander further protected those vital parts from shots coming in forward or aft, with hammocks, bags of coal, or sand, or ashes, or whatever else came to hand. The outside paint was daubed over with the yellow Mississippi mud, as being less easily seen at night; while, on the other hand, the gun-carriages and decks were whitewashed, throwing into plainer view the dark color of their equipment lying around. On some ships splinter nettings were rigged inside the bulwarks, and found of advantage in stopping the flight of larger fragments struck out by shot. Three more of the gunboats, following the example of the Pinola and Itasca, had their lower masts removed and moored to the shore. Of the four that kept them in three had their masts wounded in the fight, proving the advantage of this precaution. Thus prepared, and stripped of every spare spar, rope, and boat, in the lightest fighting trim, the ships stood ready for the night's work.

The flag-officer had at first intended to advance to the attack in two columns abreast, each engaging the fort on its own side and that only. On second thought, considering

Department not being willing to spare him from his duties. The difference was one of judgment and, perhaps, of temperament. From Higgins's character it is likely that, had he commanded the naval forces, the Louisiana would either have done more work or come to a different end. As the old proverb says, "He would have made a spoon or spoiled the horn."

that in the darkness and smoke vessels in parallel columns would be more likely to foul the hulks on either side, or else each other, and that the fleet might so be thrown into confusion, he changed his plan and directed that the starboard column should advance first, its rear vessel to be followed by the leader of the port column; thus bringing the whole fleet into single line ahead. To help this formation, after dark on the 23d, the eight vessels of the starboard column moved over from the west bank and anchored in line ahead on the other side, the Cayuga, bearing the divisional flag of Captain Theodorus Bailey, in advance. Their orders remained to engage St. Philip on the right hand, and not to use their port batteries. The signal to weigh was to be two vertical red lights.

Meanwhile, during the days that had gone by since breaking the line of hulks, some officers of the fleet had thought they could see the water rippling over a chain between the two groups; and, although the flag-officer himself could not make it out, the success of the attack so depended upon having a clear thoroughfare, that he decided to have a second examination. Lieutenant Caldwell asked to do this in person, as his work was in question. Toward nightfall of the 23d, the Hartford sent a fast twelve-oared boat to the Itasca. Caldwell and Acting-Master Edmund Jones went in the boat, which was manned from the Itasca's crew, and after holding on by the leading mortar-schooner till dark, the party started ahead. Fearing that pickets and sharpshooters on either shore might stop them, they had to pull up in the middle of the river against the heavy current, without availing themselves of the inshore eddy. Before they came up with the chain, a fire was kindled on the eastern bank throwing a broad belt of light athwart the stream. To pull across this in plain view seemed madness, so the boat was headed to the opposite side and crawled up to within a hundred yards of the hulks. Then holding on to the bushes, out of the glare of the fire, and hearing the voices of the enemy in the water battery, the party surveyed the situation. Though tangled chains hung from the bows of the outer and lower hulk it seemed perfectly plain that none reached across the river, but, after some hesitation about running the risk merely to clear up a point as to which he had himself no doubt, the necessity of satisfying others determined Caldwell; and by his orders the cutter struck boldly out and into the light. Crossing it unobserved, or else taken for a Confederate boat by any who may have seen, the party reached the outer hulk on the west side. Pausing for a moment under its shelter they then pulled up stream, abreast the inshore hulk, and Jones dropped from the bow a deep-sea lead with ten fathoms of line. The boat was then allowed to drift with the current, and the line held in the hand gave no sign of fouling anything. Then they pulled up a second time and again dropped down close to the hulk on the east shore with like favorable result; showing conclusively that, to a depth of sixty feet, nothing existed to bar the passage of the fleet. The cutter then flew on her return with a favoring current, signalling all clear at 11 P.M.

At 2 A.M. the flag-ship hoisted the appointed signal and the starboard column weighed, the heavy vessels taking a long while to purchase their anchors, owing to the force of the current. At 3.30 the Cayuga, leading, passed through the booms, the enemy waiting for the ships to come fairly into his power. In regular order followed the Pensacola, Mississippi, Oneida, Varuna, Katahdin, Kineo, Wissahickon, the Confederate fire beginning as the Pensacola passed through the breach. The Varuna, Cayuga, and Katahdin

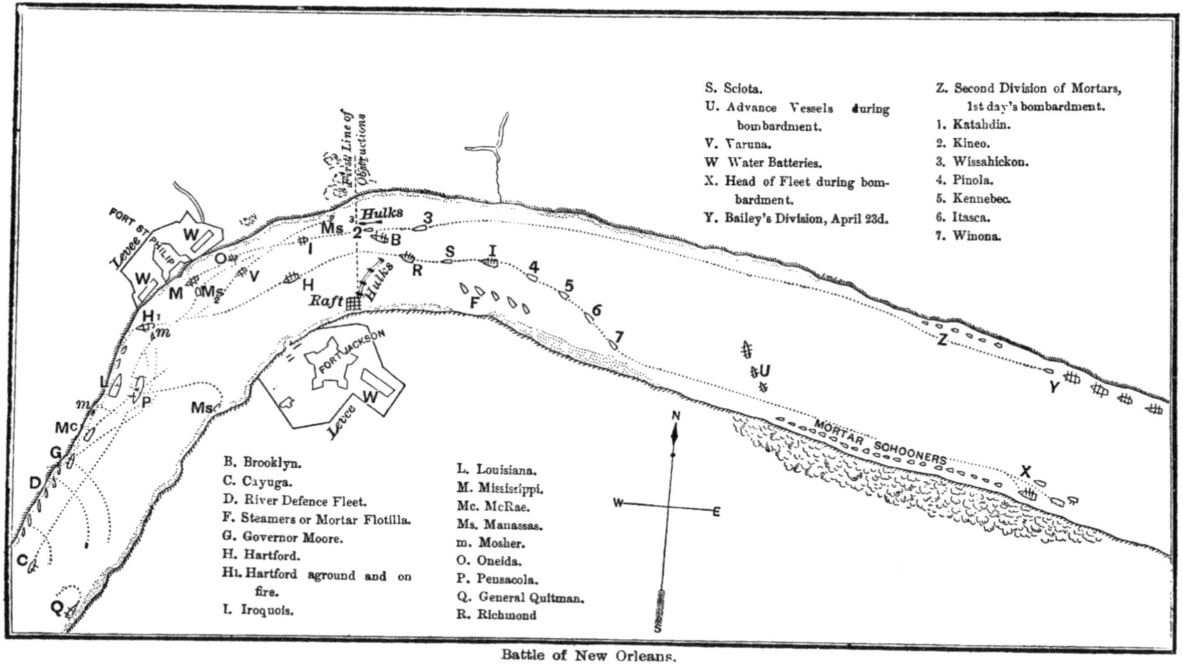
S. Sciota.
U. Advance Vessels during bombardment.
V. Varuna.
W Water Batteries.
X. Head of Fleet during bombardment.
Y. Bailey's Division, April 23d.
Z. Second Division of Mortars, 1st day's bombardment.
1. Katahdin.
2. Kineo.
3. Wissahickon.
4. Pinola.
5. Kennebec.
6. Itasca.
7. Winona.
B. Brooklyn.
C. Cayuga.
D. River Defence Fleet.
F. Steamers or Mortar Flotilla.
G. Governor Moore.
H. Hartford.
H1. Hartford aground and on fire.
I. Iroquois.
L. Louisiana.
M. Mississippi.
Mc. McRae.
Ms. Manassas.
m. Mosher.
O. Oneida.
P. Pensacola.
Q. General Quitman.
R. Richmond
FORT ST PHILIP
Levee
FORT JACKSON
Levee
First Line of Obstructions
Hulks
Hulks
Raft
MORTAR SCHOONERS
N
S
E
W

Battle of New Orleans.

steamed rapidly on, the one heavy gun of the gunboats being ill-adapted to cope with those in the works; but the heavy ships, keeping line inside the gunboats, moved slowly by, fighting deliberately and stopping from time to time to deliver their broadsides with greater effect.

The Pensacola, following the Cayuga closely and keeping a little on her starboard quarter, stopped when near Fort St. Philip, pouring in her heavy broadside, before which the gunners of its barbette battery could not stand but fled to cover; then as the big ship moved slowly on, the enemy returned to their guns and again opened fire. The Pensacola again stopped, and again drove the cannoneers from their pieces, the crew of the ship and the gunners in the fort cursing each other back and forth in the close encounter. As the ship drew away and turned toward the mid-river, so that her guns no longer bore, the enemy manned theirs again and riddled her with a quartering fire as she moved off. At about this time the ram Manassas charged her, but, by a skilful movement of the helm, Lieutenant Roe, who was conning the Pensacola, avoided the thrust. The ram received the ship's starboard broadside and then continued down, running the gauntlet of the Union fleet, whose shot penetrated her sides as though they were pasteboard.

The Mississippi, following the Pensacola and disdaining to pass behind her guns, was reduced to a very low rate of speed. As she came up with and engaged Fort St. Philip, the Manassas charged at her, striking on the port side a little forward of the mizzen-mast, at the same time firing her one gun. The effect on the ship at the time was to list her about one degree and cause a jar like that of taking the ground, but the blow, glancing, only gave a wound seven feet long and four inches deep, cutting off the heads of fifty copper bolts as clean as though done in a machine. Soon after, moving slowly along the face of the fort, the current of the river caught the Mississippi on her starboard bow and carried her over to the Fort Jackson side.

The Oneida, having shifted her port guns to the starboard side, followed the Mississippi. She shared in the delay caused by the Pensacola's deliberate passage until the Mississippi's sheer gave her the chance to move ahead. She then steamed quickly up, hugging the east bank, where the eddy current favored her advance. As she passed close under the muzzles of St. Philip's guns she fired rapidly canister and shrapnel, the fire from the fort passing for the most part harmlessly over the ship and the heads of her crew.

The two rear gunboats, the Kineo and Wissahickon, were both delayed in passing; the Kineo by a collision with the Brooklyn, the two vessels meeting between the hulks, and the Wissahickon by fouling the obstructions. The difficulty of finding the breach was already felt, and became more and more puzzling as the vessels were nearer the rear. The Wissahickon was one of the last that succeeded in getting through.

The port column was under way in time to follow close in the wake of its predecessor; indeed, it seems certain that, in impatience to be off, or from some other reason, the leading ships of this division doubled on the rear ships of the van. By the report of the captain of the Hartford, which led, that ship was engaged only twenty minutes after the enemy opened on the leading vessels of the starboard column. She steered in near to Jackson, but a fire raft coming down on her caused her to sheer across the river, where she took the ground close under St. Philip; the raft lying on her port quarter, against which it was pushed by the tug Mosher,[1] a

[1] As this feat has been usually ascribed to the Manassas, it may be well to say that the statement in the text rests on the testimony of the commander of the ram, as well as other evidence.

small affair of thirty-five tons, unarmed, with a crew of half a dozen men commanded by a man named Sherman. On that eventful night, when so many hundreds of brave men, each busy in his own sphere, were plying their work of death, surely no one deed of more desperate courage was done than that of this little band. The assault threatened the very life of the big ship, and was made in the bright light of the fire under the muzzles of her guns. These were turned on the puny foe, which received a shot in her boilers and sunk. It is believed that the crew lost their lives, but the Hartford had caught fire and was ablaze, the flames darting up the rigging and bursting through the ports; but the discipline of her crew prevailed over the fury of the element, while they were still receiving and returning the blows of their human antagonists in both forts; then working herself clear, the Hartford passed from under their fire.

The Brooklyn and Richmond followed the Hartford, and behind them the gunboat division Sciota, Iroquois, Pinola, Kennebec, Itasca, and Winona, Fleet-Captain Bell having his divisional flag flying on board the Sciota. By this the enemy had better range, and at the same time the smoke of the battle was settling down upon the face of the river. The good fortune which carried through all the vessels of the leading column therefore failed the rear. The Brooklyn lost sight of her next ahead and, as she was passing through the hulks, using both broadsides as they would bear, came violently into collision with the Kineo, next to the last ship of the starboard column—another indication that the two columns were lapping. The gunboat heeled violently over and nearly drove ashore; but the two vessels then went clear, the Brooklyn fouling the booms of the eastern hulks, breaking through them but losing her way. This caused her to fall off broadside to the stream, in which position she received a heavy fire from St. Philip. Getting clear and her head once more up river, the Manassas, which had been lying unseen close to the east bank, came butting into the starboard gangway. The blow was delivered with slight momentum against the chain armor, and appeared at the time to have done little damage; but subsequent examination showed that the Brooklyn's side was stove in about six feet below the water-line, the prow having entered between the frames and crushed both inner and outer planking. A little more would have sunk her, and, as it was, a covering of heavy plank had to be bolted over the wound for a length of twenty-five feet before she was allowed to go outside. At the same time that the Manassas rammed she fired her single gun, the shot lodging in the sand bags protecting the steam-drum. Groping on by the flash of the guns and the light of the burning rafts, the Brooklyn, just clearing a thirteen-foot shoal, found herself close under St. Philip, from whose exposed barbette guns the gunners fled at her withering fire, as they had from that of the Pensacola.

The Richmond, a slow ship at all times, was detained by her boilers foaming, and was much separated from her leaders. Still she engaged Fort Jackson and passed through the fire with small loss. The little Sciota followed with equal good fortune, having but two men wounded.

The Pinola, which had taken her place next to the Iroquois, was not so fortunate. She engaged first Fort Jackson, from whose fire she received little injury. Then she passed over to the other side within one hundred and fifty yards of St. Philip, from which she at first escaped with equal impunity; but coming then within the light of the fire-rafts, and the greater part of the squadron having passed, the enemy were able to play upon her with little to mar their aim. She was struck fourteen times, and lost three killed and eight wounded, the heaviest list of casualties among the gunboats.

The Iroquois, which was on picket duty, fell into her station behind the Sciota as the fleet went by. After passing through the obstructions, and when already some distance up the stream, as the current round the bend was throwing her bow off and setting her over on the east bank, the order "starboard" was given to the wheel. As too often happens, this was understood as "stop her," and the engines were stopped while the wheel was not moved. In consequence of this mistake the Iroquois, then a very fast ship, shot over to the east (at this point more precisely the north) bank, past the guns of St. Philip, and brought up against the ironclad steamer Louisiana that was lying against the levee a short distance above the fort. This powerful, though immovable, vessel at once opened her ports and gave the Iroquois every gun that would bear, and at the same time a number of her people ran on deck as though to repel what seemed to be an attempt to board. This gave the Iroquois an opportunity of returning the murderous fire she had received, which she did with effect. Some of the guns of the Louisiana had been double-shotted, the second shot being in two cases found sticking in the hole made by the first. This unfortunate collision made the loss of the Iroquois amount to 8 killed and 24 wounded, in proportion to her complement the heaviest of the whole fleet. It was as she slowly drew away that Commander Porter noted her as "lingering," standing out in full relief against the light of the burning rafts; then she went her way, the last to pass, and the fight was won.

The three gunboats at the rear of the second column failed to get by. The Itasca, on coming abreast of Fort Jackson, was pierced by several shot, one of them entering the boiler. The steam issuing in a dense cloud drove every one up from below, and the vessel deprived of her motive power, drifted helplessly down the stream. The Winona following her, fouled the obstructions, and before she could get clear the Itasca backed on board of her. After a half hour's delay she proceeded under a heavy fire, at first from Jackson. Thinking the burning raft, in whose light the Pinola suffered, to be on that side of the river, she tried to pass on the St. Philip side, receiving the fire of the latter fort at less than point-blank range. Shooting over to the other side again, so thick was the smoke that the ship got close to shore, and her head had to be turned down stream to avoid running on it. By this time day had broken, and the Winona, standing out against the morning sky, under the fire of both forts, and with no other vessel to distract their attention, was forced to retire. The Kennebec also fouled the rafts and was unable to get by before the day dawned.

The steamers of the mortar flotilla, and the sailing sloop Portsmouth, as soon as the flag-ship had lifted her anchor, moved up into the station which had been assigned them to cover the passage of the fleet, about five hundred yards from Jackson, in position to enfilade the water battery commanding the approach to the fort. The vessels kept their place, firing shrapnel and shell, until the last of the fleet was seen to pass the forts. They then retired, the mortar-schooners at the same time ceasing from the shelling, which had been carried on throughout the engagement.

An hour and a quarter had elapsed from the time that the Cayuga passed the obstructions. The fleet, arriving above the forts, fell in with the Confederate flotilla, but in the absence of the Louisiana the other Confederate steamers were no match for their antagonists. The Cayuga indeed, dashing forward at a rate which left her but fifteen minutes under the fire of the forts, found herself when above them in hot quarters; and in a not unequal match rendered a good account of three assailants. The Varuna, passing with yet greater rapidity, steamed through with her guns trained as far ahead as they could be, and delivered her fire as opportunity offered. She soon passed beyond them, unsupported, and continued up the river, coming close upon a steamer called the Doubloon, in which were General Lovell and some of his staff, who narrowly escaped being captured. After the Varuna came the Governor Moore, which had been down among the Union fleet, receiving there the fire of the Oneida and Pinola. Finding the berth too hot for him, and catching sight of the Varuna thus separated from her fleet, Kennon hoisted the same lights as the latter vessel and followed on up. The lights deceived the Varuna and also the Confederate steamer Jackson, which had been up the river on duty and was at quarantine as the two others drew near. Taking them for enemies the Jackson opened a long-range fire on the two impartially, one of her shots wounding the fore-mast of the Moore; she then steamed hastily away to New Orleans, where she was destroyed by her commander. The only other vessel in sight was the Stonewall Jackson[1] of the River Defence Fleet, carrying one gun. She was behind the two, trying to escape unseen to New Orleans. Kennon now opened fire, hoping that the Jackson, undeceived, would turn back to help him, but she kept on her upward course; the Varuna, however, was no longer in ignorance. Finding that the height of the Moore's forecastle out of water and the position of the bow gun would not let it be depressed enough to fire with effect, Kennon resorted to the old-time heroic treatment for such defects; loading the gun with percussion shell he fired it through the bows of his own ship, and used the hole

[1] There were two Jacksons, the naval steamer Jackson and the River Defence boat Stonewall Jackson.

thus made for a port. The next shot raked the Varuna's deck, killing three and wounding nine of the crew. Boggs then put his helm hard aport, bringing his starboard battery to bear and doubtless expecting that the enemy would follow his motion to avoid being raked, but Kennon knew too well his own broadside weakness, and keeping straight on ran into the Varuna before her head could be gotten off again. The powerful battery of the Union vessel, sweeping from stem to stern, killed or wounded a large part of the enemy's crew; but her own fate was sealed, her frame being too light for such an encounter. The Moore having rammed again then hauled off, believing the Varuna to be in a sinking condition, and tried to continue up stream, but with difficulty, having lost her wheel-ropes. The Stonewall Jackson, now coming up, turned also upon the Varuna and rammed her on the port side, receiving a broadside in return. The Union vessel then shoved her bow into the east bank and sank to her top-gallant forecastle.

The Varuna's advance had been so rapid that there seems to have been some uncertainty in the minds of Captains Bailey and Lee of the Cayuga and Oneida as to where she was. It being yet dark they were very properly inclined to wait for the rest of the fleet to come up. In a few moments, however, the Oneida moved slowly ahead as far as quarantine, whence the Varuna and her enemies were made out. The Oneida then went ahead at full speed. When she came up the Varuna was already ashore, her two opponents trying to escape, but in vain. The Stonewall Jackson ran ashore without offering resistance, on the right bank nearly opposite the Varuna; the Moore on the left bank, some distance above, where her captain set her on fire, but received the broadsides of the Oneida and Pensacola with his colors still flying, and so was taken.

The Cayuga followed the Oneida, but more slowly, and about five miles above the fort came upon a Confederate camp upon the right bank of the river. She opened with canister, and in a few moments the troops, a part of the Chalmette regiment, surrendered.

After ramming the Brooklyn, the Manassas had quietly followed the Union fleet, but when she came near them the Mississippi turned upon her. It was impossible to oppose her three hundred and eighty-four tons to the big enemy coming down upon her, so her commander dodged the blow and ran her ashore, the crew escaping over the bows, while the Mississippi poured in two of her broadsides, leaving her a wreck. Soon after, she slipped off the bank and drifted down past the forts in flames. At 8 A.M. she passed the mortar-fleet and an effort was made to secure her, but before it could be done she faintly exploded and sank.

The Iroquois, steaming up through the mêlee, saw a Confederate gunboat lying close in to the east bank. Having slowed down as she drew near the enemy, some one on board the latter shouted, "Don't fire, we surrender." This was doubtless unauthorized, for as the ship passed on, the Confederate, which proved to be the McRae, discharged a broadside of grape-shot and langrage, part of the latter being copper slugs, which were found on the Iroquois's decks in quantities after the action. The fire was promptly returned with XI-inch canister and 32-pounder shot. The McRae's loss was very heavy, among the number being her commander, Thomas B. Huger, who was mortally wounded. This gentleman had been an officer of reputation in the United States Navy, his last service having been as first-lieutenant of the very ship with which he now came into collision. This was but a few months before, under the same commission, the present being, in fact, her first cruise; and the other officers and crew were, with few exceptions, the same as those previously under his orders. There is no other very particular mention of the McRae, but the Confederate army officers, who were not much pleased with their navy in general, spoke of her fighting gallantly among the Union ships.

As for the General Quitman and the River Defence Fleet, there seems to have been but one opinion among the Confederate officers, both army and navy, as to their bad behavior before and during the fight.[1] They did not escape punishment, for their enemies were among them before they could get away. The Oneida came upon one crossing from the right to the left bank, and rammed her; but it is not possible to recover the adventures and incidents that befell each. Certainly none of them rammed a Union vessel; and it seems not unfair to say that they gave way in disorder, like any other irregular force before a determined onslaught, made a feeble effort to get off, and then ran their boats ashore and fired them. They had but one chance, and that a desperate one, to bear down with reckless speed on the oncoming ships and ram them. Failing to do this, and beginning to falter, the ships came among them like dogs among a flock of sheep, willing enough to spare, had they understood the weakness of their foes, but thinking themselves to

[1] Colonel Lovell of the Confederate army, who was ordnance and disbursing officer of the River Defence Fleet, and had been twelve years an officer in the United States Navy, testified there was no organization, no discipline, and little or no drill of the crews. He offered to employ a naval officer to drill them, but it does not appear that the offer was accepted. He also testified that he had examined the Ellet ram, Queen of the West, and considered most of the River Defence boats better fitted for their work. The night before the fight, one of them, with Grant, captain of the Quitman, went on board the Manassas, and there told Warley that they were under nobody's orders but those of the Secretary of War, and they were there to show naval officers how to fight. There is plenty of evidence to the same effect. It was impossible to do anything with them.

be in conflict with formidable iron-clad rams, an impression the Confederates had carefully fostered.

When the day broke, nine of the enemy's vessels were to be seen destroyed. The Louisiana remained in her berth, while the McRae, and the Defiance of the River Defence Squadron, had taken refuge under the guns of the forts. The two first had lost their commanders by the fire of the fleet. During the three days that followed, their presence was a cause of anxiety to Commander Porter, who was ignorant of the Louisiana's disabled condition.

The Union fleet anchored for the day at quarantine, five miles above the forts. The following morning, leaving the Kineo and Wissahickon to protect, if necessary, the landing of General Butler's troops, they got under way again in the original order of two columns, not, however, very strictly observed, and went on up the river.

As they advanced, burning ships and steamers were passed, evidences of the panic which had seized the city, whose confidence had been undisturbed up to the moment of the successful passage of the forts. Four miles below New Orleans, the Chalmette and McGehee batteries were encountered, mounting five and nine guns. The Cayuga, still leading and steaming too rapidly ahead, underwent their fire for some time unsupported by her consorts, the Hartford approaching at full speed under a raking fire, to which she could only reply with two bow guns. When her broadside came to bear, she slowed down, porting her helm ; then having fired, before she could reload, the Brooklyn, compelled to pass or run into her, sheered inside, between her and the works. The successive broadsides of these two heavy ships drove the enemy from their guns. At about the same moment the Pensacola engaged the batteries on the east bank, and the other vessels coming up in rapid succession, the works were quickly silenced.

The attack of the fleet upon the forts and its successful passage has been fitly called the battle of New Orleans, for the fate of the city was there decided. Enclosed between the swamps and the Mississippi, its only outlet by land was by a narrow neck, in parts not over three-quarters of a mile wide, running close by the river, which was at this time full to the tops of the levees, so that the guns of the fleet commanded both the narrow exit and the streets of the city. Even had there been the means of defence, there was not food for more than a few days.

At noon of the 25th, the fleet anchored before the city, where everything was in confusion. Up and down the levee coal, cotton, steamboats, ships, were ablaze, and it was not without trouble that the fleet avoided sharing the calamity. Among the shipping thus destroyed was the Mississippi, an ironclad much more powerful than the Louisiana. She was nearing completion, and had been launched six days, when Farragut came before the city. His rapid movements and the neglect of those in charge to provide tow-boats stopped her from being taken to the Yazoo, where she might yet have been an ugly foe for the fleet. This and the fate of the Louisiana are striking instances of the value of promptness in war. Nor was this the only fruit snatched by Farragut's quickness. There is very strong reason to believe that the fall of New Orleans nipped the purpose of the French emperor, who had held out hopes of recognizing the Confederacy and even of declaring that he would not respect the blockade if the city held out.

Captain Bailey was sent ashore to demand the surrender, and that the United States flag should be hoisted upon the public buildings. The rage and mortification of the excitable Creoles was openly manifested by insult and abuse, and the service was not unattended with danger. The troops, however, being withdrawn by the military commander, the mayor, with some natural grandiloquence, announced his submission to the inevitable, and Captain Bailey hoisted the flag on the mint. The next day it was hauled down by a party of four citizens; in consequence of which act, the flag-officer, on the 29th, sent ashore a battalion of 250 marines, accompanied by a howitzer battery in charge of two mid-shipmen, the whole under command of the fleet-captain. By them the flags were rehoisted and the buildings guarded, until General Butler arrived on the evening of May 1st, when the city was turned over to his care.

Meanwhile Commander Porter remained in command below the forts. The morning after the passage of the fleet he sent a demand for their surrender, which was refused. Learning that the Louisiana and some other boats had escaped the general destruction, and not aware of their real condition, he began to take measures for the safety of his mortar-schooners. They were sent down the river to Pilot Town, with the Portsmouth as convoy, and with orders to fit for sea. Six were sent off at once to the rear of Fort Jackson, to blockade the bayous that ramify through that low land; while the Miami and Sachem were sent in the other direction, behind St. Philip, to assist the troops to land.

On the 27th, Porter, having received official information of the fall of the city, notified Colonel Higgins of the fact, and again demanded the surrender, offering favorable conditions. Meanwhile insubordination was rife in the garrison, which found itself hemmed in on all sides. At midnight of the 27th, the troops rose, seized the guard and posterns, reversed the field pieces commanding the gates, and began to spike the guns. Many of them left the fort with their arms; and the rest, except one company of planters, firmly refused to fight any longer. The men were largely foreigners, and with little interest in the Secession cause; but they also probably saw that continued resistance and hardship could not result in ultimate success. The water-way above and below being in the hands of the hostile navy, all communication was cut off by the nature of the country and the state of the river; there could therefore be but one issue to a prolonged contest. The crime of the men was heinous, but it only hastened the end. To avoid a humiliating disaster, General Duncan accepted the offered terms on the 28th. The officers were permitted to retain their side arms, and the troops composing the garrison to depart, on parole not to serve till exchanged. At 2.30 P.M. the forts were formally delivered to the navy, and the United States flag once more hoisted over them.

The Confederate naval officers were not parties to the capitulation, which was drawn up and signed on board Porter's flag-ship, the Harriet Lane. While the representatives were seated in her cabin, flags of truce flying from her masthead and from the forts, the Louisiana was fired by her commander and came drifting down the river in flames. Her guns discharged themselves as the heat reached their charges, and when she came abreast Fort St. Philip she blew up, killing a Confederate soldier and nearly killing Captain McIntosh, her former commander, who was lying there mortally wounded. This act caused great indignation at the time among the United States officers present. Commander Mitchell afterward gave explanations which were accepted as satisfactory by Mr. Welles, the Secretary of the Navy. He said that the Louisiana was secured to the opposite shore from the fleet, three-quarters of a mile above, and that an attempt had been made to drown the magazine. As proof of good faith he had sent a lieutenant to notify Porter of the probable failure of that attempt. It remains, however, a curious want of foresight in a naval man not to anticipate that the hempen fasts, which alone secured her, would be destroyed, and that the vessel thus cast loose would drift down with the stream. Conceding fully the mutual independence of army and navy, it is yet objectionable that while one is treating under flag of truce, the other should be sending down burning vessels, whether carelessly or maliciously, upon an unsuspecting enemy.

When taken possession of, Fort Jackson was found to have suffered greatly. The ground inside and out was plowed by the falling shell; the levee had been cut in many places, letting water into the fort; the casemates were shattered, guns dismounted and gun-carriages destroyed; all the buildings within the walls had been burned. Yet it was far from being reduced to an indefensible condition by six days' bombardment, could it have continued to receive supplies and reinforcements. The loss of the garrison had been 14 killed and 39 wounded.

The question of the efficacy of mortar-firing was raised in this as in other instances. Granting its inability to compel the surrender, it remains certain that Fort Jackson, though the stronger work, inflicted much less damage upon the passing fleet than did St. Philip. The direct testimony of Commander De Camp of the Iroquois, and an examination of the injuries received by the ships, when clearly specified, shows this. As both posts had been under one commander, it may be inferred that the difference in execution was due partly to the exhaustion of the garrison, and partly to the constant fire of the mortar flotilla during the time of the passage; both effects of the bombardment.

The exterior line of the defences of New Orleans being thus pierced in its central and strongest point, the remaining works —Forts Pike and Macomb guarding the approaches by way of

Lake Pontchartrain, Livingston at Barrataria Bay, Berwick at Berwick Bay, and others of less importance—constituting that line were hastily abandoned. Such guns as could be saved, with others from various quarters, were hurried away to Vicksburg, which had already been selected as the next point for defence, and its fortifications begun. The whole delta of the Mississippi was thus opened to the advance of the Union forces. This was followed a few days later by the evacuation of Pensacola, for which the enemy had been preparing since the end of February, when the disaster at Donelson had made it necessary to strip other points of troops. The heavy guns had been removed, though not to New Orleans. The defenceless condition of the place was partly known to the officer commanding at Fort Pickens, but no one could spare him force enough to test it. At the time of its final abandonment, Commander Porter, who after the surrender of the forts had proceeded to Mobile with the steamers of the mortar flotilla, was lying off that bar. Seeing a brilliant light in the direction of Pensacola at 2 A.M. on the 10th of May, he stood for the entrance, arriving at daylight. The army and navy took possession the same day, and this fine harbor was now again available as a naval station for the United States.

After New Orleans had been occupied by the army, Farragut sent seven vessels, under the command of Captain Craven of the Brooklyn, up the river. Baton Rouge and Natchez surrendered when summoned ; but at Vicksburg, on the 22d of May, Commander S. P. Lee was met with a refusal. On the 9th of June the gunboats Wissahickon and Itasca, being sent down to look after some earthworks which the Confederates were reported to be throwing up at Grand Gulf, found there a battery of rifle guns completed, and were pretty roughly handled in the encounter which followed. On the 18th of June the Brooklyn and Richmond anchored below

Vicksburg, and shortly after the flag-officer came in person with the Hartford, accompanied by Commander Porter with the steamers and seventeen schooners of the mortar flotilla. The flag-officer did not think it possible to reduce the place without a land force, but the orders of the Department were peremptory that the Mississippi should be cleared. From Vicksburg to Memphis the high land did not touch the river on the east bank, and Memphis with all above it had now fallen. Vicksburg at that time stood, the sole seriously defended point.

The condition of the fleet was at this time a cause of serious concern to the flag-officer. The hulls had been much injured by the enemy's fire, and by frequent collisions in the lower river, due to the rapid current and the alarms of fire-rafts. The engines, hastily built for the gunboats, and worn in other ships by a cruise now nearing its usual end, were in need of extensive repairs. The maintenance of the coal-supply for a large squadron, five hundred miles up a crooked river in a hostile country, was in itself no small anxiety; involving as it did carriage of the coal against the current, the provision of convoys to protect the supply vessels against guerillas, and the employment of pilots; few of whom were to be found, as they naturally favored the enemy, and had gone away. The river was drawing near the time of lowest water, and the flag-ship herself got aground under very critical circumstances, having had to take out her coal and shot, and had even begun on her guns, two of which were out when she floated off. The term of enlistment of many of the crews had ended and they were clamoring for their discharge, and the unhealthy climate had already caused much illness. It was evident from the very first that Vicksburg could only be taken and held by a land force, but the Government in Washington were urgent and Farragut determined to run by

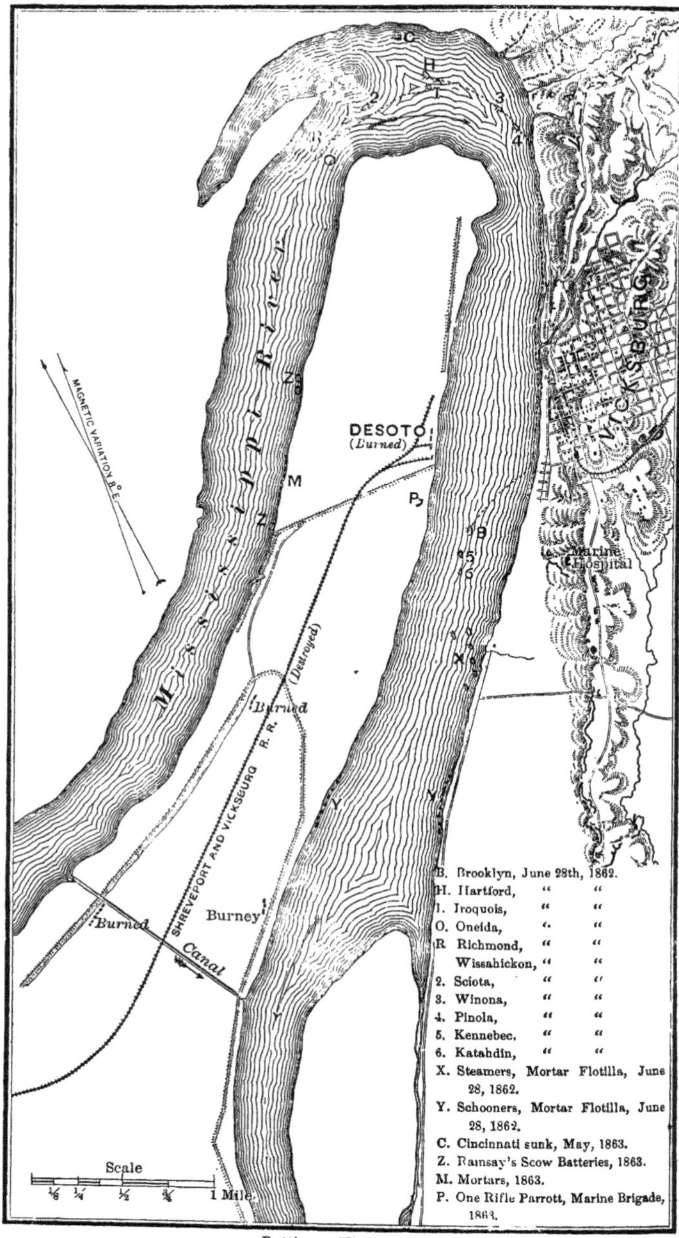
Mississippi River
VICKSBURG
DESOTO
(Burned)
Marine
Hospital
MAGNETIC VARIATION 8° E.
(Destroyed)
Burned
SHREVEPORT AND VICKSBURG R. R.
Burney
Burned
Canal
Scale
1/8 1/4 1/2 3/4 1 Mile.
B. Brooklyn, June 28th, 1862.
H. Hartford, " "
I. Iroquois, " "
O. Oneida, " "
R. Richmond, " "
Wissahickon, " "
2. Sciota, " "
3. Winona, " "
4. Pinola, " "
5. Kennebec, " "
6. Katahdin, " "
X. Steamers, Mortar Flotilla, June 28, 1862.
Y. Schooners, Mortar Flotilla, June 28, 1862.
C. Cincinnati sunk, May, 1863.
Z. Ramsay's Scow Batteries, 1863.
M. Mortars, 1863.
P. One Rifle Parrott, Marine Brigade, 1863.

Battle at Vicksburg.

the batteries. This was the first attempt; but there were afterward so many similar dashes over the same spot, by fleets or single vessels, that the scene demands a brief description.

Vicksburg is four hundred miles above New Orleans, four hundred below Memphis. The river, after pursuing its irregular course for the latter distance through the alluvial bottom lands, turns to the northeast five miles before reaching the Vicksburg bluffs. When it encounters them it sweeps abruptly round, continuing its course southwest, parallel to the first reach; leaving between the two a narrow tongue of low land, from three-quarters to one mile wide. The bluffs at their greatest elevation, just below the point where the river first touches them, are two hundred and sixty feet high; not perpendicular, but sloping down close to the water, their nearness to which continues, with diminishing elevation, for two miles, where the town of Vicksburg is reached. They then gradually recede, their height at the same time decreasing by degrees to one hundred and fifty feet.

The position was by nature the strongest on the river. The height of the banks, with the narrowness and peculiar winding of the stream, placed the batteries on the hill-sides above the reach of guns on shipboard. At the time of Farragut's first attack, though not nearly so strongly and regularly fortified as afterward, there were in position twenty six[1] guns, viz.: two X-inch, one IX-inch, four VIII-inch, five 42- and two 24-pounder smooth-bores, and seven 32-, two 24-, one 18-, and two 12-pounder rifled guns. Of these, one IX-inch, three VIII-inch, and the 18-pounder rifle were planted at the highest point of the bluffs above the town, in the bend, where they had a raking fire upon the ships before and after

[1] Quarterly Return of the ordnance officer of the post, June 30, 1862.

they passed their front. Just above these the four 24-pounders were placed.[1] Half a mile below the town was a water battery,[2] about fifty feet above the river, mounting two rifled 32s, and four 42s. The eleven other guns were placed along the crest of the hills below the town, scattered over a distance of a mile or more, so that it was hard for the ships to make out their exact position. The distance from end to end of the siege batteries was about three miles, and as the current was running at the rate of three knots, while the speed of the fleet was not over eight, three-quarters of an hour at least was needed for each ship to pass by the front of the works. The upper batteries followed them for at least twenty minutes longer. Besides the siege guns, field batteries in the town, and moving from place to place, took part in the action; and a heavy fire was kept up on the vessels from the rifle-pits near the turn.

On the 26th and 27th of June the schooners were placed in position, nine on the east and eight on the west bank. Bomb practice began on the 26th and was continued through the 27th. On the evening of the latter day Commander Porter notified the admiral that he was ready to cover the passage of the fleet.

At 2 A.M. of the 28th the signal was made, and at three the fleet was under way. The vessels advanced in two columns, the Richmond, Hartford, and Brooklyn in the order named, forming the starboard column, with intervals between them long enough to allow two gunboats to fire through. The port column was composed of the Iroquois, the leading ship, and the Oneida, ahead of the Richmond on her port

---

[1] The writer is inclined to think these were not ready on June 28th, but were the *new* battery mentioned in Union and Confederate reports of July 15th.

[2] This, known to the fleet as the hospital battery, was commanded by Captain Todd, a brother-in-law of President Lincoln.

bow, the Wissahickon and Sciota between the Richmond and the Hartford, the Winona and Pinola between the flag-ship and the Brooklyn, and in the rear, on the port quarter of the Brooklyn, the Kennebec and the Katahdin. At four o'clock the mortars opened fire, and at the same moment the enemy, the vessels of the fleet replying as their guns bore. As the Hartford passed, the steamers of the mortar flotilla, Octorara, Miami, Jackson, Westfield, Clifton, Harriet Lane, and Owasco, moved up on her starboard quarter, engaging under way the water battery, at a distance of twelve hundred to fifteen hundred yards, and maintaining this position till the fleet had passed. The leading vessels, as far as and including the Pinola, continued on, silencing the batteries when fairly exposed to their broadsides, but suffering more or less severely before and after. The prescribed order was not accurately observed, the lack of good pilots leading the ships to hug the bank on the town side, where the shore was known to be bold, and throwing them into line ahead; the distances also lengthened out somewhat, which lessened the mutual support.

The flag-ship moved slowly, and even stopped for a time to wait for the vessels in the rear; seeing which Captain Palmer, of the Iroquois, who had reached the turn, also stopped his ship, and let her drift down close to the Hartford to draw a part of the enemy's fire, and to reinforce that of the flag-officer. The upper batteries, like all the others, were silent while the ships lay in front of them; but as soon as the Hartford and Iroquois moved up they returned to their guns, and followed the rear of the fleet with a spiteful fire till out of range.

The cannonade of the enemy could at no time have been said to be discontinued along the line. The Brooklyn, with the two gunboats following, stopped when above the mortar-steamers, and engaged the batteries within range at a great disadvantage; those ahead having a more or less raking fire upon them. The three remained there for two hours and then retired, the remainder of the fleet having passed on beyond and anchored above, at 6 A.M.

Having thus obeyed his orders, the flag-officer reported that the forts had been passed and could be passed again as often as necessary, a pledge frequently redeemed afterward; but he added, "it will not be easy to do more than silence the batteries for a time." The feat had been performed with the steady gallantry that characterized all the similar attempts on the river. Notwithstanding the swift adverse current, the full power of the vessels was not exerted. The loss was 15 killed and 30 wounded, eight of the former being among the crew of the Clifton, which received a shot in her boiler, scalding all but one of the forward powder division. The Confederates reported that none of their guns had been injured, and they mention no casualties.

The action of the three commanders that failed to pass was severely censured by the flag-officer; nor is it surprising that he should have felt annoyed at finding his fleet separated, with the enemy's batteries between them. It seems clear, however, that the smoke was for a time so thick as to prevent the Brooklyn from seeing that the flag-ship had kept on, while the language of the flag-officer's written order governing the engagement was explicit. It read thus: "When the vessels reach the bend of the river, should the enemy continue the action, the ships and Iroquois and Oneida will stop their engines and drop down the river again, keeping up the fire until directed otherwise." In view of these facts, Captain Craven was certainly justified in maintaining his position until he saw that the flag-ship had passed; then it may be doubtful whether the flag-officer's action had not countermanded his orders. The question will be differently answered by different persons; probably the greater number of officers would reply that the next two hours, spent in a stationary position under the batteries, would have been better employed in running by and rejoining the fleet. The error of judgment, if it was one, was bitterly paid for in the mortification caused to a skilful and gallant officer by the censure of the most distinguished seaman of the war.

Above Vicksburg the flag-officer communicated with one of the rams under Lieutenant-Colonel Ellet, who undertook to forward his communications to Davis and Halleck. The ships were then anchored.

On the 1st of July Davis's fleet arrived. On the 9th an order was received from Washington for Commander Porter to proceed to Hampton Roads with twelve mortar-schooners. The next morning he sailed in the Octorara with the schooners in company. On the way down he not only had experience of the increasing difficulty of navigation from the falling of the water, but also his active mind ascertained the extent of the traffic by way of the Red River, and its worth to the Confederacy; as also the subsidiary value of the Atchafalaya Bayou, which, extending through the delta of the Mississippi from the Red River to the Gulf, was then an open highway for the introduction of foreign supplies, as well as the transport of native products. The object and scope of the next year's campaign are plainly indicated in a letter of his addressed to Farragut during his trip down the river. It was unfortunate that an attempt was not made to hold at once the bluffs below the point where those two highways meet, and blockade them both, instead of wasting time at Vicksburg when there was not then strength enough to hold on.

CHAPTER IV.

THE RECOIL FROM VICKSBURG.

THE position now occupied by the combined fleets of Farragut and Davis was from three to four miles below the mouth of the Yazoo River, near the neck of the long tongue of land opposite Vicksburg. The armed vessels were anchored on the east side, the transports tied up to the opposite bank. It was known that up the Yazoo was an ironclad ram, similar to one that had been building at Memphis when the capture of that city led to its destruction. The one now in the Yazoo, called the Arkansas, had been taken away barely in time to escape the same fate, and, being yet unfinished, had been towed to her present position. She was about 180 feet long by 30 feet beam, of from 800 to 1,000 tons burden, with a casemate resembling that of other river ironclads, excepting that the ends only were inclined, the sides being in continuation of the sides of the vessel. The deck carrying the guns was about six feet above water. The armor was of railroad iron dovetailed together, the rails running up and down on the inclined ends and horizontally along the sides. The iron thus arranged formed nearly a solid mass, about three inches thick, heavily backed with timber; and in the casemate between the ports there was a further backing of compressed cotton bales firmly braced. The cotton was covered within by a light sheathing of wood, as a guard against fire. Her battery of ten guns was disposed as follows: in the bow, two heavy VIII-inch columbiads; in the stern, two 6.4-inch rifles; and in broadside two 6.4-inch rifles, two 32-pounder smooth-bores and two IX-inch Dahlgren shell-guns. The hull proper was light and poorly built. She had twin screws, but the engines were too light, and were moreover badly constructed, and therefore continually breaking down. Owing to this defect, she sometimes went on shore, and the commanding officer could not feel sure of her obeying his will at any moment. Besides her battery she had a formidable ram under water. She was at this time commanded by Commander Isaac N. Brown, formerly of the United States Navy, and had a complement of trained officers.

Notwithstanding the reports of her power, but little apprehension had been felt in the Union fleet, but still a reconnoissance was ordered for the 15th of July. The vessels sent were the Carondelet, Commander Walke, the Tyler, Lieutenant-Commander Gwin, and the Queen of the West of the ram fleet; they carried with them a number of sharpshooters from the army.

The Yazoo having been entered early in the morning, the Arkansas was met unexpectedly about six miles from the mouth. At this time the ram and the Tyler were over a mile ahead of the Carondelet, the Tyler leading. The latter, having no prow and being unarmored, was wholly unfit to contend with the approaching enemy; she therefore retreated down stream toward the Carondelet.

The latter also turned and began a running fight down stream. The move was not judicious, for she thus exposed her weakest part, the unarmored stern, to the fire of the enemy, and directed her own weakest battery, two 32-pounders, against him. Besides, when two vessels are approaching on parallel courses, the one that wishes to avoid the ram may perhaps do so by a movement of the helm, as the Pensacola avoided the Manassas at the forts; but when the slower ship, as the Carondelet was, has presented her stern to the enemy, she has thrown up the game, barring some fortunate accident. The aggregate weight of metal discharged by each ironclad from all its guns was nearly the same,[1] but the Arkansas had a decided advantage in penetrative power by her four 6.4-inch rifles. Her sides, and probably her bow, were decidedly stronger than those of her opponent; but whatever the relative advantages or disadvantages under other circumstances, the Carondelet had now to fight her fight with two 32-pounders opposed to two VIII-inch shell-guns, throwing shell of 53 pounds and solid shot of 64, and with her unarmored stern opposed to the armored bow of the ram. The Tyler took and kept her place on the port bow of the Carondelet; as for the Queen of the West, she had fled out of sight. "We had an exceedingly good thing," wrote one of the Arkansas' officers; and for a long time, Walke's report says one hour, they kept it. During that time, however, a shot entered the pilot-house, injuring Commander Brown, mortally wounding one pilot and disabling another. The loss of the latter, who was pilot for the Yazoo, was seriously felt as the Arkansas came up and the order was given to ram; for the Carondelet was hugging the left bank, and as the

[1] The Carondelet, by returns made to the Navy Department in the following month, August, had four VIII-inch guns, six 32-pounders, and three rifles—one 30, one 50, and one 70-pound. Assuming her rifles to have been in the bows, the weight and distribution of battery would have been—

	Carondelet.	Arkansas.
Bow	150	106
Broadside	170	165
Stern	64	120
	384	391

The Arkansas' battery, as given, depends upon independent and agreeing statements of two of her division officers. A third differs very slightly.

enemy was drawing thirteen feet, the water was dangerously shoal. She accordingly abandoned the attempt and sheered off, passing so close that, from the decks of the Tyler, the two seemed to touch. Both fired their broadsides in passing.

After this moment the accounts are not to be reconciled. Captain Walke, of the Carondelet, says that he continued the action broadside to broadside for some minutes, till the Arkansas drew ahead, and then followed her with his bow guns until, his wheel-ropes being cut, he ran into the bank, while the ram continued down the river with her colors shot away. The colors of the Carondelet, he says, waved undisturbed throughout the fight. On the other hand, Captain Brown, of the Arkansas, states explicitly that there were no colors flying on board the Carondelet, that all opposition to his fire had ceased, and was not resumed as the ram pursued the other vessels; the Arkansas' flag-staff was shot away. The loss of the Carondelet was 4 killed and 6 wounded; that of the Arkansas cannot well be separated from her casualties during the same day, but seems to have been confined to the pilot and one other man killed.

The ram now followed the Tyler, which had kept up her fire and remained within range, losing many of her people killed and wounded. The enemy was seen to be pumping a heavy stream of water both in the Yazoo and the Mississippi, and her smoke-stack had been so pierced by shot as to reduce her speed to a little over a knot an hour, at which rate, aided by a favoring current, she passed through the two fleets. Having no faith in her coming down, the vessels were found wholly unprepared to attack; only one, the ram General Bragg, had steam, and her commander unfortunately waited for orders to act in such an emergency. "Every man has one chance," Farragut is reported to have said; "he has had his and lost it." The chance was unique, for a successful thrust would have spared two admirals the necessity of admitting a disaster caused by over-security. The retreating Tyler was sighted first, and gave definite information of what the firing that had been heard meant, and the Arkansas soon followed. She fought her way boldly through, passing between the vessels of war and the transports, firing and receiving the fire of each as she went by, most of the projectiles bounding harmlessly from her sides; but two XI-inch shells came through, killing many and setting on fire the cotton backing. On the other hand, the Lancaster, of the ram fleet, which made a move toward her, got a shot in the mud-receiver which disabled her, scalding many of her people; two of them fatally. The whole affair with the fleets lasted but a few minutes, and the Arkansas, having passed out of range, found refuge under the Vicksburg batteries.

The two flag-officers were much mortified at the success of this daring act, due as it was to the unprepared state of the fleets; and Farragut instantly determined to follow her down and attempt to destroy her as he ran by. The execution of the plan was appointed for late in the afternoon, at which time Davis moved down his squadron and engaged the upper batteries as a diversion. Owing to difficulties in taking position, however, it was dark by the time the fleet reached the town, and the ram, anticipating the move, had shifted her berth as soon as the waning light enabled her to do so without being seen. She could not therefore be made out; which was the more unfortunate because, although only pierced twice in the morning, her plating on the exposed side had been much loosened by the battering she received. One XI-inch shot only found her as the fleet went by, and that killed and wounded several of her people. All Farragut's fleet, accompanied by the ram Sumter,[1] detached for this ser-

[1] Commanded by Lieutenant Henry Erben.

vice by Flag-Officer Davis, passed down in safety; the total loss in the action with the Arkansas and in the second passage of the batteries being but 5 killed and 16 wounded. None of this fleet ever returned above Vicksburg again.

The Upper Mississippi flotilla in the same encounter had 13 killed, 34 wounded, and 10 missing. The greater part of this loss fell on the Carondelet and the Tyler in the running fight; the former having 4 killed and 10 wounded, besides two who, when a shot of the enemy caused steam to escape, jumped overboard and were drowned. The Tyler lost 8 killed and 16 wounded. The commanding officer of the Arkansas reported his loss as 10 killed and 15 badly wounded.

The ram now lay at the bend of the river between two forts. On the 22d of July, Flag-Officer Davis sent down to attack her the ironclad Essex, Commander W. D. Porter, with the ram Queen of the West, Lieutenant-Colonel Ellet. They started shortly after dawn, the Benton, Cincinnati, and Louisville covering them by an attack upon the upper batteries. As the Essex neared the Arkansas the bow fasts of the latter were slacked and the starboard screw turned, so that her head swung off, presenting her sharp stem and beak to the broad square bow of the assailant. The latter could not afford to take such an offer, and, being very clumsy, could not recover herself after being foiled in her first aim. She accordingly ran by, grazing the enemy's side, and was carried ashore astern of him, in which critical position she remained for ten minutes under a heavy fire; then, backing and swinging clear, she ran down the river under fire of all the batteries, but was not struck. When Porter saw that he would be unable to ram, he fired into the Arkansas' bows, at fifty yards distance, three solid IX-inch shot, one of which penetrated and raked her decks, killing 7 and wounding 6 of her small crew, which then numbered only 41; the rest having been taken away as she was not fit for immediate service. The Queen of the West rammed, doing some injury, but not of a vital kind. She then turned her head up stream and rejoined the upper fleet, receiving much damage from the batteries as she went back.

Two days later, Farragut's fleet and the troops on the point opposite Vicksburg, under the command of General Williams, went down the river; Farragut going to New Orleans and Williams to Baton Rouge. This move was made necessary by the falling of the river and the increasing sickliness of the climate. Porter, on his passage down a fortnight before, had expressed the opinion, from his experience, that if the heavy ships did not come down soon they would have to remain till next season. But the health of the men, who had now been three months up the river, was the most powerful cause for the change. On the 25th of July forty per cent. of the crews of the upper flotilla were on the sick list. The troops, who being ashore were more exposed, had but 800 fit for duty out of a total of 3,200. Two weeks before the Brooklyn had 68 down out of 300. These were almost all sick with climatic diseases, and the cases were increasing in number and intensity. The Confederates now having possession of the point opposite Vicksburg, Davis moved his fleet to the mouth of the Yazoo, and finally to Helena. The growing boldness of the enemy along the banks of the Mississippi made the river very unsafe, and supply and transport vessels, unless convoyed by an armed steamer, were often attacked. One had been sunk, and the enemy was reported to be establishing batteries along the shores. These could be easily silenced, but to keep them under required a number of gunboats, so that the communications were seriously threatened. The fleet was also very shorthanded, needing five hundred men to fill the existing vacancies. Under these circumstances Flag-Officer Davis decided to withdraw to Helena, between which point and Vicksburg there was no high land on which the enemy could permanently establish himself and give trouble. By these various movements the ironclad Essex and the ram Sumter, now permanently separated from the up-river fleet, remained charged with the care of the river below Vicksburg; their nearest support being the Katahdin and Kineo at Baton Rouge.

On the 5th of August the Confederates under the command of Breckenridge made an attack upon General Williams's forces at Baton Rouge. The Arkansas, with two small gunboats, had left Vicksburg on the 3d to co-operate with the movement. The Union naval force present consisted of the Essex, Sumter, Cayuga, Kineo, and Katahdin. The attack was in superior force, but was gallantly met, the Union forces gradually contracting their lines, while the gunboats Katahdin and Kineo opened fire as soon as General Williams signalled to them that they could do so without injuring their own troops. No Confederate gunboats came, and the attack was repelled; Williams, however, falling at the head of his men.

The Arkansas had been prevented from arriving in time by the failure of her machinery, which kept breaking down. After her last stop, when the order to go ahead was given, one engine obeyed while the other refused. This threw her head into the bank and her stern swung down stream. While in this position the Essex came in sight below. Powerless to move, resistance was useless; and her commander, Lieutenant Stevens, set her on fire as soon as the Essex opened, the crew escaping unhurt to the shore. Shortly afterward she blew up. Though destroyed by her own officers the act was due to the presence of the vessel that had gallantly attacked her under the guns of Vicksburg, and lain in wait for her ever since. Thus perished the most formidable Confederate iron-clad that had yet been equipped on the Mississippi.

By the withdrawal of the upper and lower squadrons, with the troops under General Williams, the Mississippi River, from Vicksburg to Port Hudson, was left in the undisputed control of the Confederates. The latter were not idle during the ensuing months, but by strengthening their works at the two ends of the line, endeavored to assure their control of this section of the river, thus separating the Union forces at either end, maintaining their communication with the Western States, and enjoying the resources of the rich country drained by the Red River, which empties into the Mississippi in this portion of its course. On the 16th of August, ten days after the gallant repulse of the Confederate attack, the garrison was withdrawn from Baton Rouge to New Orleans, thus abandoning the last of the bluffs above the city; the Confederates, however, did not attempt to occupy in force lower than Port Hudson. Above Vicksburg, Helena on the west side was in Union hands, and the lower division of the Mississippi flotilla patrolled the river; but Memphis continued to be the lowest point held on the east bank. The intercourse between the Confederates on the two sides, from Memphis to Vicksburg, though much impaired, could not be looked upon as broken up. Bands of guerillas infested the banks, firing upon unarmed vessels, compelling them to stop and then plundering them. There was cause for suspecting that in some cases the attack was only a pretext for stopping, and that the vessels had been despatched by parties in sympathy with the Confederates, intending that the freight should fall into their hands. Severe retaliatory measures upon guerilla warfare were instituted by the naval vessels.

Flag-Officer Davis and General Curtis also arranged that combined naval and military expeditions should scour the banks of the Mississippi from Helena to Vicksburg, until a healthier season permitted the resumption of more active hostilities. One such left Helena on the 14th of August, composed of the Benton, Mound City, and General Bragg, with the Ellett rams Monarch, Samson, and Lioness, and a land force under Colonel Woods. Lieutenant-Commander Phelps commanded the naval force. The expedition landed at several points, capturing a steamer with a quantity of ammunition and dispersing parties of the enemy, and proceeded as far as the Yazoo River. Entering this, they took a newly erected battery twenty miles from the mouth, bursting the guns and destroying the work. Going on thirty miles farther, the rams were sent twenty miles up the Big Sunflower, one of the principal tributaries of the Yazoo. The expedition returned after an absence of eleven days, having destroyed property to the amount of nearly half a million.

The lull during the autumn months was marked by similar activity on the Tennessee and Cumberland, for which a squadron of light vessels was specially prepared. During the same period the transfer of the flotilla from the army to the navy was made, taking effect on the 1st of October, 1862. From this time the flotilla was officially styled the Mississippi Squadron.

During the rest of the summer and the autumn months Admiral Farragut's attention was mainly devoted to the seaboard of his extensive command. The sickly season, the low stage of the river, and the condition of his squadron, with the impossibility of obtaining decisive results without the co-operation of the army, constrained him to this course. Leaving a small force before New Orleans, he himself went to Pensacola, while the other vessels of the squadron were dispersed on blockading duty. Pursuing the general policy of the Government, point after point was seized, and the blockade maintained by ships lying in the harbors themselves. On the 15th of October, Farragut reported that Galveston, Corpus Christi, and Sabine Pass, with the adjacent waters, were in possession of the fleet, without bloodshed and almost without firing a shot. Later on, December 4th, he wrote in a private letter that he now held the whole coast except Mobile ; but, as so often happens in life, the congratulation had scarcely passed his lips when a reverse followed.

On the 1st of January, 1863, a combined attack was made upon the land and naval forces in Galveston Bay by the Confederate army and some cottonclad steamers filled with sharpshooters, resulting in the capture of the garrison, the destruction of the Westfield by her own officers, and the surrender of the Harriet Lane after her captain and executive officer had been killed at their posts. The other vessels then abandoned the blockade. This affair, which caused great indignation in the admiral, was followed by the capture of the sailing vessels Morning Light and Velocity off Sabine Pass, also by cottonclad steamers which came out on a calm day. Both Sabine Pass and Galveston thenceforth remained in the enemy's hands. An expedition sent to attempt the recovery of the latter failed in its object and lost the Hatteras, an iron side-wheel steamer bought from the merchant service and carrying a light battery. She was sent at night to speak a strange sail, which proved to be the Confederate steamer Alabama, and was sunk in a few moments. The disproportion of force was too great to carry any discredit with this misfortune, but it, combined with the others and with yet greater disasters in other theatres of the war, gave a gloomy coloring to the opening of the year 1863, whose course in the Gulf and on the Mississippi was to see the great triumphs of the Union arms.

The military department of the Gulf had passed from General Butler to General Banks on the 17th of December, shortly before these events took place. It was by Banks that the troops were sent to Galveston, and under his orders Baton Rouge also was reoccupied at once. These movements were followed toward the middle of January by an expedition up the Bayou Teche, in which the gunboats Calhoun, Estrella, and Kinsman took part. The enterprise was successful in destroying the Confederate steamer Cotton, which was preparing for service ; but Lieutenant-Commander Buchanan, senior officer of the gunboats, was killed.

CHAPTER V.

THE MISSISSIPPI OPENED.

Flag-Officer Davis had been relieved in command of the Mississippi flotilla on the 15th of October, by Commander David D. Porter, holding the local rank of acting rear-admiral. The new commander was detained in Cairo for two months, organizing and equipping his squadron, which had been largely increased. A division of vessels was still stationed at Helena, patrolling the lower river, under the command of Captain Henry Walke.

During the fall of 1862 and the following winter, two new types of vessels were added to the squadron. The first, familiarly called tinclads, but officially light-draughts, were river stern-wheel steamers purchased for the service after the suggestion of Flag-Officer Davis, and covered all round to a height of eleven feet with iron from half to three-quarters of an inch thick, which made them proof against musketry. The protection around the boilers was increased to resist the light projectiles of field artillery. They quartered their crew comfortably, and could on a pinch, for an expedition, carry 200 men. The usual battery for these vessels was six or eight 24-pound brass howitzers, four on each side, with sometimes two light rifled guns in the bows. This armament was of little use against works of any strength, but with canister or shrapnel could keep off the riflemen, and meet on equal terms the field artillery brought against them on the banks of the narrow streams, often thickly timbered or covered with underbrush, into which they were called to penetrate and engage in that kind of warfare significantly called bushwhacking. For this service their light draught, not exceeding three feet when deep, and diminishing to eighteen or twenty inches when light, peculiarly fitted them ; but they were also useful in connection with the operations of the larger vessels, and some of them generally went along as a kind of light force fitted for raids and skirmishing.

The other vessels, which were not completed till later, were of an entirely different kind, being intended to supply a class of fighting ships of superior power, armor, and speed to those which had fought their way down to Vicksburg from Cairo. The fighting power of the Confederates had increased, and the successes of the Union arms, by diminishing the extent of their line to be defended, had enabled them to concentrate their men and guns. The defences of Vicksburg, both on the Mississippi and Yazoo, had become greatly stronger. The new armored vessels that were ready for some part of the coming operations were the Lafayette, Tuscumbia, Indianola, Choctaw, and Chillicothe. Of these the Tuscumbia, of 565 tons, the Indianola, of 442, and the Chillicothe, of 303, were specially built for the Government at Cincinnati. They were side-wheel, flat-bottomed boats, without keels ; the wheels being carried well aft, three-fourths of the entire length from the bow, and acting independently of each other to facilitate turning in close quarters. The Indianola and Tuscumbia had also two screw propellers. On the forward deck there was a rectangular casemate, twenty-two feet long in each vessel, but of differing widths, as the vessels were of different size. Thus that of the Tuscumbia was sixty-two feet wide, that of the Chillicothe only forty-two. The sides of the casemate sloped at an angle of thirty degrees from the perpendicular, and they, as well as the hull before the wheels, were plated with two- or three-inch iron, according to the locality; the heaviest plating being on the forward end of the casemate. In the Tuscumbia this forward plating was six inches thick. The casemates were pierced with ports for all their guns at the forward end only; on each beam one port, and two aft. The ports were closed with two three-inch iron shutters which slid back on tracks on either side. In these casemates the Tuscumbia carried three XI-inch guns, the Indianola and Chillicothe each two XI-inch. In the two larger vessels there was also, between the wheels, a stern casemate seventeen feet long, built of thick oak, not armored on the forward end, but having two-inch plating aft and one-inch on each side. In this stern casemate, pointing aft and capable of being trained four points (45°) on each quarter, the Tuscumbia carried two 100-pound rifles, and the Indianola two IX-inch guns. The hulls inside and abaft the wheels, and the decks, except inside the main casemate, were plated, but more lightly than the forward parts. In the Tuscumbia and Indianola, iron bulwarks, half an inch thick and pierced with loop-holes for musketry, extended all round the boats, except against the wheelhouses; they were so arranged as to let down on deck when desired. When ready for service, with guns and stores on board, these boats drew from five to seven feet of water; but they were so weakly built as to be dangerous and comparatively inefficient vessels, quickly "disabled," as is apt to be the case with such preparations for war as are postponed to the time of its outbreak. The contingency of civil war on our inland waters was not indeed to be anticipated nor prepared for; but what was the history of the ocean navy, on whose hasty creation such harmful boasts and confidence were and are based? They served their turn, for that enemy had no seamen, no navy, and few mechanics; but they were then swept from the list, rotten and broken down before their time. At this day nearly every ship that can carry the United States flag was built before the war or long after it.

The Lafayette and Choctaw, of one thousand tons each, were purchased by the Government and converted into ironclad gunboats with rams. Built deliberately, they were strong and serviceable vesssels, but not able to carry as much armor as had originally been intended. They were side-wheel steamers, the wheels acting independently, but had no screws. The Choctaw had a forward turret with inclined sides and curved top, armored with two inches of iron on twenty-four inches of oak, except on the after end and crown, where the iron was only one inch. Just forward of the wheels was a thwartship casemate containing two 24-pound howitzers pointing forward and intended to sweep the decks if boarders should get possession. Over this casemate was the pilot-house, conical, with two inches of iron on twenty-four of oak. From turret to wheelhouses the sides were inclined like casemates and covered with one-inch iron, as was the upper deck. Abaft the wheels there was another thwartship casemate, sides and ends also sloping, in which were two 30-pound Parrott rifles training from aft to four points on the quarter. It had been at first proposed to carry in the forward casemate two guns on a turn-table; but as this did not work, four stationary guns were placed, three IX-inch and one 100-pound rifle, two of which pointed ahead and one on each beam. The Lafayette had a sloping casemate carried across the deck forward, and as far aft as the wheels, covered in the lower part with one inch of iron over one inch of indiarubber; the upper part of the bulwarks had three-quarter-inch plating, and the deck half-inch. She carried two XI-inch bow guns, four IX-inch in broadside but well forward, two 24-pound brass howitzers, and two 100-pound stern guns. The draught of these two boats was about nine feet.

Besides these vessels may be mentioned the Black Hawk, a fine steamer, unarmored, but with a battery of mixed guns, which had been remodelled inside and fitted as a schoolship with accommodations for five hundred officers and men. She carried also syphon-pumps capable of raising any vessel that might sink. The old ram Sampson had been fitted as a floating smithery. The two accompanied the fleet, the former taking her place often in battle and serving as a swift flag-ship on occasions.

Active operations again began toward the end of November, when the rivers were rising from the autumnal rains. The great object of the combined Union forces was the reduction of Vicksburg, upon which the authorities at Washington preferred to move by way of the river, as it gave, under the convoy of the navy, an easy line of communication not liable to serious interruptions. The Confederate line of which Vicksburg was the centre then faced the river, the right resting on Haines's Bluff, a strongly fortified position twelve miles away, near to and commanding the Yazoo; while the left was on the Mississippi at Grand Gulf, sixty miles below Vicksburg by the stream, though not over thirty by land. The place, in the end, was reduced much in the same way as Island No. 10; the troops landing above it on the opposite bank, and marching down to a point below the works. The naval vessels then ran by the batteries and protected the crossing of the army to the east bank. A short, sharp campaign in the rear of the city shut the Confederates up in their works, and the Union troops were able to again secure their communications with the river above the town. There were, however, grave risks in this proceeding from the time that the army abandoned its water-base, adding to

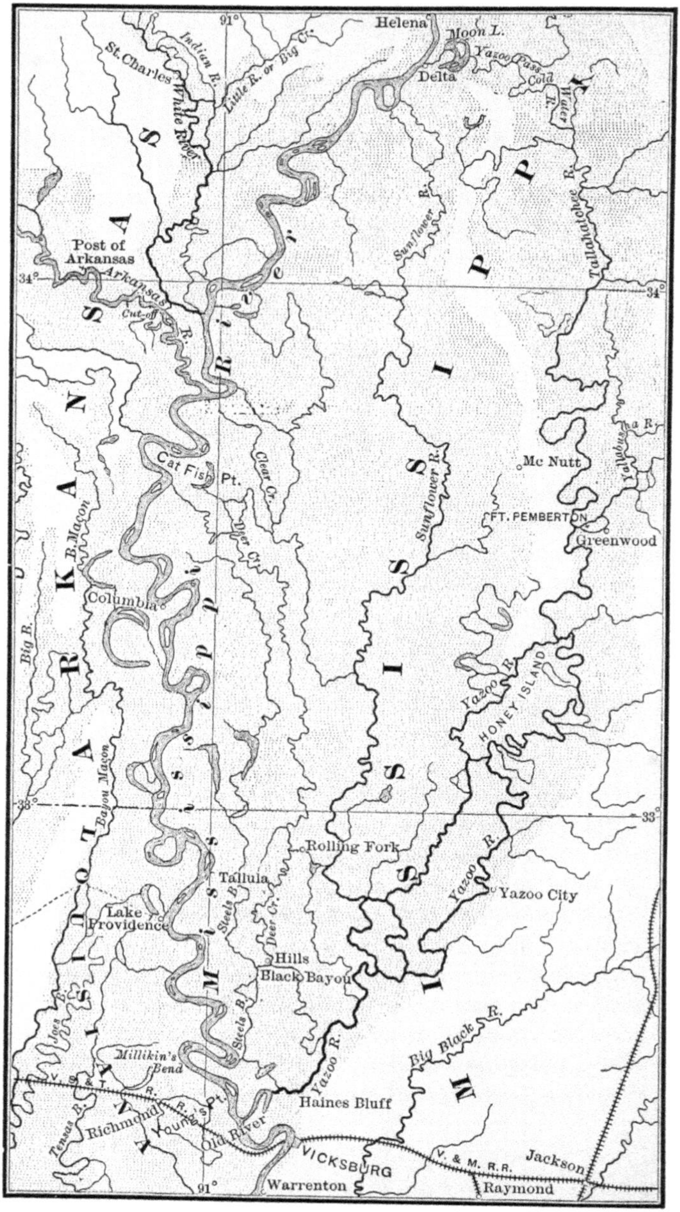

MISSISSIPPI VALLEY—HELENA TO VICKSBURG.

its line of communication thirty miles of bad roads on the river bank, and then throwing itself into the enemy's country, leaving the river behind it. It was therefore preferred first to make every effort to turn the position from the north, through the Yazoo country.

The Yazoo Valley is a district of oval form, two hundred miles long by sixty wide, extending from a short distance below Memphis to Vicksburg, where the hills which form its eastern boundary again reach the Mississippi. The land is alluvial and, when not protected by levees, subject to overflow in ordinary rises of the river, with the exception of a long narrow strip fifteen miles from and parallel to the eastern border. It is intersected by numerous bayous and receives many streams from the hills, all of which, from the conformation of the ground, find their way first to the Yazoo River, and by it to the Mississippi. The Yazoo is first called, in the northern portion of the basin, the Cold Water, then the Tallahatchie, and, after receiving the Yallabusha from the east, the Yazoo. In the latter part of its course it is a large stream with an average width of three hundred yards, and navigable always, for vessels drawing three feet of water, as far as Greenwood, a distance of two hundred and forty miles. It flows in a southerly direction along the eastern side of the basin, between the hills and the narrow strip of dry land before mentioned, receiving the streams from the former, which it does not touch except at Yazoo City, eighty miles from its mouth. After passing Yazoo City the river makes several successive bends to the west, and then begins to receive the various bayous which have been pursuing their own southerly course on the other side of the strip of dry land, the principal one of which is the Big Sunflower. At the present day the Yazoo enters the Mississippi eight miles above Vicksburg, but formerly did so by another bed, now a blind lead known as the Old River, which diverges from the existing channel about six miles above its mouth.

Neither rivers nor bayous are the simple streams thus described. Separating at times into two or more branches which meet again lower down, having perhaps undergone further subdivisions in the meanwhile, connected one with the other by lateral bayous, they form a system of water-courses, acquaintance with which confers the same advantage as local knowledge of a wild and desolate country. Opposite Helena, in the natural state of the ground is a large bayou called Yazoo Pass, leading from the Mississippi to the Cold Water, by which access was formerly had to Yazoo City; but before the war it had been closed by the continuation of the levees across its mouth.

When not under cultivation, the land and the banks of the streams are covered with a thick growth of timber. Where the troops or gunboats penetrated, it was found that there was abundance of live stock, stores of cotton, and rich harvests of grain. The streams carried on their waters many steamers, the number of which had been increased by those that fled from New Orleans when the city fell; and at Yazoo City the Confederates had established a navy yard, where at least three powerful war vessels were being built for the river service.

The first step by the navy was undertaken early in December, when the autumn rains had caused the rivers to rise. Admiral Porter issued orders, dated November 21st, to Captain Walke to enter the Yazoo with all his gunboats, except the Benton and General Bragg left at Helena, and to destroy any batteries that he could. The object was to get possession of as much of the river as possible and keep it clear for General McClernand, who was to land and make the first attempt on Vicksburg by that way.

In accordance with his orders, Walke, on arriving off the mouth of the river, sent two light-draught gunboats, the Signal and Marmora, which made a reconnoissance twenty miles up, where they fell in with a number of torpedoes, one of which exploded near them. Having received their report, Captain Walke determined, as the river was rising, to send them up again with two of the heavy boats, the Cairo and Pittsburg, to cover them while they lifted the torpedoes. The ram Queen of the West also went with them.

These vessels left the main body at 8 A.M., December 12th. When the torpedoes were reached they began removing them, the two light-draughts in advance, the ram next, the two heavy boats bringing up the rear. While thus engaged the Marmora began firing musketry, and Lieutenant-Commander Selfridge, in the Cairo, pushed ahead to support her. It was found that she was firing at an object floating in the water, which turned out to be a torpedo that had already been exploded. The Marmora was then ordered to proceed slowly again, the Cairo following; but before the latter had gone her length two sharp explosions occurred in quick succession, one under the bow and one under the stern, the former so severe as to lift the guns from the deck. The ship was at once shoved into the bank, and hawsers run out to keep her from slipping off into deep water; but all was useless. She filled and sank in twelve minutes, going down in a depth of six fathoms, the tops of her chimneys alone remaining visible. The work of destroying the torpedoes was continued after the accident, in which no lives were lost. Thus, at the very beginning of operations, the flotilla was deprived of one of its best vessels, the first to go of the original seven.

The torpedoes by which the Cairo was sunk were merely demijohns filled with powder and ignited by a common friction primer rigidly secured inside. To the primer was fastened a wire passing through a water-tight cork of gutta percha and plaster of Paris. The first very primitive idea was to explode them by pulling from the shore, and it is possible that the first to go off near the light-draughts was thus fired. The matter was then taken in hand by a Confederate naval officer, who arranged them in pairs, anchored twenty feet apart, the wire leading from the primer of one to that of the other. Torpedoes had hardly yet come to be looked on as a respectable mode of warfare, especially by seamen, and the officer who laid these, and was looking on when the Cairo went down, describes himself as feeling much as a schoolboy might whose practical joke had taken a more serious shape than he expected.

The work of removing the torpedoes was continued by the boats under Lieutenant-Commander John G. Walker, of the Baron de Kalb, formerly the St. Louis. Two landing-places were at the same time secured. After the arrival of the admiral the work went on still more vigorously from the 23d to the 26th of December. A bend in the river was then reached, which brought the vessels under fire of the forts on Drumgoold's Bluff. Every step of the ground so far gained had been won under a constant fire of musketry, which the armored portion of the light-draught gunboats resisted, but their upper works were badly cut up. The batteries of the enemy being now only twelve hundred yards off, the flag-ship Benton took position to cover the lighter vessels, having to tie up to the bank because the wind blowing up stream checked the current and threw her across it. She remained in this position for two hours, receiving the enemy's fire and being struck thirty times, but without serious injury. Unfortunately her captain, Lieutenant-Commander William Gwin, a valuable officer, who had distinguished himself at

Shiloh and in the fight with the Arkansas, was mortally wounded; having, in his anxiety to see how effective was the fire of the vessels, left the armored pilot-house, saying, with a noble rashness, that the captain's place was on his quarter-deck.

The army, 32,000 strong, under General W. T. Sherman, had arrived on the 26th, and landed on the low ground above the old mouth of the Yazoo, the gunboats occupying the sweep of river around them for a length of eight miles. Heavy rains had set in, making the ground almost impassable and causing the water to rise. After various preliminary operations the troops assaulted the works on the hills in front on the 29th, but the attack failed entirely. Sherman considered the works too strong to justify its renewal at the same point, but determined to hold his ground and make a night assault with 10,000 men higher up the river, upon the right of the Confederate works at Haines's Bluff, where the navy could get near enough to try and silence the batteries. Colonel Charles Rivers Ellet,[1] of the ram fleet, volunteered to go ahead with the ram Lioness and attempt to blow up a raft which was laid across the stream. Everything was ready on the night of the 31st, but a dense fog setting in prevented the movement.

The continued rains now rendered the position of the army dangerous, and it was re-embarked on the 2d of January. The enemy apparently did not discover the movement till it was nearly finished, when they sent down three regiments with field pieces to attack the transports, a movement quickly checked by the fire of the gunboats.

When Sherman's army was embarked, the transports moved out into the Mississippi and anchored five miles

[1] A son of Colonel Charles Ellet, Jr., the first commander of the ram fleet.

above Vicksburg, where General McClernand joined and assumed the chief command. Soon after his arrival he determined upon a movement against Fort Hindman, on the Arkansas River, fifty miles from its mouth. This point, better known as Arkansas Post, commanded the approach to Little Rock, the capital of Arkansas, but was specially obnoxious to the Union forces at this time, as being the base from which frequent small expeditions were sent out to embarrass their communications by the line of the Mississippi, from which it was but fifteen miles distant in a straight line. A few days before, the capture of the Blue Wing, a transport loaded with valuable stores, had emphasized the necessity of destroying a work that occupied such a menacing position upon the flank and rear of the projected movement against Vicksburg.

The admiral detailed the three ironclads, De Kalb, Louisville, and Cincinnati, and all the light-draught gunboats to accompany the expedition; the gunboats, on account of their low speed, being taken in tow by the transports. Passing by the mouth of the Arkansas, to keep the enemy as long as possible uncertain as to the real object of the movement, the fleet entered the White River and from the latter passed through the cut-off which unites it with the Arkansas.

On the 9th of January the army landed about four miles below the fort. This was a square bastioned work of three hundred feet on the side, standing on ground elevated above the reach of floods on the left bank, at the head of a horseshoe bend. It had three casemates, one in the curtain facing the approach up the bend, and one in the face of the northeast and southeast bastions looking in the same direction. In each bastion casemate was a IX-inch, and in that of the curtain an VIII-inch shell-gun. These were the special antagonists of the navy, but besides them there were four rifled and four smooth-bore light pieces on the platform of the fort, and six similar pieces in a line of rifle-pits exterior to and above it. Some trenches had been dug a mile and a half below the fort, but they were untenable in presence of the gunboats, which enfiladed and shelled them out.

While the army was moving round to the rear of the fort the admiral sent up the ironclads to try the range, and afterward the light-draught Rattler to clear out the rifle-pits, which was done at 5.30 P.M. Hearing from General McClernand that the troops were ready, the Louisville, Lieutenant-Commander Owen; De Kalb, Lieutenant-Commander Walker, and Cincinnati, Lieutenant Bache, advanced to within four hundred yards of the work and opened fire; the Louisville in the centre, the De Kalb on the right and the Cincinnati on the left, each having one of the enemy's casemate guns assigned to it. The vessels fought bows on, three guns each; the odds being thus three guns afloat to one in casemate on shore, leaving the advantage by the old calculation, four to one, rather with the fort, without counting the light pieces in the latter. When the ironclads were hotly engaged the admiral brought up the light-draught vessels, with the Black Hawk and Lexington, to throw in shrapnel and light rifled shell. Later, when the battery was pretty well silenced, the Rattler, Lieutenant-Commander Watson Smith, was ordered to pass the fort and enfilade it, which he did in handsome style, suffering a good deal from the enemy's fire; when above, however, he became entangled in snags and was obliged to return. No assault was made this day by the army.

The following day, at 1.30 P.M., the army again being reported ready, the attack was renewed in the same order by the navy, the artillery on shore in rear of the fort opening at the same time. The guns opposed to the fleet were silenced by 4 P.M., when the Rattler and Glide, with the ram Monarch, Colonel Ellet, pushed by the fort and went up the river, destroying a ferry ten miles above, so that not over thirty or forty of the enemy escaped by it. At 4.30 P.M., when the army had worked its way close to the intrenchments and orders had been issued for a general assault, but before it could be made, white flags were displayed on the face of the works. The commanding officer of the fort, Colonel Dunnington, formerly an officer in the United States Navy, surrendered to Admiral Porter; General Churchill, commanding the troops, to General McClernand. The total number of Confederate troops taken was 5,000.

It was impossible that the work of the navy could be done more thoroughly than in this instance. Every gun opposed to it was either destroyed or dismounted, and the casemates were knocked to pieces, the fire of the X-inch guns of the De Kalb being in the opinion of the enemy most injurious. In performing this service the vessels did not come off scatheless. The De Kalb had one 32-pounder gun dismounted and one X-inch destroyed, besides undergoing severe damage to the hull. The other vessels were repeatedly struck, but none were rendered unfit for immediate service. The armor was found to protect them well, the injuries to the crew being by shot entering the ports. The casualties, confined to the Louisville and De Kalb, were 6 killed and 25 wounded.

The next morning, January 12th, the admiral despatched the De Kalb and Cincinnati, under Lieutenant-Commander Walker, to the White River; transports and troops, under General Gorman, accompanying. St. Charles was reached at 11 A.M. of the 14th, and found to be evacuated; the garrison having left on the evening of the 12th, in the Blue Wing, taking with them two VIII-inch guns and a field battery.

Leaving the Cincinnati here, the De Kalb with the troops pushed on to Duvall's Bluff, fifty miles further up, where is the crossing of the railroad to Little Rock, on the Arkansas River. The transports were left four miles below, while the De Kalb steamed up to the bluff, arriving there at 3 P.M. of the 16th. She was close on the heels of the Blue Wing, which got away fifteen minutes before her arrival, but the two VIII-inch guns were seized in the act of being loaded on the cars for Little Rock. At this point of his progress, the orders issued by General Grant for the return of McClernand's forces to before Vicksburg were received. The dépôt buildings and captured rolling stock having been destroyed, the gunboats and transports rejoined the main body in the Mississippi.

The naval vessels, on the 24th of January, lay off the mouth of the Yazoo, and from there to the neck of land opposite Vicksburg, where the army under Grant's orders was disembarking. A few days before Porter had been obliged to withdraw the gunboats, because the coal supply of the fleet was exhausted. During their absence eleven Confederate transports that had been employed on the river between Vicksburg and Port Hudson went up the Yazoo for supplies, and were there caught by the unexpected return of the squadron, a serious embarrassment to the enemy.

At this time the vessels of the squadron near Vicksburg, or within easy reach, were: The Benton, Cincinnati, De Kalb, Louisville, Mound City, Pittsburg, and Chillicothe, ironclads; Rattler, Glide, Linden, Signal, Romeo, Juliet, Forest Rose, Marmora, light-draughts; the Tyler and Black Hawk, wooden armed steamers; Queen of the West, Monarch, Switzerland, Lioness, rams. During the following month the Carondelet and Indianola, ironclads, joined the fleet. The heavy vessels remained near the army and the principal scene of operations, but some of these lighter vessels and rams, with others farther up, were scattered at intervals along the river from Island No. 10 downward, cruising up and down, keeping off guerillas, preventing contraband traffic, and convoying transports and supply boats; in a word, keeping open the communications of the army. A small squadron of five light-draughts performed the same service constantly in the Tennessee and Cumberland Rivers.

General Grant arrived on the 30th of January. The army were busy digging on the canal across the neck, which had been begun the previous summer, and the various plans as yet discussed had mainly reference to turning the right flank of the Confederates. Meantime there was no hindrance to the complete control of the river between Vicksburg and Port Hudson by the enemy, who continued their traffic across it and by the Red River unmolested.

Porter, therefore, determined to send some vessels below. The batteries were much stronger than when Farragut had last passed, but the importance of the step justified the risk. Once below, the possession of the west bank by the Union troops gave a safe base to which to retreat. The honor of leading in such an enterprise was given to Colonel Charles R. Ellet, of the ram fleet, a man of tried daring. Many considerations pointed to the rams being the fittest to make such an attempt. They had greater speed, were well able to cope with any vessel they were likely to meet, their greater height gave them more command of the levees, and they were not needed to fight batteries, which the heavier boats might be. The Queen of the West was chosen and prepared with two thicknesses of cotton bales. Her commander received minute orders as to his undertaking, and was directed to proceed by night, under low speed until near the town, or discovered, to ram a steamer called the Vicksburg lying at the wharf, at the same time firing turpentine balls into her, and then to pass on down under the guns of the army. She started on what was to prove a chequered career at 4.30 A.M. of the 2d of February. Unfortunately it was found that a recent change in the arrangement of her wheel kept her from being steered as nicely as was needful, and the delay to remedy this defect brought daylight upon her as she rounded the point. A heavy fire opened at once, but still she went straight on, receiving three shots before she reached the Vicksburg. Rounding to partly, she succeeded in ramming, and at the same time firing the enemy with her turpentine balls. Just then two shells from the Confederate batteries passed through her cotton armor, one of them setting it on fire near the starboard wheel, while the discharge of her own bow guns produced the same effect forward. The flames spread rapidly, and the dense smoke was suffocating the men in the engine-room. Seeing that, if he delayed longer in order to ram again, he would probably lose his vessel, Ellet turned her head down stream and arrived safely abreast the army below. The fire was subdued by cutting her burning bales adrift and throwing them overboard.

In this gallant affair the Queen of the West was struck twelve times by heavy shot, besides undergoing a steady fire from the Confederate sharpshooters. One of her guns was dismounted, but the other harm was trifling, and none of her company were hurt. The Vicksburg was badly injured.

The ram was at once sent down the river, starting at 1 P.M. of the same day. At Warrenton, just below Vicksburg, she encountered two batteries, which fired upon without hurting her. The following day, when fifteen miles below the mouth of the Red River, she captured two Confederate steamers, one of which was loaded down with provisions for the army;

and when returning up stream, a third, similarly loaded, was taken coming out of the Red River. The coal supply running short, it became necessary to burn them. A quantity of meal on a wharf, awaiting transportation, was also destroyed, and seven Confederate officers captured. The Queen returned from this raid on the 5th.

On the night of the 7th a barge, with coal enough to last nearly a month, was set adrift from the fleet above and floated safely by the batteries to the ram. Having filled up, she took the barge in tow and again went down the river on the 10th, accompanied by the De Soto, a small ferryboat which the army had seized below and turned over to the navy; she was partly protected with iron and cotton. At 10.15 P.M. of the 12th the admiral sent down the ironclad steamer Indianola, Lieutenant-Commander George Brown. Taking with her two coal barges, she proceeded slowly and quietly, and was not discovered till she had passed the uppér batteries. When the first gun was fired, she started ahead full speed, and, though under fire for twenty minutes longer, was not struck. With justifiable elation the admiral could now write: "This gives us complete control of the Mississippi, except at Vicksburg and Port Hudson. We have now below two XI-inch guns, two IX-inch, two 30-pounder rifles, six 12-pounders, and three vessels." Yet, with the same mockery of human foresight that followed Farragut's satisfaction when he felt he controlled the whole Gulf coast, on the same day that these lines were penned two of the three passed out of Union hands, and the third had but a few days' career before her.

The Queen of the West went down the Mississippi, destroying skiffs and flatboats whenever found, as far as the Red River, which was reached on the morning of the 12th. Going up the Red River to the point where the Atchafalaya

Bayou branches off on its way to the Gulf, the De Soto and barge were secured there, while the Queen went down the bayou destroying Confederate Government property. In performing this service one of her officers was wounded by a party of guerillas. Returning to the De Soto, the two started up Red River. On the morning of the 14th a transport, called the Era No. 5, was captured with two Confederate officers. Hearing that there were three large boats lying, with steam down, at Gordon's Landing, thirty miles higher up (about seventy-five miles from the mouth of the river), Colonel Ellet decided to attempt their capture. On rounding the bluff above which they were lying, the Queen was fired upon by a battery of four 32-pounders. Orders were immediately given to back down behind the bluff, but by some mishap she ran aground on the right side, in plain view of the battery, within easy range and powerless for offence. Here she received several shots, one of which, cutting the steam-pipe, stopped the engines, that had been backing vigorously. Nothing further in the way of escape was tried, and the commanding officer was deterred from setting fire to the ship by the impossibility of removing the wounded officer.

The Queen and the De Soto each had but one boat, and in the panic that followed the explosion a party took possession of the Queen's and made off with it to the De Soto, under the pretext of hurrying that vessel up to the assistance of her consort; so the remainder of the ship's company, including her commander, made their escape to the other steamer on cotton bales. The De Soto sent up her yawl, which took off one load, getting away just before the Confederates boarded their prize.

The De Soto now started on a hurried retreat down the river, but running into the bank she lost her rudder. Deprived of the power of directing her motions, she was allowed to drift with the stream, picking up, from time to time, a fugitive on a bale, and was rejoined by her yawl about ten miles lower down. Shortly after this the parties fell in with the prize of the morning, when the De Soto was burned and the hasty flight continued in the Era. The following morning the Mississippi was reached, and the day after, the 16th, they met the Indianola eight miles below Natchez.

The Queen of the West had thus passed practically unhurt into Confederate hands, the manner of her loss giving another instance of how lack of heed in going into action is apt to be followed by a precipitate withdrawal from it and unnecessary disaster. Colonel Ellet's only reason for not burning the Queen was that he could not remove one of her officers, who had been wounded the day before. If he had transferred him to the De Soto before going under the battery with the Queen, the fighting ship, this difficulty would not have existed. No one seems to have been hurt, by the Union and Confederate reports, and it is hard to avoid the conclusion that Ellet's rashness in exposing his vessel, though he knew the Indianola was to be sent down, was not atoned for by sticking to her until he had destroyed her. The accidents were of a kind most likely to happen, and very simple appliances that might have been all ready would have ensured her burning. It is to be remembered, however, that Colonel Ellet was at this time not twenty years old.

On receiving the news of the disaster, Lieutenant-Commander Brown decided to go down as far as the mouth of the Red River. The same day was met off Ellis's Cliff the Confederate gunboat Webb, which had been lying at Alexandria and had started in hot pursuit of the fugitives from the Queen of the West. Upon making out the Indianola, which she had not expected, the Webb at once turned, and having greater speed easily escaped; the Indianola following down to the mouth of the Red River. Here she anchored and remained three days, while the Era, on the 18th, returned to the neck below Vicksburg.

Brown now learned that the Queen of the West had not been so much injured as her late commander had thought, and that a combined attack would probably be made by her and the Webb upon the Indianola. Two cottonclad boats were also in preparation by the Confederates for the same purpose. In view of these facts he determined to go up the Mississippi and get cotton, with which better to protect the Indianola against boarders by filling up the gangways between the casemates and the wheels. By the time this was done, having as yet met no other vessel of the squadron, though he had hoped for reinforcements when the loss of the Queen became known, he had reached the decision to return and communicate with the admiral.

With two barges alongside, the progress of the Indianola against the current was slow—too slow, for the swift rams of the enemy were already on her track; but although Brown had kept the bunkers of the Indianola full, he confidently expected to meet another boat which would need the coal, and was unwilling to sink it. The smoke of the pursuers had been seen throughout the day, and at 9.30 P.M. of the 24th four steamers were made out. These were the rams Queen and Webb, the former in charge of Captain McCloskey, the latter of Captain Pierce; Major J. L. Brent, of General Taylor's staff, having command of this part of the expedition, which was fitted out in Alexandria and accompanied by a tender called the Grand Era. These had been joined before leaving the Red River by the cottonclad steamer Batey from Port Hudson, carrying 250 riflemen under Lieutenant-Colonel Brand, whose rank entitled him to command the whole.

The enemy used the advantage of their greatly superior speed to choose the night for attacking, that the Indianola might not fire with the certainty of clear sight. They first saw her near Palmyra Island, a little above New Carthage, and were themselves made out at the same instant. The Indianola at once went to quarters and cleared for action, continuing up stream till her preparations were made; then she turned and stood down. The channel above Palmyra Island at that time hugged the eastern shore, crossing to the western just above the island, and the Indianola seems to have been in this place when the enemy coming up describes her as "with her head quartering across and down river," presenting the port bow to their approach. The order of advance was with the Queen leading, the Webb five hundred yards astern, and the two other boats lashed together some distance in the rear. The Queen dashed up, firing her light pieces to no purpose when one hundred and fifty yards off, and endeavored to ram the Indianola abaft the port wheel; but the latter, backing, received the blow on the barge, through which the enemy's sharp bow passed but without injuring her opponent. The barge went adrift and sunk. The Webb followed, and, the Indianola standing for her at full speed, the two came together bows on with a crash that knocked down most of their crews. The Webb's bow was cut in for a distance of eight feet, extending from two feet above the water-line to the keelson, but as she was filled in solid for more than eight feet she did not sink. The Indianola received no damage.

A third blow was delivered on the starboard side by the Webb, in what manner does not appear precisely, with the effect of crushing the other barge, leaving it hanging by the lashings, which were then cut adrift. The Webb passed up following the Queen. The latter, having gained sufficient distance, turned and charged down, but as the Indianola was turning up at the same moment the blow on the starboard bow glanced, the vessels rasping by each other; and as the Queen cleared the stern of her enemy, the latter planted two IX-inch shot successfully, killing 2 and wounding 4 of her crew and disabling two guns. During all this time the Indianola kept firing her guns whenever they could be made to bear, but, as the enemy had calculated, the darkness of the night prevented them from doing as much execution as they otherwise would. The rams also kept up a constant firing with their musketry and light guns. In the uncertain light it was very difficult to watch the two assailants through the peep-holes in the pilot-house of the gunboat, but yet a fifth blow was received forward of the wheels without injury. At last, however, the Queen was able to strike just abaft the starboard wheel-house, crushing the wheel, disabling the starboard rudder, and starting a number of leaks abaft the shaft. The starboard engine was thus useless and the Indianola helpless to avoid the onset of the Webb, which struck her fair in the stern, starting the timbers and starboard rudder-box so that the water poured in in large volumes. This settled the fight, and Brent reported to Colonel Brand that the enemy was disabled. The Batey then dashed up to board, but the Indianola, after delaying a few moments in mid river, till the water had risen nearly to the grate-bars, to assure her sinking, had run her bows into the west bank, and surrendered as soon as the cottonclads came alongside. The enemy, finding that she must sink and not willing that this should happen on the side where the Union army was, made fast at once two steamers and towed her down and over to the east bank, where she sank in ten feet of water near the plantation of the President of the Confederacy. The loss of the Indianola was 1 killed, 1 wounded, and 7 missing. The latter probably got ashore on the west bank, for 3 were captured there the following day and more than one got through to Porter's squadron. The loss of the enemy was officially stated at 3 killed and 5 wounded, but a Confederate officer admitted to the commander of the Indianola that it was much greater.

This ended Porter's sanguine hopes of blockading the river by detached vessels while he kept the body of the fleet above. After being harassed and stirred up during three weeks, the Confederates again found themselves masters of the line from Vicksburg to Port Hudson for a few days longer, and with two Union vessels in their hands, one of which was serviceable, while the other, badly damaged and partly sunk, it is true, had still her armament intact and was possibly not beyond repair. Their possession of the Indianola, however, was of short duration. The second day after the capture, a detail of 100 men with a lieutenant was sent to try and save her, by the army officer commanding near by, while the Queen of the West went up to Warrenton, to act as picket for the fleet, and with despatches to General Stevenson, commanding at Vicksburg, asking for pumps and other help. In a short time, the Queen returned in great haste and reported a gunboat approaching. All the vessels that had behaved so gallantly two nights before got under way in a panic and went hurriedly down, leaving the working party and the lieutenant. The gunboat did not come nearer than two miles and a half, and seemed very apprehensive of an attack herself, sticking close to the bank. The lieutenant stood his ground for one day; but then finding himself deserted by his own fleet, which by this time was up Red River, and the gunboat still lying, terrible though inert, just above him, he, the next evening, laid the two XI-inch guns muzzle to muzzle, and so fired them. One was burst, the other apparently only kicked over. He next threw overboard two field pieces he had with him, made an attempt to blow up the vessel, which resulted in destroying the forward casemate and burning most of the wreck above water, and then fled with his command.

The gunboat which caused all this consternation with such happy results to the Union fleet was a mock monitor, built upon the hull of an old coal barge, with pork barrels piled to resemble smoke-stacks, through which poured volumes of smoke from mud furnaces. She went down swiftly with the current, passing the Vicksburg batteries just before daylight, and drawing from them a furious cannonade. As day broke she drifted into the lower end of the canal, and was again sent down stream by the amused Union soldiers, who as little as the admiral dreamed of the good service the dummy was to do. Such was the end of the Indianola, a striking instance of the moral power of the gunboats. The Queen of the West was subsequently sent through the Bayou Atchafalaya to Grand Lake, and there destroyed two months later by the gunboats of the Gulf Squadron.

When the news of these reverses reached New Orleans, Admiral Farragut, who had for some time contemplated a movement up the river, felt that the time was come. On the 12th of March he was at Baton Rouge, where he inspected the ships of the squadron the next day; and then moved up to near Profit's Island, seven miles below the bend on which Port Hudson is situated. On the 14th, early, the vessels again weighed and anchored at the head of the island, where the admiral communicated with Commander Caldwell, of the Essex, who for some time had occupied this station with a half dozen mortar-schooners.

As one ascends the river to Port Hudson, the course pursued is nearly due north; then it takes a sharp turn to the west-southwest for a distance of one or two miles. The little town of Port Hudson is on the east bank just below the bend. The bluffs on which the batteries were placed begin at the bend, extending for a mile and a half down the river, and are from eighty to one hundred feet high. From the opposite bank, at and just below the point, a dangerous shoal spot makes out. At the time of the passage of the fleet there were mounted in battery nineteen heavy guns,[1] viz.: two X-inch and two VIII-inch columbiads; two 42-, two 32-, and three 24-pound smooth-bores; and eight rifles, varying from 80- to 50-pounders.

The object of the admiral was simply to pass the batteries with his fleet, so as to blockade the river above. The vessels he had with him were the Hartford (flag-ship), twenty-four guns, Captain James S. Palmer; Monongahela, ten guns, Captain J. P. McKinstry; Mississippi, seventeen guns, Captain Melancton Smith; Richmond, twenty-four guns, Commander James Alden; Genesee, eight guns, Commander William H. Macomb; Albatross, six guns, Lieutenant-Commander John E. Hart; Kineo, six[2] guns, Lieutenant-Commander John Watters.

The larger ships, except the Mississippi, were directed to take a gunboat on the port side, securing her well aft, so as to leave as much of the port battery as possible clear. Each was to keep a little to starboard of her next ahead, so as to be free to use her bow guns as soon as possible with the least danger from premature explosions of projectiles. In accordance with this order, the Hartford took the Alba-

---

[1] Confederate Return of March 27, 1863. A large number of field pieces, reported to be as many as 35, took part in the action of the 15th.

[2] Of these, four were 24-pounder brass howitzers, usually not counted in ships' batteries.

tross, the Monongahela the Kineo, and the Richmond the Genesee; the Richmond being the slowest ship and the Genesee the most powerful gunboat. The ships were prepared as at the passage of the lower forts, and in the Hartford the admiral had placed his pilot in the mizzen-top, where he could see more clearly, and had arranged a speaking-tube thence to the deck. The Essex and Sachem were not to attempt the passage, but with some mortar-boats to engage the lower batteries to cover the movement.

Shortly before 10 P.M. the ships weighed and advanced in the following order: Hartford, Richmond, Monongahela, Mississippi. At eleven, as they drew near the batteries, the lowest of which the Hartford had already passed, the enemy threw up rockets and opened their fire. Prudence, and the fact of the best water being on the starboard hand, led the ships to hug the east shore of the river, passing so close under the Confederate guns that the speech of the gunners and troops could be distinguished. Along the shore, at the foot of the bluffs, powerful reflecting lamps, like those used on locomotives, had been placed, to show the ships to the enemy as they passed; and for the same purpose large fires, already stacked on the opposite point, were lit. The fire of the fleet and from the shore soon raised a smoke which made these precautions useless, while it involved the ships in a danger greater than any from the enemy's guns. Settling down upon the water, in a still damp atmosphere, it soon hid everything from the eyes of the pilots. The flag-ship, leading, had the advantage of pushing often ahead of her own smoke; but those who followed ran into it and incurred a perplexity which increased from van to rear. At the bend of the river the current caught the Hartford on her port bow, sweeping her round with her head toward the batteries and nearly on shore, her stem touching the ground slightly; but by her own efforts and the assistance of the Albatross she was backed clear. Then, the Albatross backing and the Hartford going ahead strong with the engines, her head was fairly pointed up the stream, and she passed by without serious injury. Deceived possibly by the report of the howitzers in her top, which were nearly on their own level, the Confederates did not depress their guns sufficiently to hit her as often as they did the ships that followed her. One killed and two wounded is her report; and one marine fell overboard, his cries for help being heard on board the other ships as they passed by, unable to save him.

The Richmond, with the Genesee alongside, following the Hartford, had reached the last battery and was about to make the turn when a plunging shot entering about four feet above the berth-deck, passed through a barricade of clothes-bags and hawsers into the engine-room, upsetting the starboard safety-valve; then glancing a little upward, it displaced the port safety-valve weight and twisted the lever, leaving the valve partly opened. The steam escaped so rapidly as to reduce the pressure at once to nine pounds, while filling the fire-room and berth-deck. Deprived thus of her motive force, it was found that the Genesee was not able to drag both vessels up against the strong current then running. Commander Alden was therefore compelled to turn down stream, and after some narrow escapes from the fire of his own fleet, was soon carried by the gunboat out of range. The two vessels lost 3 killed and 15 wounded; among the latter the first lieutenant of the Richmond, A. Boyd Cummings, mortally.

The Monongahela and Kineo were third in line. While under the fire of the principal batteries, musketry opened upon them from the west bank, which was soon silenced by shrapnel and grape from the Kineo. A few moments later a chance shot lodged between the stern-post and rudder-post of the gunboat, wedging the rudder and making it completely useless. The density of the smoke, complained of by all the officers of the fleet that night, caused the pilots to miss their way; and the larger ship took the ground on the spit opposite the town. The Kineo, not touching, with the way she had tore clear of her fasts, and, ranging a short distance ahead, grounded also. Both vessels received considerable though not serious damage from the violence of the separation. The Kineo was soon able to back clear and, though disabled, managed to get a hawser from the Monongahela and pull that ship off after she had been twenty-five minutes aground. The latter then went ahead again, while the Kineo, unable to steer properly, drifted down stream out of range. While aground a shot came in, cutting away the bridge under Captain McKinstry's feet, and throwing him to the deck below; the fall incapacitated him from remaining at his station, and Lieutenant-Commander N. W. Thomas took command of the Monongahela. Meanwhile the Mississippi had passed, unseen and unseeing, in the smoke, and had herself grounded a little farther up near the head of the spit. She was observed to be on fire as the Monongahela again drew near the bend, and at the same moment the latter vessel's engines ceased to move, a crank-pin being heated. Thus unmanageable she drifted down within thirty yards of the batteries, and had to anchor below. Her loss was 6 killed and 21 wounded; the Kineo, though repeatedly struck, had no one hurt.

The Mississippi had passed the lower batteries and had reached the bend, going fast, when she struck, heeling at once three streaks to port. The engines were reversed and backed to the full extent of their power, and the port battery run in to bring the ship on an even keel. After working for thirty-five minutes it was found impossible to get her off. The port battery and pivot gun were then ordered to be thrown overboard, but before that was done Captain Smith decided that the ship would have to be abandoned, as three batteries had her range and were hulling her constantly.

The sick and wounded were brought up, and three small boats, all that were left, were employed in landing the crew. The fire of the starboard battery had been kept up until this time, but now ceased. The ship was then set on fire in the forward store-room ; but before the fire had gained sufficient headway, three shot entering there let in water and put it out. She was then fired in four different places aft, and as soon as it was sure that she would be destroyed, the captain and first lieutenant left her, passing down to the Richmond in safety. The Mississippi remained aground till 3 A.M., when she floated off and drifted down the river, passing the other ships without injuring them. At 5.30, being then some distance below, she blew up, thus meeting the same fate that had befallen her sister ship, the Missouri, twenty years before, in the harbor of Gibraltar.

From the circumstances of the case the exact number of killed and wounded of the Mississippi could not be ascertained. Upon mustering the ship's company after the action, 64 were found missing out of a total of 297. Of these 25 were believed to have been killed.

It is sufficiently apparent, from the above accounts of the experiences of each vessel, that the failure of the greater part of the fleet to pass was principally due to other circumstances than the Confederate fire. The darkness of the night, the stillness of the air, which permitted the smoke to settle undisturbed, the intricacy of the navigation, the rapidity of the current, then running at the rate of five knots, the poor speed of the ships, not over eight knots, were known beforehand, and were greater elements of danger than the simple fire of the enemy. To these is to be added the difficulty of making the turn, with the swift current of the river round the bend tending to throw the ship bodily on to the hostile shore before she could be brought to head in the new direction. The Hartford and her consort alone reached this final trial, and were by it nearly involved in the common disaster.

Nearly, but not quite; and the success of the two vessels, though it placed them in a trying and hazardous position, ensured the attainment of the object for which the risk had been run. The Red River was blockaded, not again to be open to the Confederates during the war; and though nearly four months were still to elapse before the Mississippi would be freely used throughout its length by Union vessels, it slipped finally from the control of the enemy as Farragut with his two ships passed from under the batteries at Port Hudson.

The morning after the action the flag-ship dropped down nearly within range of the enemy, to communicate, if possible, by signal with the fleet below, but they could not be seen from her mast-heads; therefore after firing three guns, as before concerted with General Banks, the admiral went on up the river. The following morning he anchored off the mouth of the Red River, remaining twenty-four hours; and then went on to below Vicksburg to communicate with Porter, arriving there on the 20th. On the way the ships engaged a battery of four rifled pieces at Grand Gulf, losing 2 men killed and 6 wounded, but met with no other opposition. Porter was absent in Deer Creek, one of the bayous emptying into the Yazoo, when Farragut's messenger arrived, but communication was held with General Grant, Captain Walke, the senior naval officer present, and General A. W.

Ellet, commanding the ram flotilla. Farragut, deprived of the greater part of his own fleet, was very desirous of getting reinforcements from above; asking specially for an iron-clad and a couple of rams to assist him in maintaining the blockade of Red River and to patrol the Mississippi. In the absence of Porter he was not willing to urge his request upon the subordinate officers present, but General Ellet assumed the responsibility of sending down two rams, without waiting to hear from the admiral, of whose concurrence he expressed himself as feeling assured; an opinion apparently shared by the others present at the consultation. It would seem, however, that Porter did not think the rams actually sent fit to be separated from a machine-shop by enemies' batteries; and his ironclads could not be spared from the work yet to be done above. The rams Switzerland and Lancaster, the former under command of Colonel Charles R. Ellet, late of the Queen of the West, the latter under Lieutenant-Colonel John A. Ellet, were detailed for this duty and started during the night of the 24th, but so late that they did not get by before the sun had risen. The batteries opened upon them between 5.30 and 6 A.M. of the 25th. The Lancaster, an old and rotten boat, received a shell in her boilers; and her hull was so shattered by the explosion that she went to pieces and sank, the officers and crew escaping on cotton bales. The Switzerland was hulled repeatedly and received two shots in her boilers; but being a stronger boat survived her injuries and drifted down safely to her destination, where a week's labor put her again in fighting condition. The recklessness of the daring family whose name is so associated with the ram fleet had thus caused the loss of two of them, and led Porter to caution Farragut to keep the one now with him always under his own eye.

Soon after the coming of General Grant, while the army was digging canals at two or three different points, with the view of opening new waterways from above to below Vicksburg, Admiral Porter had suggested that by cutting the levee across the old Yazoo Pass, six miles below Helena, access might be had to the Yazoo above Haines's Bluff and Vicksburg turned by that route. Grant ordered the cutting, and Porter sent the light-draught Forest Rose to stand by to enter when open.

There are two entrances from the Mississippi to the pass, the upper one direct, the lower one turning to the left and running parallel to the course of the river. Just within their junction the levee, built in 1856, crosses the pass, which is here only seventy-five feet wide between the timber on either side. At the distance of a mile from the great river the pass enters the northern end of Moon Lake, a crescent-shaped sheet of water, probably an old bed of the Mississippi. The lake is seven or eight miles long and from eight hundred to a thousand yards wide, with a uniform depth enough to float the largest steamboats. Two or three plantations were then on the east shore, but the rest was unbroken forest, quiet and isolated, abounding in game as the waters did in fish. The pass issues again half way down the eastern side, through an opening so shut in with trees that it can scarcely be seen a hundred yards away, and pursues a tortuous course of twelve or fourteen miles to the Coldwater River, the upper portion of the Yazoo. In this part of the route, which never exceeds one hundred feet in width and often narrows to seventy-five or less, the forest of cyprus and sycamore trees, mingled with great cottonwoods and thickly twining wild grape-vines, formed a perfect arch overhead, shutting out the rays of the sun; and, though generally high enough to allow the tall smoke-stacks to pass underneath, sometimes grazed their tops and again swept them down to the deck as the swift current bore the vessels along.

Digging on the levee was begun on the 2d of February, under the direction of Lieutenant-Colonel James H. Wilson, of the Engineers. At this time the difference of level between the water inside and out of the levee was eight and a half feet. At seven the next evening, the digging having gone far enough, a mine was exploded and the water rushed in. By eleven the opening was forty yards wide and the water pouring in like a cataract, tearing aways logs, trees, and great masses of earth with the utmost ease. Owing to the vast tract of country to be flooded before the waters could attain their level, it was not possible to enter for four or five days; during that time they were spreading north and south and east, driving the wild animals from their lairs and the reptiles to take refuge in the trees.

Meanwhile news of the project had reached the Confederates, who, though they could have little idea of the magnitude of the force which intended to penetrate where few but flat-boats had gone before, had taken the easy precaution of felling large trees across the stream. On the 10th Colonel Wilson had passed through Moon Lake and into the pass beyond. Then it took three days of constant labor to get through five miles of felled timber and drifted wood. Some of the trees reached quite across the stream, and were four feet in diameter. To add to the difficulties of the pioneers, the country all around was overflowed, except a mere strip a few inches out of water on the very bank. Still they persevered, and the way was opened through to the Coldwater.

Porter detailed for this expedition the ironclads Chillicothe, Lieutenant-Commander James P. Foster, and De Kalb, Lieutenant-Commander John G. Walker; light-draught steamers Rattler, Marmora, Signal, Romeo, Petrel, and Forest Rose; rams Lioness and Fulton; the whole being under Lieutenant-Commander Watson Smith, of the Rattler. The expedition went through Yazoo Pass, meeting many obstructions and difficulties, despite the work of Wilson's corps.

Three and a half days were consumed in making the twelve miles from the lake to the Coldwater; for, though the current ran swiftly—five or six miles an hour—the low, overhanging trees threatened the chimneys, and big projecting limbs would come sweeping and crashing along the light upper works, making a wreck of anything they met. The great stern-wheels were constantly backing, and a small boat lay on either quarter in readiness to run a line to the trees to check the way of the vessels and to ease them round the sharp bends, which were so frequent it was impossible to see ahead or astern one hundred yards in any part of the route. Huge rafts of driftwood still remained to be dislodged.

On the 28th of February the vessels entered the Coldwater. Here the stream was wider and the current slacker, the trees rarely meeting overhead; but the channel was nearly as crooked, and accidents almost as frequent. Six days were consumed in advancing thirty miles through an almost unbroken wilderness. The stream widened and the country became more promising in the lower part of the Coldwater and the upper part of the Tallahatchie, into which the vessels steamed on the evening of the 6th in a sorely damaged condition. The Petrel had lost her wheel and was wholly disabled; both smoke-stacks of the Romeo were gone; the Chillicothe had run upon the stump of a tree and started a plank in her bottom, which was now kept in place by being shored down from the beams of the deck above; and though none, except the Petrel, were unfit for fighting, all had suffered greatly in hull and upper works.

The transports, which had joined with 6,000 troops, were yet more roughly handled.

The lower part of the Tallahatchie again became narrow and crooked, and for forty or fifty miles no break appeared in a wild and forbidding wilderness until they began to draw near Fort Pemberton, when the stream grew to a fair size. Tokens of the enemy now were seen in burning piles of cotton, and a Confederate steamer, which was picking up what she could, was so closely pressed as to be burned by her crew. The position of the Confederates had been chosen but a few days before, and the works were only partially up. The Tallahatchie here sweeps sharply to the east, and then returns again, forming a horseshoe bend thirteen miles long, the two parts of the stream approaching each other so closely that the neck of the enclosed peninsula is less than a quarter of a mile wide. It is in this bend that the Yallabusha enters, the river then taking the name of Yazoo; so that the works erected across the neck were said to be between the Tallahatchie and Yazoo, though the stream is one. The fort, which was called Pemberton, was built of cotton and earth; in front of it was a deep slough, and on its right flank the river was barricaded by a raft and the hull of the ocean steamer Star of the West, which, after drawing the first shots fired in the war, when the batteries in Charleston stopped her from reinforcing Fort Sumter in January, 1861, had passed by some chance to New Orleans, where she was seized by the Government of Louisiana when that State seceded. When Farragut took New Orleans, she, with many river steamers, was taken to the Yazoo, and now met her end sunk in the swollen waters of a Southern creek. The cannon mounted in the works were one six-and-a-half-inch rifled gun, three 20-pounder Parrott rifles, and some field pieces, among which was a Whitworth rifle. Lieutenant F.

E. Shepperd, of the Confederate Navy, who had been busy felling trees in the upper river, was put in charge of these pieces because none of the army officers present, except General Loring, were familiar with the use of great guns. The heavy rifle, the main reliance of the fort, was only got into position by blocking it up from the ground, no other appliances being at hand; and as there was not enough blocking, the attempt had nearly failed. It was in place barely in time to meet the gunboats.

The Chillicothe, at 10 A.M. of the 11th of March, steamed round the bend above and engaged the battery. She was twice struck on the turret, being materially injured, and withdrew to fortify with cotton bales. At 4.25 P.M. she again went into action, at a distance of eight hundred yards, with the De Kalb, but after firing four times, a shell from the Confederate battery struck in the muzzle of the port XI-inch just as the loaders had entered a shell and were stripping the patch from the fuze; both projectiles exploded, killing 2 and wounding 11 of the gun's crew, besides injuring the gun. The Chillicothe was then withdrawn, after receiving another shot, which killed one of her ship's company, and showing her unfitness for action through scamped work put upon her. The stream was so narrow that two vessels could with difficulty act, and therefore a 30-pound rifled gun was landed from the Rattler on the 13th and an VIII-inch from the De Kalb on the 15th. The action was renewed again on the 13th, by both ironclads at 10.45 A.M., at a distance of eight hundred yards, and was severe until 2 P.M., when the Chillicothe was forced to retire, her ammunition running short. The De Kalb remained in position until dark, firing every fifteen minutes, but receiving no reply from the enemy. In this day's fight the fort was much damaged, the earth covering and bales being knocked away and the cotton set on fire in many places. None of the guns were dismounted, but the large rifle was struck on the side of the muzzle. The greater part of the powder was in a powder-boat a mile away in the Yazoo, but small supplies for the immediate service of the battery were kept in temporary receptacles in the fort. One of these was struck by a shot and the cotton bale covering it knocked off; before it could be replaced a bursting shell exploded the powder, killing and wounding a number of the garrison.

On the 16th another attack was made by the two boats, but the Chillicothe was disabled in a few minutes and both were withdrawn. The difficulty of handling when fighting down stream prevented the vessels from getting that nearness to the enemy which is so essential in an attack by ships upon fortifications. Besides the damage sustained by the Chillicothe, the De Kalb was much cut up, losing ten gun-deck beams and having the wheel-house and steerage badly knocked to pieces, but was not rendered unfit for service as the Chillicothe was. The latter lost 4 killed and 16 wounded; the De Kalb 3 killed and 3 wounded. On the 17th, the troops being unable to land because the country was overflowed and the ships unable to silence the fort, the expedition fell back. On the 22d General Quimby and his command was met coming down, and at his desire the whole expedition returned to Fort Pemberton; but after remaining twelve days longer without effect the attempt was finally abandoned.

Though thus inconclusive, the attempt by Yazoo Pass has an interest of its own from the unique character of the difficulties encountered by the ships. Although forewarned, the enemy were taken unawares, and there is reason to believe, as we have seen, that had a little more feverish energy been displayed the vessels might have got possession of Fort

Pemberton before its guns were mounted. As it was, by the Confederate reports, "notwithstanding every exertion the enemy found us but poorly prepared to receive him." There was no other favorable position for defensive works down to Yazoo City.

While the result of the Yazoo Pass expedition was uncertain and the vessels still before Fort Pemberton, an enterprise of similar character was undertaken by Admiral Porter in person, having for its object to reach the Yazoo below Yazoo City but far above the works at Haines's Bluff. The proposed route was from the Yazoo up Steele's Bayou, through Black Bayou to Deer Creek, and thence by Rolling Fork, a crooked stream of about four miles, to the Big Sunflower, whence the way was open and easy to the Yazoo River. Fort Pemberton would then be taken between two divisions of the fleet, and must fall; while the numerous steamers scattered through the streams of the Yazoo country would be at the mercy of the gunboats.

After a short preliminary reconnoissance as far as Black Bayou, which indicated that the enterprise was feasible, though arduous, and having received encouraging accounts of the remainder of the route, the admiral started on the 16th of March with five ironclads: the Louisville, Lieutenant-Commander E. K. Owen; Cincinnati, Lieutenant George M. Bache; Carondelet, Lieutenant J. M. Murphy; Mound City, Lieutenant Byron Wilson; Pittsburg, Lieutenant W. R. Hoel; four mortars, and four tugs. All went well till Black Bayou was reached. This is about four miles long, narrow, and very crooked, and was then filled with trees. Here the crews had to go to work, dragging the trees up by the roots, or pushing them over with the ironclads, and cutting away the heavy overhanging branches. Having done this the ironclads were able to force their way through the bushes and trees which lined the banks and clung closely to the bows and sides of the vessels, but the way remained impracticable for transports and wooden boats. In twenty-four hours the ironclads had gotten through these four miles to Hill's plantation, at the junction of Black Bayou and Deer Creek.

General W. T. Sherman had been directed to support the movement with one division of his corps and a body of pioneers. The number of steamers fit for the bayou navigation being limited, the division was landed on the east bank of the Mississippi and crossed by land to Steele's Bayou, which there approaches to within a mile of the river. The pioneers followed the admiral up Black Bayou, and when the gunboats entered Deer Creek remained to further clear the bayou. On the 20th the work had progressed so that two transports entered as far as a mile and a half below Hill's, where was the first piece of dry land between that point and the mouth of the Yazoo, the country generally being under water.

Meanwhile the admiral had pushed on up Deer Creek, where the water was deep but the channel narrow, crooked, and filled with young willows, which bound the boats and made progress very difficult. The bends were sharp, and much trouble was experienced in heaving the vessels around them, while the banks were lined with heavy trees and overhanging branches that would tear down the chimneys and demolish boats and light woodwork. Still they worked on, making from half a mile to a mile an hour. The enemy, notwithstanding what had been done at Yazoo Pass, were taken by surprise, not having believed that even gunboats would try to penetrate by those marshy, willowy ditches. On the night of the 17th, Colonel Ferguson, commanding the district, first received word at his headquarters on Deer Creek, forty miles above Rolling Fork, that the gunboats had entered the creek.

He at once hurried a battalion of sharpshooters and some artillery on board a steamer and hastened down to Rolling Fork, being so lucky as to get there before the vessels, on the afternoon of the 19th. A small detached body of cavalry were ahead of him, and, acting on their own account, had begun to cut down trees across the stream. Anticipating this, the admiral had sent Lieutenant Murphy ahead in a tug and he had come up in time to stop the felling of the first; but the horsemen galloped across country faster than the tug could force her way through the channel and at last got down a large tree, which arrested the tug till the rest of the force came up. Then the slaves, with muskets to their breasts, were compelled to ply their axes to stop the advance of those to whom they looked for freedom.

The situation was critical, and the crews turned to with a will, working night and day to clear away these obstacles, without sleep and snatching their food. They were now five or six miles from Rolling Fork, and hearing that the enemy were landing, Lieutenant Murphy was sent forward with 300 men and two howitzers to hold the stream until the gunboats could cover it with their guns; which he did, occupying an Indian mound sixty feet high. After working all night and the next day, the 19th, the squadron had hewed its way by sundown to within eight hundred yards of Rolling Fork. They rested that night, and the morning of the 20th again started to work through the willows, but the lithe trees resisted all their efforts to push through, and had either to be pulled up one by one or cut off under water both tedious processes. Meanwhile Ferguson, having collected 800 men and six pieces of artillery, attacked Murphy's little body of men, who had to be recalled. At three in the afternoon Featherstone's brigade, with a section of artillery, arrived from Vicksburg to reinforce the enemy, and toward sundown opened a sharp fire upon the gunboats from a distance. Though this was easily silenced by the vessels, the difficulty of throwing out working parties in the presence of the enemy's force was apparent. Word was at once sent to Sherman of the state of things, and reached him at 3 A.M. of the 21st; but before that time the admiral, learning that some of the enemy had reached his rear and had begun felling trees behind him to prevent his retreat, had decided to withdraw. Advance through Rolling Fork was no longer possible, it having been so obstructed that two or three days' labor would have been needed to clear it, even if unopposed.

Having but ten or twelve feet to spare on either side it was impossible to turn the boats, so the rudders were unshipped and they began that night to back down, rebounding from tree to tree on either bank as they struck them. The country from Rolling Fork to Black Bayou was mostly a chain of plantations, in which the trees at few points came down to the bank of the stream thickly enough to afford cover for troops in numbers; but yet there was shelter for sharpshooters at such a distance as enabled them to pick off any of the crews that exposed themselves. The guns were three feet below the levee, depriving them of much of their power to annoy the assailants. At 4 P.M. of the 21st, however, Colonel Giles A. Smith, of Sherman's command, arrived with 800 men; Sherman, as soon as he heard of the admiral's dilemma, having sent every man he had by the east bank of Deer Creek, remaining himself alone at Hill's until nightfall. Three steamboat loads of troops then arrived below and were conducted by him, with lighted candles, through two and a half miles of dense cane-brake to the plantation.

When Smith reached the vessels, they had been stopped

for an hour or two by a coal barge sunk across the creek, and were kept from sending out working parties by the enemy's sharpshooters. Smith now took charge of the banks, being reinforced with 150 men and two howitzers from the fleet, and before midnight the barge was blown up. The retreat continued next day, the boats backing, and the Louisville, which was the farthest down, clearing away the obstructions while the troops kept the enemy from molesting the workers. Owing to the number of trees to be removed, only six miles had been gained by 3 P.M., at which hour a large body of the enemy were seen passing by, along the edge of the woods, and taking position about a mile ahead of the advance of the troops. The gunboats opened upon them, and at this time General Sherman himself opportunely came up with his reinforcements and drove the Confederates well back to the north and rear of the squadron, thus finally freeing it from a very anxious and critical dilemma. On the 24th Hill's plantation was reached, and the vessels returned without further adventure to the mouth of the Yazoo, where Porter communicated with Farragut, who still remained near the lower end of the canal.

On the 29th and 30th it blew a gale of wind from the north, during which the steamer Vicksburg, that had been rammed two months before by the Queen of the West, broke adrift from her moorings at the city, and went ashore on the bank opposite the Hartford. Upon examination it was found that her machinery had been removed, and before any further action had been taken by Farragut, the Confederates sent down and burned her. Meanwhile coal from the army and provisions from the upper squadrons were floated down in barges, and on the 31st, having waited for the completion of the repairs on the Switzerland, the admiral got under way, with the Albatross and the ram in company, and went down the river. At Grand Gulf the batteries again opened on the ships, striking the Switzerland twice and the Hartford once; the latter losing one man killed. On the evening of April 1st the little squadron reached Red River, having destroyed on its passage down a large number of skiffs and flat-boats, available for the transport of stores across the Mississippi from the western country, on which Vicksburg now mainly depended for supplies.

In their isolated condition, and occupying a position so obnoxious to the enemy, there was reason to expect a repetition on a larger scale of the attack made upon the Indianola. The Hartford was specially prepared for such a meeting. The lower yards were lowered down to the rail and the stream-chain, lashed to the bowsprit end, was carried aft, clove-hitched to the yard-arms and brought in again at the warping-chocks. This barrier, while it remained intact, would keep an assailant fifteen to twenty feet from the ship; then, if it were passed, as a further protection against boarders, hawsers were stretched along fore and aft by the lower rigging, thirty feet above the deck, carrying a heavy boarding netting which extended from that height to the ship's rail. The hammock-cloths were kept triced up, and the poop-deck and topgallant-forecastle, which were flush with the rail of the ship, were barricaded with hammocks and sails. For protection against rams large cypress logs were slung around the vessel, a foot above the water line. During the time they were thus alone the guns' crews always slept by the guns and the ship was kept in a constant state of preparation for instant action.

On the 6th Farragut went down again to Port Hudson, anxious for news about his other ships, from which he had now been for three weeks separated, and desiring to communicate with General Banks. The ordinary methods of signalling having failed to attain these objects, the admiral's secretary, Mr. Gabaudan, volunteered to pass Port Hudson in a skiff by night. The boat was covered with twigs, arranged to resemble one of the floating trees not uncommon in the Mississippi.

At a quarter past eight on the evening of the 7th Mr. Gabaudan stepped into his ark, and lying down in the bottom of it, with a paddle and revolver by his side, was committed to the current. This bore him safely by; but once grazing the shore, the sentinels were heard commenting on the size of the log, and a boat put out to make an examination. Fortunately the men were contented with a glance, which satisfied them that the object was what it seemed; and Gabaudan's safe arrival was signalled from the vessels below at 10 P.M.

The next morning the admiral returned to Red River and caught two steamers outside, one of which managed to get in again; but the other was captured, and with her a Confederate commissary, who was making arrangements for crossing a large number of cattle from the West at various points. Red River was effectually closed, but the smallness of his force made it necessary to keep them all together, in case of attack, and though intercourse across the Mississippi was seriously impaired, it was not wholly checked. On the 15th the admiral again returned to the bend above Port Hudson, and communicated by signal with the Richmond, which had come up in accordance with instructions transmitted through Mr. Gabaudan. This officer at the same time returned to the ship, under protection of an escort, overland, there being no regular Confederate force on the right bank.

Meanwhile General Grant had been maturing his plans

for the movement by which Vicksburg was eventually reduced. The bayou expeditions had failed, and with them every hope of turning the enemy's right flank. The idea had been entertained of opening a water route by cutting a channel from the west bank of the Mississippi, seventy-five miles above Vicksburg, to Lake Providence, from which there was communication by bayous to the Tensas, Wachita, and Red Rivers, and so to the Mississippi below Vicksburg. Yet another water-way by bayous was contemplated from Milliken's Bend, twenty miles above, through the Tensas, to New Carthage, thirty miles below, Vicksburg. Work was done upon both these routes by the army; but the rapid falling of the river toward the middle of April at once made them less desirable and the roads on the west bank passable. Three army corps had already moved, one after the other, beginning on the 29th of March, toward New Carthage on the west bank; but though not over twenty miles by land in a straight line, the condition of the country from broken levees and bad roads made necessary a circuit of thirty-five miles to reach this point. As soon as the movement was definitely decided upon, Admiral Porter made his preparations for running the batteries of Vicksburg with the greater portion of his fleet. To assure a supply of fuel below, the vessels detailed for the duty took each a coal barge on the starboard side, leaving the port guns, which would bear upon the batteries, clear for firing. There being no intention to engage the enemy except for the purpose of covering the passage, every precaution was taken to avoid being seen or heard. All lights were extinguished, ports carefully covered, and the fires well lighted before starting, so as to show, if possible, no smoke; while to lessen the noise, the steam, as with the Carondelet at Island No. 10, was to exhaust into the wheel, and the vessels were to proceed at low speed. To avoid collisions, fifty yards were prescribed as the interval to be observed, and each boat was to keep a little to one side of its next ahead, so that, in case of the latter stopping, the follower would be able to pass without change of course. The sterns of the vessels—their weakest part—were to be specially protected against raking shots, which was done by piling wet bales of hay and slinging heavy logs near the water line.

At a quarter past nine of the night of April 16th, the fleet destined for this service got under way from the mouth of the Yazoo River, the flag-ship Benton, sixteen guns,[1] Lieutenant-Commander James A. Greer, leading, and the other vessels in the following order: Lafayette, eight guns, Captain Henry Walke; Louisville, twelve guns, Lieutenant-Commander Elias K. Owen; Mound City, fourteen guns, Lieutenant Byron Wilson; Pittsburg, thirteen guns, Lieutenant W. R. Hoel; Carondelet, eleven guns, Lieutenant J. McLeod Murphy; Tuscumbia, five guns, Lieutenant-Commander James W. Shirk. The Lafayette carried with her, lashed to the other side of her coal barge, the ram General Price, Lieutenant S. E. Woodworth, which had continued in the service after being taken from the Confederates at Memphis. After the Carondelet, between her and the Tuscumbia, came three army transports, the Silver Wave, Henry Clay, and Forest Queen, unprotected except by bales of hay and cotton round the boilers. They carried stores, but no troops.

A month later, and probably at this time also, the river batteries before which the fleet was to pass contained thirty-one pieces of heavy artillery and thirteen of light.[2] Among

[1] For particulars of batteries of Mississippi Squadron of 1862 and 1863, see Appendix.

[2] Report of Colonel Higgins, C. S. A., commanding the river batteries.

them were eight X-inch, one IX-inch, and one VIII-inch columbiad, smooth-bore guns; and eleven rifled guns of a calibre of 6.5 inches and upward.

At 11.10 P.M., the fleet then moving at a speed scarcely exceeding the drift of the current, a musketry fire began from the upper batteries of the enemy. At 11.16 the great guns began, slowly at first, but soon more rapidly. A few moments later a large fire was lit on the point, bringing the vessels, as they passed before it, into bold relief, and serving to confuse, to some extent, the pilots of the fleet. Each ship as she brought her guns to bear on rounding the point, opened her fire, first from the bow and then from the port battery. The engagement thus soon became general and animated. The confusion of the scene was increased by the eddying currents of the river, which, catching the slowly moving steamers, now on the bow, now on the quarter, swung them round with their broadside to the stream, or even threw the bow up river again. Unable to see through the smoke and perplexed by the light of the fire, the majority of the vessels, thus cut around, made a full turn in the stream under the guns of the enemy, and one, at least, went round twice. The flag-ship Benton, though heavily struck, passed through without special adventure escaping this involuntary wheel. The Lafayette, in the smoke, found her nose nearly on shore on the enemy's side, and her coal barge received a shell in the bow which reduced it to a sinking condition. The Louisville, next astern, coming up, fouled the Lafayette's consort, the General Price; which, being already badly cut up by shot and shell, cast off her fasts and made the rest of the journey alone. The Lafayette then let go her barge and went down without further adventure. The Louisville also lost her barge, apparently, at this time, but picked it up again while still under fire. The Mound City following came down upon the three vessels thus sported with by the current and the difficulties of the night, and to avoid a like disaster passed them by. The Pittsburg came next in her appointed station; like the Mound City, she escaped the pranks of the eddy, and both vessels, steaming leisurely on, used their guns with good effect; receiving, while passing the burning pile ashore, several shot from the enemy. The Pittsburg was struck on the quarter, where the logs alone prevented the shot from entering the magazine. The Carondelet met with no other mishap than making an involuntary circle in the river. The Tuscumbia remained in rear of the transports, which had a hard time. Either swung by the eddy, or daunted by the tremendous fire which they were certainly ill-fitted to resist, two of them at one time pointed up stream. The Tuscumbia stopped, prepared to compel their passage down; but force was not needed. The Henry Clay caught fire, was burnt and sank; the other resumed her course. When rounding the point, the Tuscumbia touched, and as she backed off fouled the Forest Queen, causing great hurrahs among the enemy. The vessels soon got apart, but the transport had a shot through her steam-pipe; so the Tuscumbia stuck to her, the two drifting down together until out of range, when the gunboat towed the other ashore. The Tuscumbia had a shot in the bows under water, starting seven planks and causing her to leak badly.

Though repeatedly hulled, the armed vessels received no injury unfitting them for instant service, and of their crews lost only 13 wounded. By three o'clock in the morning they were all anchored twelve miles above New Carthage, ready to co-operate with the movements of the army.

Encouraged by the comparative success of the transports on the 16th, Grant directed six more to run the batteries, which was done on the night of the 22d. One got a shot under water, and sank after getting by; the others were more or less damaged, but were repaired by the orders of Admiral Porter. Still the number was so limited, in proportion to the amount of transportation required, that the general decided to move the troops by land to Hard Times Landing, twenty-five miles below New Carthage by the course of the river. The ships of war and transports followed, the latter carrying as many men as they could.

Five miles below Hard Times, on the opposite shore, is Grand Gulf, where a battery had fired upon Farragut, both on his passage to Vicksburg and return from there, after the fight at Port Hudson. The Confederates had begun to strengthen the works immediately after that time to prevent him from going by with impunity; but as he considered his task limited to the blockade of the Red River and the Mississippi below, to which alone his force was adequate, he had not again come within their range. Immediately above Grand Gulf is the mouth of the Big Black River, a considerable stream, by which supplies from the Red River country were transported to the interior of the Confederacy on the east of the Mississippi.

Eight hundred yards below the mouth of the Big Black is the Point of Rocks, rising about seventy-five feet above the river at its then height. On this was the upper battery, mounting, at the time of attack, two VII-inch rifles, one VIII-inch smooth-bore, and a 30-pound rifled gun on wheels. A line of rifle-pits and a covered way led from there to the lower fort, three-quarters of a mile farther down, in which were mounted one 100-pound rifle, one VIII-inch smooth-bore, and two 32-pounders. There were in addition five light rifled guns, 10- and 20-pounders, in different parts of the works. The Point of Rocks battery was close over the river, but the bluffs below receded so as to leave a narrow strip of

Battle at Grand Gulf.

land, three to four hundred yards wide, along the water and in front of the lower fort. All the fortifications were earthworks.

The intention was to silence the works by the fleet, after which the army was to cross in transports, under cover of the gunboats, and carry the place by storm. The orders prescribing the manner of attack were issued by the admiral on the 27th. On the 29th, at 7 A.M., the fleet got under way, the Pittsburg leading; her commander, Lieutenant Hoel, a volunteer officer, being himself a pilot for the Mississippi, obtained the honor of leading through his local knowledge. The Louisville, Carondelet, and Mound City followed in the order named, firing upon the upper fort so long as their guns bore, but passing by it to attack the lower work, which was allotted to them. The Pittsburg rounded to as she reached her station, keeping up her fire all the time, and took position close into the bank with her head up stream. The Louisville, following the Pittsburg's motions, passed her, rounded to and took her station immediately astern. The Carondelet and Mound City successively performed the same manœuvre. All four then went into close action with the lower fort, at the same time directing any of their guns that would bear upon other points of the works. The remaining vessels, Lafayette, Tuscumbia, and flag-ship Benton, followed the first four, but rounded to above the town to engage the upper fort; the Lafayette taking position at first in an eddy of the river, and using her two stern guns, 100-pound rifles. The Benton and Tuscumbia fought their bow and starboard guns; all the vessels keeping under way during the engagement, and being at times baffled by the eddies in the stream. At eleven o'clock, the admiral signalled the Lafayette to change her position to the lower battery, which she did. About eleven, a shot came into the Benton's pilot-house, wounding the pilot and shattering the wheel. The vessel was for a moment unmanageable, got into an eddy, and was carried down three-quarters of a mile before she could again be brought under control; but her place was promptly supplied by the Pittsburg, which had just moved up with that division of the fleet, the lower fort being silenced. The whole squadron now concentrated its fire upon the Point of Rocks battery, keeping under way, and from the difficulties of the stream and the eddying current, at varying ranges. The Lafayette took again her position in the eddy to the north of the battery. Half an hour after noon, the Tuscumbia's port engine was disabled, and being unable to stem the stream with her screws, she was compelled to drop down below Grand Gulf. The action was continued vigorously until 1 P.M., when the enemy's fire, which had not been silenced in the upper fort, slackened materially. The admiral then passed up the river to consult with Grant, who had seen the fight from the deck of a tug and realized, as did Porter, that the works had proved themselves too high and too strong to be taken from the water side. He therefore decided to land the troops, who were already on board the transports waiting to cross, and march down to the point immediately below Grand Gulf, while Porter signalled his ships to withdraw, which they did, after an action lasting four hours and a quarter, tying up again to the landing at Hard Times. The limitation to the power of the vessels was very clearly shown here, as at Fort Donelson; the advantage given by commanding height could not be overcome by them. On a level, as at Fort Henry, or with slight advantage of command against them, as at Arkansas Post, the chances were that they would at close quarters win by disabling or silencing the guns; but when it came to a question of elevation the guns on shore were too much sheltered. Even so, it may be looked upon as an unusual misfortune that after tearing the works to pieces as they did, no gun of the Confederates was seriously injured. On the other hand, though the gunboats were roughly handled, it could be claimed for them, too, that they were not silenced, and that, like the earthworks, they were not, with one exception, seriously injured. The loss of the fleet was: the Benton, 7 killed and 19 wounded; Tuscumbia, 5 killed and 24 wounded; Pittsburg, 6 killed and 13 wounded. The Lafayette had one man wounded, while the remaining vessels lost none.

In the afternoon the Confederates were observed to be repairing their works, so the Lafayette was ordered down to stop them. She soon drove off the working parties, and then kept up a steady fire at five-minute intervals against the upper battery until 8 P.M., getting no reply from a work which had responded so vigorously in the morning.

That evening the fleet got under way at 8 P.M., the Benton leading, followed by the other gunboats and the transports, the Lafayette joining as they reached her station. The armed vessels again engaged the batteries and the transports slipped safely by under cover of this attack, receiving no injury; in fact, being struck not more than two or three times. As soon as they had passed, the gunboats followed, and tied up again on the Louisiana shore, four miles below Grand Gulf. One life only was lost in the night action, on board the Mound City.

At daylight the following morning the work of carrying the army across the Mississippi to Bruinsburg began, the gunboats as well as the transports aiding in the operation.

The same day, April 30th, a feigned attack was made at Haines's Bluff by the vessels of the squadron remaining above

Vicksburg, under Lieutenant-Commander K. R. Breese, in conjunction with the Fifteenth Army Corps, under General W. T. Sherman. The object of General Grant in ordering this demonstration was to hinder the Confederates at Vicksburg from sending heavy reinforcements to Grand Gulf to oppose the troops on their first landing. The expedition was most successful in attaining this end, but the vessels were very roughly handled, having been much exposed with the wish to make the attack appear as real as possible. The Choctaw, Lieutenant-Commander F. M. Ramsay, was struck as often as forty-six times. Despite the heavy fire of the enemy, no serious casualties occurred on board the fleet in an action which lasted three hours, from 11 A.M. to 2 P.M. The demonstration was continued during the following day, but at 8 P.M. General Sherman withdrew his troops to the other side of the Mississippi, taking up his march to join the main body of the army; and the vessels returned to their anchorage off the mouth of the Yazoo.

On the morning of the 3d Porter advanced upon Grand Gulf with his fleet below, intending to attack if the enemy were still there; but the place was found to be evacuated, as had been expected, the march of the army inland having rendered it untenable. The earthworks were torn to pieces by the fire of the fleet, and Colonel Wade, the commandant, had been killed; but the guns were still in position, except two 32-pounders in the lower battery, which were dismounted and broken. A large quantity of ammunition was also obtained, showing that lack of it was not the cause of the fire slackening on the 29th of April. The same day General Grant arrived, and made the necessary arrangements for transferring his base of supplies to Grand Gulf instead of Bruinsburg.

On the day that Porter ran by the batteries of Vicksburg,

April 16th, Farragut, having received his secretary and the despatches brought by him, went back from Port Hudson to the mouth of the Red River. During the next fortnight he kept up the blockade of the Mississippi between those two points, twice catching stores crossing in flat-boats, besides destroying a number of boats along the river and a large quantity of commissary stores at Bayou Sara. Besides cutting off Port Hudson from the west bank of the Mississippi, his presence in this position prevented reinforcements from that place being sent by the Red River, as they otherwise might have been, to the Confederate General Taylor, who was now being pressed by Banks toward Alexandria. Farragut had also in view blockading the Black River, a tributary of the Red, which enters it from the north and northwest about thirty miles from the Mississippi and by which it was reported that reinforcements to Taylor were expected to arrive from Arkansas.

These military movements in Western Louisiana were due to the operations of General Banks, who had abandoned the demonstration made from Baton Rouge against Port Hudson, at the time Farragut passed, and resumed his operations by the Bayous Teche and Atchafalaya. This expedition was accompanied by four light gunboats, the Calhoun, Clifton, Arizona, and Estrella, under the command of Lieutenant-Commander A. P. Cooke, of the latter vessel. The land forces reached Opelousas near the Teche, sixty miles from Alexandria, on the 20th of April; and the same day the gunboats took Butte-à-la-Rose, on the Atchafalaya, sixty miles from Brashear City, a fortified place, mounting two heavy guns. Banks continued his advance upon Alexandria, and the gunboats pushed on through the Atchafalaya for the mouth of the Red River.

On the evening of the 1st of May the Arizona arrived

where the Hartford was then lying, bringing with her despatches from Banks to Farragut, asking his co-operation against Alexandria. The Estrella coming a few hours later, the admiral sent the two, with the Albatross, under Lieutenant-Commander John E. Hart, senior officer, up the Red River on the 3d. The little detachment reached the mouth of the Black River that afternoon, and there learned that none of the Confederate reinforcements expected by that stream had as yet passed. At sunset they anchored thirteen miles below Gordon's Landing. The next day, at 5 A.M., they again went up the stream, reaching, at 8.40, the bluff and bend which had been the scene of the capture of the Queen of the West ten weeks before. When the Albatross, which was leading, looked out from behind the bluff her people saw a battery with three casemates, now called Fort De Russey, commanding the river, covering two river steamers with steam up; alongside one of these was a flatboat loaded with a heavy gun, believed to be one of those taken from the Indianola. Below the battery was a heavy raft, stretching across the stream and secured by chains to both banks. The Albatross went at once into action at a distance of five hundred yards, having, at that distance, to deal not only with the battery but with sharpshooters sheltered behind cotton barricades on board the steamers. The ship was much embarrassed by the eddies and the intricacy of the channel, touching several times; but the fight was maintained for forty minutes, after which she withdrew, having been hulled eleven times, her spars and rigging seriously injured, and having lost two men killed and four wounded. The force was too small to grapple successfully with the work, so Lieutenant-Commander Hart gave the order to return.

On the way down the vessels met Admiral Porter, who had

delayed at Grand Gulf no longer than was necessary to take possession. Leaving there at noon of the day of its occupation he reached the mouth of the Red River on the 4th, and communicated with Farragut. The next day he went up the Red River, taking with him, besides the flag-ship Benton, the Lafayette, Pittsburg, and Price. The ram Switzerland, which Farragut no longer needed, and the tug Ivy accompanied him.

When he fell in with Hart's expedition, Porter took the Estrella and Arizona in addition to his own force, leaving the Albatross to rejoin Farragut alone. On the 5th, toward sundown, Fort DeRussey was reached, but found to be abandoned and the guns removed, except one 64-pounder. Losing no time in destroying the abandoned works, the squadron pushed on at once for Alexandria; a passage through the raft being opened by the Price's ram. The Arizona having speed was sent ahead to surprise any steamer that might be at the town, where she arrived the evening of the 6th, the rest of the vessels coming up the following morning. Most of the Confederate public property had been already removed to Shreveport, three hundred and fifty miles farther up, in the northwest corner of Louisiana, where the gunboats in that stage of the river could not follow. General Banks arrived on the evening of the 7th from Opelousas.

As the river was beginning to fall, Porter went down again on the 8th with all the vessels but the Lafayette, Captain Walke, who was left at Alexandria to co-operate with the army. The Benton stopped for a short time at Fort De Russey, while a detached expedition consisting of the Price, Switzerland, Pittsburg, and Arizona was sent up the Black River. They got as far as Harrisonburg, seventy miles up, where were found batteries on high hills too heavy for the force, which was recalled after communicating with the admiral, having succeeded in destroying $300,000 worth of the enemy's provisions. The Switzerland, Estrella, and Arizona were now sent up to Captain Walke at Alexandria, and the admiral returned to Grand Gulf on the 13th. The Black River expedition was in itself of no great consequence; but, taken in connection with others of the same character through these waters, after the fall of Vicksburg, and the expected reinforcements of Taylor by the same route, it illustrates the facilities for rapidly traversing the enemy's country afforded by the navigable streams, and the part played by them in the conduct of the war by either party.

Farragut now felt that his personal presence was no longer required above Port Hudson, and returned to New Orleans by one of the bayous; leaving Commodore Palmer with the Hartford, Albatross, Estrella, and Arizona to maintain the blockade above until Porter was ready to assume the entire charge. The Hartford, however, did not come down till after the surrender of Port Hudson, two months later.

After the capture of Alexandria and the dispersal of the enemy in that quarter, General Banks moved down with his army to Simmesport, on the Atchafalaya Bayou, five miles from the Red River, and thence across the Mississippi at Bayou Sara, five or six miles above Port Hudson. General Augur of his command at the same time moved up from Baton Rouge. The two bodies met on the 23d of May, and Port Hudson was immediately invested. An assault was made on the 27th, but proved unsuccessful, and the army settled down to a regular siege. A battery of four IX-inch shell-guns from the navy was efficiently served throughout the siege by a detachment of seamen from the Richmond and Essex under Lieutenant-Commander Edward Terry, executive officer of the former vessel. The Essex, Commander Caldwell, and the half dozen mortar-schooners under his orders maintained a constant bombardment and succession of artillery fights with the river batteries of the enemy, being exposed to the fire of four VIII- and X-inch columbiads and two heavy rifles. Between the 23d of May and 26th of June Caldwell estimated that one thousand shot and shell had been fired at him from these guns. During these daily engagements the Essex was hulled twenty-three times, besides being frequently struck above her decks, and had received severe injury. The mortar-schooners also came in for their share of hard knocks, and their captains were all specially commended both by Caldwell and Farragut.

On the 15th of May Porter went to the Yazoo and there awaited news from the army. On the 18th heavy firing in the rear of the city assured him of Grant's approach. That afternoon the advance of Sherman's corps came in below Snyder's Bluff, between the city and Haines's Bluff. The works at the latter point had been abandoned the evening before on the approach of the army ; a small party only being left to destroy or remove whatever they could. Upon the appearance of the troops the admiral sent up a force of gunboats under Lieutenant-Commander K. R. Breese, whereupon the party ran off, leaving everything in good order. The works mounted fourteen heavy guns, VIII- and X-inch smooth-bores, and VII½-inch rifles; the carriages of these were burned, as were the Confederate encampments, and the magazines blown up. Porter now received letters from Grant, Sherman, and Steele, informing him of the entire success of the campaign in the rear of Vicksburg, and asking that provisions might be sent up, the army having lived off the country almost entirely during a fortnight of constant marching and fighting. Lieutenant-Commander J.

G. Walker in the De Kalb was sent up to Yazoo City with sufficient force to destroy the enemy's property which he might find, and the gunboats below Vicksburg were moved up to fire on the hill batteries, an annoyance to the garrison which they kept up off and on during the night. On the 19th six mortar-boats were got into position, with orders to fire night and day as rapidly as possible.

Grant, having completed the investment of Vicksburg, sent word on the evening of the 21st that he intended to make a general assault upon the enemy's works at 10 A.M. the following day, and asked that the fleet might shell the batteries from 9.30 to 10.30. Porter complied by keeping up his mortar fire all night and sending up the gunboats to shell the water batteries, and other places where he thought the enemy might find rest. At 7 A.M. the next day the Mound City, followed at eight by the Benton, Tuscumbia, and Carondelet, moved up abreast the lower end of the canal, opening upon the hill batteries; then they attacked the water batteries, the duel between them and the ships at a range of four hundred and fifty yards being maintained incessantly for two hours. The Tuscumbia proved, as before, too weak to withstand such close action and had to drop down. The admiral wrote that this was the hottest fire that the gunboats had yet endured, but the water batteries having little elevation, the ships contended on more even terms than at Grand Gulf, and fighting bows on, received little damage.

The fire was maintained for an hour longer than Grant had asked, when the vessels dropped out of range, having lost only a few wounded. The assault of the army was not successful and regular siege operations were begun. Vicksburg and Port Hudson, the two extremes of the Confederate line, were thus formally invested by the 27th of May. On that day, Porter, having received a request from Grant and

Sherman to try whether the enemy had moved from the batteries the guns on their extreme left, as they had from many of the other hill batteries, sent down the gunboat Cincinnati, Lieutenant George M. Bache, to draw their fire if still there; and, if possible, to enfilade the enemy's rifle-pits in that quarter and drive them out. The Cincinnati started from the upper division of the squadron at 7 A.M.; the vessels of the lower division, Price, Benton, Mound City, and Carondelet, steaming up at the same time to cover her movement by engaging the lower batteries, which might have played upon her. General Sherman took a position upon a hill at the extreme right of the Union lines, overlooking the river, so as to see the affair and take advantage of any success gained by the Cincinnati's attack. The gunboat, protected as usual by logs and hay, came within range shortly after nine o'clock, and the enemy began firing rapidly from all their batteries, the guns whose position had been doubted proving to be in their old place. When abreast the position assigned her for enfilading the rifle-pits the Cincinnati rounded to, and as she did so a shot pierced her side and entered the shell-room, capsizing nearly all the boxes on one side of the alley. As she came to with her head up stream, another ball entered the shell-room below the water-line, and a third pierced her stern, always the weakest part of these vessels, going into the magazine, also below the water-line, flooding it instantly and causing the vessel to fill rapidly. A heavy shot drove through the pilot-house, and shortly afterward the starboard tiller was carried away. The plunging fire of many big guns, concentrated on a single vessel, wrought great injury in a short time; penetrating her light deck, five of her guns were disabled by it. All three flag-staffs were shot away, carrying the colors down with them; upon which, a quartermaster, Frank Bois by name, went out and nailed a flag to the stump that was left of the forward staff. Finding the vessel must sink, Lieutenant Bache kept running up stream, hugging the east bank to be as far as possible out of the enemy's range, and about ten minutes before she went down sheered in, ran out a hawser, and a plank by which the wounded were landed. Unfortunately the men who went ashore with the hawser did not secure it properly, the boat began drifting out into the stream, and the officers and crew had to swim for their lives. She sank in three fathoms of water within range of the enemy's batteries, the second to go down of the seven first built. The loss was 5 killed, 14 wounded, and 15 missing; supposed to have been drowned.

The detached expedition to Yazoo City, under Lieutenant-Commander Walker, had returned on the evening of the 23d. On the approach of the vessels, the Confederates had set fire to the navy yard and three steamers on the stocks building for ships of war, one a very large vessel, 310 feet long by 70 feet beam and intended to carry 4½-inch plating. All that had not been destroyed or removed by the enemy the gunboats finished, the loss being estimated at two million dollars. An attack was made upon the gunboats at a bend of the river by a small force of riflemen with three field pieces, but was repelled without trouble, one man only being killed and eight slightly wounded. The morning after their return the same vessels were again sent up. One of the light-draughts, the Signal, met with the curious accident of knocking down her smoke-stacks, an incident which again illustrates the peculiar character of this bayou warfare. Sending her back, and leaving his own vessel, the De Kalb, to follow as rapidly as possible, Walker pushed on with the Forest Rose, Linden, and Petrel to within fifteen miles of Fort Pemberton, by which the Yazoo Pass expedition had been baffled. Here four fine steamers had been sunk on a bar, stopping farther progress. Having no means of raising them, they were fired and burned to the water's edge. The vessels then passed down the Yazoo, burning a large saw-mill twenty-five miles above Yazoo City, till they came to the Big Sunflower River. They ascended this stream one hundred and eighty miles, branch expeditions being sent into the bayous that enter it, destroying or causing the destruction of four more steamers. Transportation on the Yazoo by the Confederates was now broken up below Fort Pemberton, while above it a few steamers only remained.

From this time until the surrender of Vicksburg little occurred to vary the routine siege operations. Thirteen heavy cannon, from IX-inch to 32-pounders, were landed from the fleet to take their place in the siege batteries, in charge, at different points of the lines, of Lieutenant-Commander T. O. Selfridge, and Acting-Masters C. B. Dahlgren and J. F. Reed; and as many officers and men as could be spared were sent with them. Three heavy guns, a X-inch, IX-inch, and 100-pound rifle, under the command of Lieutenant-Commander F. M. Ramsay, of the Choctaw, were placed in scows close to the point opposite the town, but where they were protected by the bank, enfilading the batteries and rifle-pits on the enemy's left, against which the Cincinnati had made her unsuccessful attack. The gunboats below were constantly under fire and the mortars steadily shelling. On the 19th of June Grant notified the admiral that he intended to open a general bombardment at 4 A.M. the following day and continue it till 10 A.M. The lower division, the scow battery, and the mortars joined in this, shelling the hill batteries and the city, but no reply was made by the enemy from the water front.

The great service of the navy during the siege was keeping open the communications, which were entirely by the river from the time that Sherman's corps reached Snyder's Bluff. The danger of Vicksburg thrilled from the heart of the Confederacy through every nerve to its extremities. It was felt that its fall would carry down Port Hudson also, leave the Mississippi open, and hopelessly sever the East and West. Every man, therefore, that could be moved was in motion, and though the enemy had no vessel on the river, the banks on either side swarmed with guerillas, moving rapidly from spot to spot, rarely attempting to attack any body of troops, but falling back into the interior and dispersing when followed up. Provided with numerous field pieces, they sought to cut off the transports carrying reinforcements and the steamers carrying supplies. The tortuous course of the stream in many places enabled those who knew the ground to move rapidly across the country and attack the same vessel a second time if she escaped the first assault. On several occasions batteries were built, and a large force attempted the destruction of transports. From these dangers the navy was the only, as it was the best protection. The long line from Cairo to Vicksburg was patrolled by the smaller class of gunboats, and, thanks to their skilful distribution and the activity and courage of the individual commanders, no serious interruption of travel occurred. One steamer only was badly disabled and a few men killed or wounded.

On the 4th of July, 1863, Vicksburg surrendered, and on the 9th the garrison of Port Hudson also laid down its arms. The Mississippi was now open from Cairo to the Gulf, and the merchant steamboat Imperial, leaving St. Louis on the 8th, reached New Orleans on the 16th of this month without molestation.

The Navy Department now directed that the command of the river as far down as New Orleans should be assumed by Porter, Farragut to confine himself henceforth to the coast operations and blockade. Toward the end of July the two admirals met in New Orleans, and, the transfer having been made, Farragut sailed on the 1st of August for the North to enjoy a short respite from his labors. Porter then returned to Cairo, where he at once divided the long line of waterways under his command into eight districts,[1] of which six were on the Mississippi. The seventh extended on the Ohio from Cairo to the Tennessee, and thence through the course of the latter river, while the eighth embraced the upper Ohio and the Valley of the Cumberland. Each district had its own commander, who was responsible to the admiral, but was not to interfere with another unless in case of great need. For the present all was quiet, but there were already rumors of trouble to come when the enemy should recover from the stunning blows he had just received.

[1] The number of districts was afterward increased to ten.

CHAPTER VI.

MINOR OCCURRENCES IN 1863.

On the 4th of July, the same day that Vicksburg surrendered, an attack was made upon Helena, in Arkansas, by the Confederates in force. The garrison at the same time numbered 4,000 men, the enemy were variously estimated at from 9,000 to 15,000. Having attacked the centre of the position, the Confederates carried the rifle-pits and a battery upon the hills, in rear of the town, which commanded all the other defensive works as well as the town itself. They then began pushing masses of troops down the hill, while their sharpshooters were picking off the artillerists in the main fort, called Fort Curtis. Guns had also been placed in commanding positions near the river, both above and below the town, and opened fire upon the line of defensive works across the river bottom, there about a thousand yards in width. Lieutenant-Commander Pritchett, of the Tyler, seeing how the assault was about to be made, placed his vessel in front of the town, so that her broadside played upon the enemy descending the hills, while their artillery above and below were exposed to her bow and stern guns. From this advantageous position the Tyler opened fire, and to her powerful battery and the judgment with which it was used must be mainly attributed the success of the day; for though the garrison fought with great gallantry and tenacity, they were outnumbered two to one. The enemy were driven back with great slaughter. General Prentiss, commanding the post, took occasion to acknowledge, in the fullest and most generous manner, Pritchett's care in previously acquainting himself with the character of the ground, as well as the assistance afterward rendered by him in the fight. Four hundred of the enemy were buried on the field and 1,100 were made prisoners.

While Grant was occupied at Vicksburg and Banks at Port Hudson, General Taylor, commanding the Confederate forces in West Louisiana, had concentrated, on the morning of the 6th of June, a force of three brigades at Richmond, about ten miles from Milliken's Bend and twenty from Young's Point. At Milliken's there was a brigade of negro troops, with a few companies of the Twenty-third Iowa white regiment, in all 1,100 men; and at Young's a few scattered detachments, numbering 500 or 600. Taylor determined to try a surprise of both points, having also a vague hope of communicating with Vicksburg, or causing some diversion in its favor. At sundown of the 6th one brigade was moved toward Milliken's, and one toward Young's Point, the third taking a position in reserve six miles from Richmond. The force directed against Young's Point blundered on its way, got there in broad daylight, and, finding a gunboat present, retired without making any serious attempt. The other brigade, commanded by McCulloch, reached its destination about 3 A.M. of the 7th, drove in the pickets and advanced with determination upon the Union lines. The latter were gradually forced back of the levee, the Iowa regiment fighting with great steadiness, and the negroes behaving well individually; but they lacked organization and knowledge of their weapons. Accordingly when the enemy, who were much superior in numbers, charged the levee and came hand to hand, the colored troops, after a few moments of desperate struggle, broke and fled under the bank of the river. Nothing saved them from destruction but the presence of the Choctaw, which at 3.30 A.M. had opened her fire and was now able to maintain it without fear of injuring her friends. The Confederates could not, or would not face it, and withdrew at 8.30 A.M. What the fate of these black troops would have been had the Confederates come upon them in the flush of a successful charge seems somewhat doubtful, in view of Taylor's suggestive remark that "*unfortunately* some fifty of them had been taken prisoners."

Immediately after the surrender of Vicksburg, Porter followed up the discomfiture of the Confederates by a series of raids into the interior of the country through its natural water-ways. Lieutenant-Commander Walker was again sent up to Yazoo City, this time in company with a force of troops numbering 5,000, under Major-General Herron. During the month that had passed since Walker's last visit, the enemy had been fortifying the place, and the batteries were found ready to receive the vessels. General Herron was then notified, and when his men were landed, a combined attack was made by the army and navy. The Confederates made but slight resistance and soon fled, abandoning everything. Six heavy guns and one vessel fell into the Union hands, and four fine steamers were destroyed by the enemy. Unfortunately, while the De Kalb was moving slowly along she struck a torpedo, which exploded under her bow and sunk her. As she went down another exploded under her stern, shattering it badly. This gunboat, which at first was called the St. Louis, was the third to be lost of the seven. The Cincinnati was afterward raised; but the De Kalb was so shattered as to make it useless to repair her.

At this same time Lieutenant-Commander Selfridge, with a force of light-draught gunboats, entered the Red River, turned out of it into the Black, and from the latter again into the Tensas; following one of the routes by which Grant had thought to move his army below Vicksburg. This water-line runs parallel with the Mississippi. Selfridge succeeded in reaching the head of navigation, Tensas Lake and Bayou Macon, thirty miles above Vicksburg, and only five or six from the Mississippi. The expedition was divided at a tributary of the Black, called Little Red River; two going up it, while two continued up the Tensas. Afterward it went up the Washita as far as Harrisonburg, where the batteries stopped them. Four steamers were destroyed, together with a quantity of ammunition and provisions.

A few weeks later, in August, Lieutenant Bache, late of the Cincinnati, went up the White River with three gunboats, the Lexington, Cricket, and Marmora. At a second Little Red River, a narrow and crooked tributary of the White, the Cricket was sent off to look for two steamers said to be hidden there. Bache himself went on to Augusta, thirty miles further up the White, where he got certain news of the movements of the Confederate army in Arkansas; thus attaining one of his chief objects. He now returned to the mouth of the Little Red, and, leaving the Marmora there, went up himself to see how the Cricket had fared. The little vessel was met coming down; bringing with her the two steamers, but having lost one man killed and eight wounded in a brush with sharpshooters. On their return the three vessels were waylaid at every available point by musketry, but met with no loss. They had gone two hundred and fifty miles up the White, and forty up the Little Red River.

During a great part of 1863, Tennessee and Kentucky, beyond the lines of the Union army, were a prey not only to raids by detached bodies of the enemy's army, but also to the operations of guerillas and light irregular forces. The ruling feeling of the country favored the Confederate cause, so that every hamlet and farm-house gave a refuge to these marauders, while at the same time the known existence of some Union feeling made it hard for officers to judge, in all cases, whether punishment should fall on the places where the attacks were made. The country between the Cumberland and Tennessee Rivers early in the year harbored many of these irregular bodies, having a certain loose organization and a number of field-pieces. The distance between the two streams in the lower part of their course being small, they were able to move from the banks of one to the other with ease. It was necessary, therefore, to keep these rivers patrolled by a force of gunboats; which, though forming part of Porter's fleet, were under the immediate orders of Captain Alexander M. Pennock, commanding the naval station at Cairo. West of the rivers, between them and the great river, the western parts of Kentucky and Tennessee and the northern part of Mississippi were under control of the Union troops, though inrcads of guerillas were not unknown. Nashville was held by the Union forces; but the Confederates were not far away at Shelbyville and Tullahoma. The fights between the gunboats and the hostile parties on these rivers do not individually possess much importance, but have an interest in showing the unending and essential work performed by the navy in keeping the communications open, aiding isolated garrisons, and checking the growth of the guerilla war.

On the 30th of January Lieutenant-Commander S. L. Phelps, having been sent by Captain Pennock in the Lexington to make a special examination of the condition of affairs on the Cumberland River, reported that, a transport having been fired upon twenty miles above Clarksville, he had landed and burned a storehouse used as a resort by the enemy. As he returned the vessel was attacked with some Parrott rifles and struck three times; but the heavy guns of the Lexington drove the enemy off. Going down to Clarksville he met there a fleet of thirty-one steamers, having many barges in tow, convoyed by three light-draught gunboats. These he joined, and the enemy having tested the power of the Lexington, did not fire a shot between Clarksville and Nashville. As a result of his enquiries he thought that no transport should be allowed to go without convoy higher than Fort Henry or Donelson, situated on either river on the line separating Kentucky and Tennessee. The Lexington was therefore detained, and for a time added to the flotilla on those rivers.

Four days later, Lieutenant-Commander Le Roy Fitch, in active charge of the two rivers, was going up the Cumberland with a fleet of transports, convoyed by the Lexington and five light-draughts. When twenty-four miles below Dover, the town on the west bank near which Fort Donelson was situated, he met a steamer bearing a message from Colonel Harding, commanding the post, to the effect that his pickets had been driven in and that he was attacked in force. Fitch at once left the convoy and pushed ahead as fast as he could. A short distance below the town he met a second steamer with the news that Harding was surrounded. At 8 P.M. he arrived, and found the Union forces not only surrounded by overwhelming forces but out of ammunition.

The enemy, not thinking about gunboats, had posted the main body of his troops in a graveyard at the west end of the town, the left wing resting in a ravine that led down to the river, thus enabling the vessels to rake that portion of his line. The gunboats opened fire simultaneously up the ravine, into the graveyard and upon the valley beyond. Taken wholly by surprise, the Confederates did not return a shot, but decamped in haste. Leaving two boats to maintain the fire through the ravine, Fitch hastened up with the other four to shell the main road, which, after leaving the upper end of the town, follows nearly the bank of the stream for some distance. The attacking force in this case was 4,500 strong, composed of regular Confederate troops under Generals Wheeler, Forrest, and Wharton. By 11 P.M. they had disappeared, leaving 140 dead. The garrison, which numbered only 800, had defended itself gallantly against this overwhelming force since noon, but was *in extremis* when the gunboats arrived.

On the 27th of March, Fitch was at Fort Hindman, on the Tennessee, where he took on board a force of 150 soldiers and went up the river. On reaching Savanna he heard of a cotton-mill four miles back being run for the Confederate army. The troops and a force of sailors were landed and took the mill, although a regiment of the enemy's cavalry was but two or three miles away. Finding no sure proof of its working for the army, they did not destroy the building, but removed some of the essential parts of the machinery. Going on to Chickasaw, south of the Tennessee line, as the water was too low for the Lexington, he sent on two light-draughts as far as Florence, where they shelled a camp of the enemy. The rapid falling of the river obliged them to return. On the way a quantity of food and live stock belonging to a noted abettor of guerilla warfare were seized.

Having returned to the mouth of the Cumberland to coal, Fitch received a telegram on the 3d of April that a convoy had been attacked at Palmyra, thirty miles above Dover, and the gunboat St. Clair disabled. He at once got under way, took five light-draughts besides his own vessel, the Lexington, and went up the river. When he reached Palmyra he burned every house in the town, as a punishment for the firing on unarmed vessels and harboring guerillas. A quick movement followed against a body of the enemy higher up the stream, but they had notice of his approach, and had disappeared.

On the 24th a steamer was fired upon in the Tennessee, and three men badly wounded. Fitch went at once to the scene, but the enemy were off. On the 26th, cruising up the river, he found the vessels of General Ellet, commanding what was now called the Marine Brigade, fighting a battery and body of infantry 700 strong. Fitch joined in, and the enemy were of course repulsed. The Marine Brigade landed and pursued the enemy some distance, finding their commander mortally wounded.

On the 26th of May Lieutenant-Commander Phelps, with the Covington and two other gunboats, was at Hamburg, on the Tennessee, a few miles from the Mississippi State line. Here he ferried across 1,500 cavalry and four light field-pieces from Corinth, in Mississippi, under Colonel Cornyn. This little body made a forced march upon Florence, forty miles distant, in rear of the left of the Confederate army at Columbia, captured the place and destroyed a large amount of property, including three cotton-mills. An attempt was made by the enemy to cut this force off on its return to the boats, but without success.

Early in July a very daring raid was made by General J. H. Morgan of the Confederate army into the States of Kentucky, Indiana, and Ohio. Crossing the Ohio River at Brandenburg, he moved in an easterly direction through the southern part of Indiana and Ohio, burning bridges, tearing up railroads, destroying public property, capturing small bodies of troops, and causing general consternation. Fitch heard of him, and at once started up the river with his lightest vessels to cut off the retreat of the raiders. Leaving some boats to patrol the river below, he himself, in the Moose, came up with them on the 19th, at a ford a mile and a half above Buffington Island, and two hundred and fifty miles east of Cincinnati. The retreating enemy had placed two field-pieces in position, but the Moose's battery of 24-pound howitzers drove them off with shell and shrapnel. The troops in pursuit had come up, so the Confederates, finding their retreat stopped, broke and ran up the stream in headlong flight, leaving their wounded and dismounted men behind. The Moose followed, keeping always on their right flank, and stopping two other efforts made to cross. Only when the water became too shoal for even his little paddle steamer of one hundred and sixty tons to go on, did Fitch stop the chase, which had led him five hundred miles from his usual station. His efforts and their useful results were cordially acknowledged by Generals Burnside and Cox, at Cincinnati.

During the siege of Port Hudson the enemy on the west bank of the Mississippi made several demonstrations against Donaldsonville and Plaquemine, with a view to disturbing General Banks's communications; threatening also New Orleans, which was not well prepared for defence. Farragut stationed the Princess Royal, Commander Woolsey, at Donaldsonville; the Winona, Lieutenant-Commander Weaver, above at Plaquemine, and the Kineo, Lieutenant-Commander Watters, some distance below. The Confederates attacked the fort at Donaldsonville in force at midnight of June 27th. The Princess Royal kept under way above the fort, engaging the assailants, the Winona arriving at 4 A.M. and joining with her. The Kineo also came up from below, but not in time to take part. The storming party of the enemy succeeded in getting into the fort, but the supports broke and fled under the fire of the gunboats, leaving the advance, numbering 120, prisoners in the hands of the garrison. On the 7th of July, as the Monongahela was coming up the river, some field batteries of the enemy attacked her, and her commander, Abner Read, an officer of distinguished activity and courage, was mortally wounded. Her other loss was 1 killed and 4 wounded; among the latter being Captain Thornton A. Jenkins, on his way to assume command of the Richmond and of the naval forces off Port Hudson.

CHAPTER VII.

TEXAS AND THE RED RIVER.

Upon the fall of Vicksburg and Port Hudson two objects in the Southwest were presented to the consideration of the Government at Washington—Mobile and Texas. General Banks, commanding the Department of the Gulf, was anxious to proceed against the former; a desire fully shared by the navy, which knew that sooner or later it must be called upon to attack that seaport, and that each day of delay made its defences stronger. Considerations of general policy, connected with the action of France in Mexico and the apparent unfriendly attitude of the Emperor Napoleon III. toward the United States, decided otherwise. On the 10th of June, 1863, just a month before the fall of the strongholds of the Mississippi, the French army entered the city of Mexico. On the 24th of July General Banks was instructed to make immediate preparations for an expedition to Texas. This was speedily followed by other urgent orders to occupy some point or points of Texan territory, doubtless as an indication that the course of interference begun in the weaker republic would not be permitted to extend to lands over which the United States claimed authority, though actually in revolt. The expectation that France would thus attempt to interfere was far from lacking foundation, and was shared, with apprehension, by the Confederate Government. A year before, M. Theron, a French consul in Texas, acting in his official capacity, had addressed a letter to the Governor of the State, suggesting that the re-establishment of the old republic of Texas, in other words, the secession of the State from the Confederacy, might be well for his "beloved adopted country;" and ended by saying that the Governor's answer would be a guide to him in his political correspondence with the government he represented. In consequence of this letter, M. Theron and the French consul at Richmond, who had also been meddling with Texan affairs, were ordered to leave the Confederate States. The object evidently was to set up an independent republic between the new empire in Mexico and whichever power, Union or Confederacy, should triumph in the Civil War.

The Commander-in-Chief, General Halleck, expressed his own preference for a movement by the Red River to Shreveport, in the northwest corner of Louisiana, and the military occupation from that point of northern Texas, but left the decision as to taking that line of operation, or some other, to General Banks. The latter, for various reasons, principally the great distance of Shreveport, seven hundred miles from New Orleans, and the low state of the Red River, which entirely precluded water transportation, chose to operate by the sea-coast, and took as the first point of attack Sabine Pass and city, three hundred miles from Southwest Pass, where the river Sabine, separating the States of Louisiana and Texas, enters the Gulf. If he could make good his footing here at once, he hoped to be able to advance on Beaumont, the nearest point on the railroad, and thence on Houston, the capital and railway centre of the State, which is less than one hundred miles from Sabine City, before the enemy could be ready to repel him.

Owing to lack of transportation, all the troops for the destined operations could not go forward at once. The first division of 4,000, under Major-General Franklin, sailed from New Orleans on the 5th of September. Commodore Henry H. Bell, commanding the Western Gulf Squadron in the absence of Farragut, detailed the gunboats Clifton, Sachem, Arizona, and Granite City to accompany the expedition, Lieutenant Frederick Crocker of the Clifton being senior officer. With the exception of the Clifton they were all of very light armament, but were the only available vessels of sufficiently small draught, the naval-built gunboats of the Cayuga class drawing too much water to cross the bar.

The transports arrived off the Pass on the morning of the 7th, the gunboats coming in the same evening. The next morning at eight the Clifton, followed soon after by the other gunboats and the transports, crossed the bar and anchored inside about two miles from the fort. At 3.30 P.M. the Clifton, Sachem, and Arizona advanced to attack the works. At four the Sachem received a shot in her boilers and was at once enveloped in steam. A few minutes later the Clifton grounded and also was struck in the boilers, but kept up her fire for twenty or thirty minutes longer; then both the disabled vessels hauled down their flags. The army now abandoned the expedition, and the transports with the remaining gunboats withdrew during the night. In this unfortunate affair the Clifton lost 10 killed and 9 wounded, the Sachem 7 killed, the wounded not being given. There were 39 missing from the two vessels, many of whom were drowned.

The hopes of success being dependent upon a surprise, this route was now abandoned. Banks entertained for a little while the idea of advancing from Berwick Bay by land, crossing the Sabine at Niblett's Bluff; but the length of the communication and difficulty of the country deterred him. The Red River Route would not be available before the spring rise. To carry out the wish of the Government he next determined to land at the extreme end of the Texas coast line, near the Rio Grande, and work his way to the eastward. A force of 3,500 men, under General Dana, was organized for this expedition, which sailed from New Orleans on the 26th of October, Banks himself going with it. The transports were convoyed by the ships-of-war Monongahela, Owasco, and Virginia, Captain James H. Strong of the Monongahela being senior officer. The fleet was somewhat scattered by a norther on the 30th, but on the 2d of November a landing was made on Brazos Island at the mouth of the Rio Grande. The next day another detachment was put on shore on the main-land, and Brownsville, thirty miles from the mouth of the river, was occupied on the 6th. Leaving a garrison here, the troops were again embarked on the 16th and carried one hundred and twenty miles up the coast to Corpus Christi, at the southern end of Mustang Island, where they landed and marched to the upper end of the island, a distance of twenty-two miles. Here was a small work, mounting three guns, which was shelled by the Monongahela and surrendered on the approach of the army. The troops now crossed the Aransas Pass and moved upon Pass Cavallo, the entrance to Matagorda Bay. There was here an extensive work called Fort Esperanza, which the army invested; but on the 30th the enemy withdrew by the peninsula connecting with the main-land, thus leaving the control of the bay in the hands of the Union forces. The light gunboats Granite City and Estrella were sent inside.

So far all had gone well and easily; the enemy had offered little resistance and the United States flag had been raised in Texas. Now, however, Banks found powerful works confronting him at the mouth of the Brazos River and at Galveston. To reduce these he felt it necessary to turn into the interior and come upon them in the rear, but the forces of the enemy were such as to deter him from the attempt unless he could receive reinforcements. Halleck had looked with evident distrust upon this whole movement, by which a small force had been separated from the main body by the width of Louisiana and Texas, with the enemy's army between the two, and the reinforcements were not forthcoming; but recurring to his favorite plan of operating by the Red River and Shreveport, without giving positive orders to adopt it, the inducement was held out that, if that line were taken up, Steele's army in Arkansas and such forces as Sherman could detach should be directed to the same object. The co-operation of the Mississippi squadron was also promised.

It was necessary, however, that this proposed expedition should be taken in hand and carried through promptly, because both Banks's own troops and Sherman's would be needed in time to take part in the spring and summer campaigns east of the Mississippi; while at the same time the movement could not begin until the Red River should rise enough to permit the passage of the gunboats and heavy transports over the falls above Alexandria, which would not ordinarily be before the month of March.

The two months of January and February were spent in inactivity in the Department of the Gulf, but frequent communications were held between the three generals whose forces were to take part in the movement. On the 1st of March Sherman came to New Orleans to confer with Banks, and it was then arranged that he should send 10,000 men under a good commander, who should meet Porter at the mouth of the Red River, ascend the Black, and strike a hard blow at Harrisonburg, if possible, and at all events be at Alexandria on the 17th of March. Banks on his part was to reach there at the same date, marching his army from Franklin by way of Opelousas, and to conduct his movement on Shreveport with such celerity as to enable the detachment from Sherman's corps to get back to the Mississippi in thirty days from the time they entered the Red River. General Steele was directed by Grant to move toward Shreveport from Little Rock, a step to which he was averse, and his movements seem to have had little, if any, effect upon the fortunes of the expedition. Having finished his business, Sherman went back at once, resisting the urgent invitation of General Banks, whose military duties seem to have been somewhat hampered by civil calls, to remain over the 4th of March and participate in the inauguration of a civil government for Louisiana, in which the Anvil Chorus was to be played by all the bands in the Army of the Gulf, the church bells rung, and cannons fired by electricity.

General Franklin, who was to command the army advancing from Franklin by Opelousas, did not receive his orders to move till the 10th, which was too late to reach Alexandria, one hundred and seventy-five miles away, by the 17th. Moreover, the troops which had been recalled from the Texas coast, leaving only garrisons at Brownsville and Matagorda, had just arrived at Berwick Bay and were without transportation; while the cavalry had not come up from New Orleans. The force got away on the 13th and 14th and reached Alexandria on the 25th and 26th.

Meanwhile, Sherman, having none but military duties to embarrass him, was in Vicksburg on the 6th, and at once issued his orders to General A. J. Smith, who was to command the corps detached up the Red river. On the 11th Smith was at the mouth of the River, where he met Porter, who had been there since the 2d, and had with him the following vessels: Essex, Commander Robert Townsend; Eastport, Lieutenant-Commander S. L. Phelps; Black Hawk, Lieutenant-Commander K. R. Breese; Lafayette, Lieutenant-Commander J. P. Foster; Benton, Lieutenant-Commander J. A. Greer; Louisville, Lieutenant-Commander E. K. Owen; Carondelet, Lieutenant-Commander J. G. Mitchell; Osage, Lieutenant-Commander T. O. Selfridge; Ouachita, Lieutenant-Commander Byron Wilson; Lexington, Lieutenant G. M. Bache; Chillicothe, Lieutenant S. P. Couthouy; Pittsburg, Lieutenant W. R. Hoel; Mound City, Lieutenant A. R. Langthorne; Neosho, Lieutenant Samuel Howard; Ozark, Lieutenant G. W. Browne; Fort Hindman, Lieutenant John Pearce; Cricket, Master H. H. Gorringe; Gazelle, Master Charles Thatcher.

Most of these vessels will be recognized as old acquaintances. The last three were light-draughts, the Cricket and Gazelle being but little over 200 tons. The Ouachita was a paddle-wheel steamer, carrying in broadside, on two decks, a numerous battery of howitzers, eighteen 24-pounders and sixteen 12-pounders (one of the latter being rifled); and besides these, five 30-pounder rifles as bow and stern guns. The Ozark, Osage, and Neosho, were ironclads of very light draught, having a single turret clad with 6-inch armor in which were mounted two XI-inch guns. They were moved by stern paddle-wheels covered with an iron house, of ¾-inch plates, which was higher than the turret, and from a broadside view looked like a gigantic beehive. The Essex did not go farther than the mouth of the river.

Early on the morning of March 12th the gunboats started up, the transports following. There was just enough water to allow the larger boats to pass. The transports, with the Benton, Pittsburg, Louisville, Mound City, Carondelet, Chillicothe, Ouachita, Lexington, and Gazelle turned off into the Atchafalaya, the admiral accompanying this part of his squadron; while Lieutenant-Commander Phelps with the other vessels continued up the Red River to remove obstructions, which the enemy had planted across the stream eight miles below Fort de Russy.

The army landed at Simmesport on the 13th, taking possession there of the camping-ground of the enemy, who retreated on Fort de Russy. The next day at daylight they were pursued, and Smith's corps, after a march of twenty-eight miles, in which it was delayed two hours to build a bridge, reached the fort in time to assault and take it before sundown. The Confederate General Walker had withdrawn the main body of his troops, leaving only 300 men, who could offer but slight resistance. Eight heavy guns and two field-pieces were taken.

The detachment of vessels under Lieutenant-Commander Phelps were at first delayed by the difficulty of piloting the Lafayette and Choctaw, long vessels of heavy draft, through the narrow and crooked river. The 13th thus wore away slowly, and on the 14th they reached the obstructions. Two rows of piles had been driven across the channel, braced, and tied together; immediately below them was a raft well secured to either bank and made of logs which did not float. Finally a great many trees had been cut and floated down upon the piles from above. The Fort Hindman removed a portion of the raft, and then the Eastport got to work on the piles, dragging out some and starting others by ramming. By four o'clock in the afternoon a large enough gap had been made, and the Eastport, followed by the Hindman, Osage, and Cricket, hastened up the river. Rapid artillery firing was heard as they drew near the works, but being ignorant of the position of the Union troops, few shots were fired for fear of injuring them. The slight engagement was ended by the surrender, a few moments after the boats came up. An order from the admiral to push on at once to Alexandria was delayed five hours in transmission. When it was received, the fastest vessels, the Ouachita and Lexington, were sent on, followed by the Eastport, but got there just as the last of the Confederate transports passed over the Falls. One of them grounded and was burnt.

These advance vessels reached Alexandria on the evening of the 15th, the admiral with the rest on the 16th; at which time there had also come up from 7,000 to 8,000 of Smith's corps, the remainder being left at Fort de Russy.

Alexandria was the highest point reached by the fleet the May before. Shreveport, the object of the present expedition, is three hundred and forty miles farther up the Red River. It was the principal dépôt of the Confederates west of the Mississippi, had some machine-shops and dockyards, and was fortified by a line of works of from two to three miles radius, commanding the opposite bank. Between the two places the river, which gets its name from the color of its water, flows through a fertile and populous country, the banks in many places being high, following in a very crooked channel a general southeasterly direction. In this portion of its course it has a width of seven hundred to eight hundred feet, and at low water a depth of four feet. The slope from Shreveport to Alexandria at high water is a little over a hundred feet, but immediately above the latter place there are two small rapids, called the Falls of Alexandria, which interrupt navigation when the water is low. The annual rise begins in the early winter, and from December to June the river is in fair boating condition for its usual traffic; but water enough for the gunboats and transports to pass the Falls could not be expected before the spring rise in March. The river, however, can never be confidently trusted. For twenty years before 1864 it had only once failed to rise, in 1855; but this year it was exceptionally backward, and so caused much embarrassment to the fleet.

General Banks came in on the 26th of March and the last of Franklin's corps on the 28th. Smith's command was then moved on to Bayou Rapides, twenty-one miles above Alexandria. The slow rise of the river was still detaining the vessels. There was water enough for the lighter draughts, but, as the enemy was reported to have some ironclad vessels not far above, the Admiral was unwilling to let them go up until one of the heavier gunboats had passed. The Eastport was therefore sent up first, being delayed two or three days on the rocks of the rapids, and at last hauled over by main force. She at once passed ahead of Smith's corps. The Mound City, Carondelet, Pittsburg, Louisville, Chillicothe, Ozark, Osage, Neosho, Lexington, and Hindman also went above the Falls, as did some thirty transports. At this time the Marine Brigade, which was now under the army and formed part of Smith's command, was summoned back to Vicksburg, taking 3,000 men from the expedition. The river continuing to rise slowly, it was thought best to keep two lines of transports, one above and one below the Falls, and to transship stores around them. This made it necessary to establish a garrison at Alexandria, which further reduced the force for the field.

Banks's own army marched by land to Natchitoches, eighty miles distant, arriving there on the 2d and 3d of April; but Smith's command went forward on transports convoyed by the gunboats and reached Grand Ecore, four miles from Natchitoches, on the 3d. Here it landed, except one division of 2,000 men under General T. Kilby Smith, who took charge of the transports, now numbering twenty-six, many of them large boats. These Smith was directed to take to the mouth of Loggy Bayou, opposite Springfield, where it was expected he would again communicate with the army. So far the water had been good, the boats having a foot to spare ; but as the river was rising very slowly, the admiral would not take his heavy boats any higher. Leaving Lieutenant-Commander Phelps in command at Grand Ecore, with instructions to watch the water carefully and not be caught above a certain bar, a mile lower down, Porter went ahead with the Cricket, Hindman, Lexington, Osage, Neosho, Chillicothe, and the transports, on the 7th of April.

The army marched out on the 6th and 7th, directed upon Mansfield. The way led through a thickly wooded country by a single road, which was in many places too narrow to admit of two wagons passing. On the night of the 7th Banks reached Pleasant Hill, where Franklin then was ; the cavalry division, numbering 3,300 mounted infantry, being eight miles in advance, Smith's command fifteen miles in the rear. The next day the advance was resumed, and, at about fifteen miles from Pleasant Hill, the cavalry, which had been reinforced by a brigade of infantry, became heavily engaged with a force largely outnumbering it. After being pushed back some little distance, this advanced corps finally gave way in confusion. Banks had now been some time on the field. At 4.15 P.M. Franklin came up, and, seeing how the affair was going, sent word back to General Emory of his corps, to form line of battle at a place he named, two miles in the rear. The enemy came on rapidly, and as the cavalry train of one hundred and fifty wagons and some eighteen or twenty pieces of artillery were close in rear of the discomfited troops, it was not possible, in the narrow road, to turn and save them. Emory, advancing rapidly in accordance with his orders, met flying down the road a crowd of disorganized cavalry, wagons, ambulances, and loose animals, through which his division had to force its way, using violence to do so. As the enemy's bullets began to drop among them, the division reached a suitable position for deploying, called by Banks Pleasant Grove, three miles in rear of the first action. Here the line was formed, and the enemy, seemingly not expecting to meet any opposition, were received when within a hundred yards by a vigorous fire, before which they gave way in about fifteen minutes. By this time it was dark, and toward midnight the command fell back to Pleasant Hill, where it was joined by A. J. Smith's corps.

The following day, at 5 P.M., the enemy again attacked at Pleasant Hill, but were repulsed so decidedly that the result was considered a victory by the Union forces, and by the Confederates themselves a serious check; but for various reasons Banks thought best to fall back again to Grand Ecore. The retreat was continued that night, and on the night of the 11th the army reached Grand Ecore, where it threw up intrenchments and remained ten days. As yet there was no intention of retreating farther.

Meanwhile the navy and transports had pressed hopefully up the river. The navigation was very bad, the river crooked and narrow, the water low and beginning to fall, the bottom full of snags and stumps, and the sides bristling with cypress logs and sharp, hard timbers. Still, the distance, one hundred and ten miles, was made in the time appointed, and Springfield Landing reached on the afternoon of the 10th. Here the enemy had sunk a large steamer across the channel, her bow resting on one shore and her stern on the other, while the body amidships was broken down by a quantity of bricks and mud loaded upon her. Porter and Kilby Smith were consulting how to get rid of this obstacle, when they heard of the disaster and retreat of the army. Smith was ordered by Banks to return, and there was no reason for Porter to do otherwise. The following day they fell back to Coushattee

Chute, and the enemy began the harassment which they kept up throughout the descent to, and even below, Alexandria. The first day, however, the admiral was able to keep them for the most part in check, though from the high banks they could fire down on the decks almost with impunity. The main body of the enemy was on the southern bank, but on the north there was also a force under a General Liddell, numbering, with Harrison's cavalry, perhaps 2,500 men.

On the 12th a severe and singular fight took place. At four in the afternoon the Hastings, transport, on which Kilby Smith was, having disabled her wheel, had run into the right bank for repairs. At the same moment the Alice Vivian, a heavy transport, with four hundred cavalry horses, was aground in the middle of the stream; as was the gunboat Osage, Lieutenant-Commander Selfridge. Two other transports were alongside the Vivian, and a third alongside the Osage, trying to move them. Another transport, called the Rob Roy, having on her decks four siege guns, had just come down and was near the Osage. The Lexington, gunboat, Lieutenant Bache, was near the northern shore, but afloat. The vessels being thus situated, a sudden attack was made from the right bank by 2,000 of the enemy's infantry and four field pieces. The gunboats, the Rob Roy with her siege guns, and two field pieces on the other transports all replied, the Hastings, of course, casting off from her dangerous neighborhood. This curious contest lasted for nearly two hours, the Confederate sharpshooters sheltering themselves behind the trees, the soldiers on board the transports behind bales of hay. There could be but one issue to so ill-considered an attack, and the enemy, after losing 700 men, were driven off; their commander, General Thomas Green, a Texan, being among the slain. The large loss is accounted for by the fact that besides the two thousand actually engaged there were five thousand more some distance back, who shared in the punishment.

The following day an attack was made from the north bank, but no more from the south before reaching Grand Ecore on the 14th and 15th. The admiral himself, being concerned for the safety of his heavy vessels in the falling river, hurried there on the 13th, and on his arrival reported the condition of things above to Banks, who sent out a force to clear the banks of guerillas as far as where the transports lay. Lieutenant-Commander Phelps had already moved all the vessels below the bar at Grand Ecore, but had recalled four to cover the army when it returned. The admiral now sent them all below to move slowly toward Alexandria. His position was one of great perplexity. The river ought to be rising, but was actually falling; there was danger if he delayed that he might lose some of the boats, but on the other hand he felt it would be a stain upon the navy to look too closely to its own safety, and it was still possible that the river might take a favorable turn. He had decided to keep four of the light-draughts above the bar till the very last moment, remaining with them himself, when he received news that the Eastport had been sunk by a torpedo eight miles below. The accident happened on the 15th, the vessel having been previously detained on the bar nearly twenty-four hours. The admiral left Lieutenant-Commander Selfridge in charge at Grand Ecore and at once went to the scene, where he found the Eastport in shoal water but sunk to her gun-deck, the water on one side being over it. The Lexington and a towboat were alongside helping to pump her out. Giving orders that she should be lightened, he kept on down to Alexandria to start two pump-boats up to her and to look after the affairs of the squadron both along the Red River and in the Mississippi. On his return, two days later, he found her with her battery and ammunition out and the pump-boats alongside. By this time it was known that the army would not advance again, and that Banks was anxious to get back to Alexandria. The officers and crew of the Eastport worked night and day to relieve her, and on the 21st she was again afloat, with fires started, but as yet they had not been able to come at the leak. That day she made twenty miles, but at night grounded on a bar, to get over which took all the 22d. Four or five miles farther down she again grounded, and another day was spent in getting her off. Two or three times more she was gotten clear and made a few more miles down the river by dint of extreme effort; but at last, on the 26th, she grounded on some logs fifty miles below the scene of the accident, in a position evidently hopeless.

Selfridge's division of light ironclads had been compelled by the falling water to drop below the bar at Grand Ecore, and, as they were there of no further use to the army, had continued down to Alexandria, except the Hindman, which was kept by the Eastport. On the 22d the army evacuated Grand Ecore and marched for Alexandria. On this retreat the advance and rear-guard had constant skirmishing with the enemy. At Cane River the Confederates had taken position to dispute the crossing, and the advance had a serious fight to drive them off. The rear-guard also had one or two quite sharp encounters, but the army reached Alexandria without serious loss on the 26th.

The Eastport and Fort Hindman were now in a very serious position, aground in a hostile river, their own army sixty miles away, and between it and them the enemy lining the banks of the river. The admiral, having seen the rest of his fleet in safety, returned to the crippled boat, taking with him only two tinclads, the Cricket and Juliet; but the Osage and Neosho were ordered to move up forty miles, near the mouth of Cane River, so as to be in readiness to render assistance. On the 26th, the commander of the Eastport, whose calmness and hopefulness had won the admiral's admiration and led him to linger longer than was perhaps prudent, in the attempt to save the vessel, was obliged to admit that there was no hope. The river was falling steadily, the pilots said there was already too little water for her draught on the bars below, and the crew were worn out with six days of incessant labor. The attempt was made to remove her plating, but it was not possible to do so soon enough. Orders were therefore given to transfer the ship's company to the Fort Hindman, whose captain, Lieutenant Pearce, had worked like her own to save her, and to blow the Eastport up. Eight barrels of powder were placed under her forward casemate, a like number in the stern, and others about the machinery, trains were laid fore and aft, and at 1.45 P.M. Phelps himself lit the match and left the vessel. He had barely time to reach the Hindman before the explosions took place in rapid succession; then the flames burst out and the vessel was soon consumed.

The three remaining gunboats and the two pump-boats now began a hazardous retreat down the river. Just as the preparations for blowing up the Eastport were completed, a rush was made by twelve hundred men from the right bank to board the Cricket, which was tied up. Her captain, Gorringe, backed clear, and opening upon them with grape and canister, supported by a cross fire from the other boats, the attack was quickly repelled. They were not again molested until they had gone twenty miles farther, to about five miles above the mouth of Cane River. Here they came in sight of a party of the enemy, with eighteen pieces of artillery, drawn up on the right bank. At this time the Cricket was leading with the admiral's flag; the Juliet following, lashed to one pump-boat; the Hindman in the rear. The Cricket opened at once, and the enemy replied. Gorringe stopped his vessel, meaning to fight and cover those astern, but the admiral directed him to move ahead. Before headway was gained the enemy was pouring in a pelting shower of shot and shell, the two broadside guns' crews were swept away, one gun disabled, and at the same instant the chief engineer was killed, and all but one of the men in the fire-room wounded. In these brief moments the Juliet was also disabled by a shot in her machinery, the rudder of the pump-boat lashed to her was struck, and the boiler of the other was exploded. The captain of the latter, with almost the entire ship's company, numbering two hundred,[1] were scalded to death, while the boat, enveloped in steam, drifted down and lodged against the bank under the enemy's battery, remaining in their power. The pilot of the boat towing the Juliet abandoned the wheel-house—an act unparalleled among a class of men whose steadiness and devotion under the exposure of their calling elicited the highest praise from Porter and others; the crew also tried to cut the hawsers, but were stopped by Watson, the captain of the gunboat. A junior pilot named Maitland, with great bravery and presence of mind, jumped to the wheel and headed the two boats up river. This confusion in the centre of the line prevented the Hindman from covering the admiral as Phelps wished, but he now got below the Juliet and engaged the enemy till she was out of range. Meanwhile the admiral had found the pilot of the Cricket to be among the wounded, and taking charge of the vessel himself, ran by the battery under the heaviest fire[2] he ever ex-

[1] These were mostly slaves who were running from their masters.

[2] Colonel Brent, Taylor's Chief of Artillery, reported that there were only four Confederate pieces, two 12-pounders and two howitzers, in this attack; instead of

perienced. When below he turned and engaged the batteries in the rear, but seeing that the Hindman and the others were not coming by he continued down to the point where he expected to meet the Osage and Neosho.

In this truly desperate fight the Cricket, a little boat of one hundred and fifty-six tons, was struck thirty-eight times in five minutes, and lost 25 killed and wounded, half her crew. Soon after passing below she ran aground and remained fast for three hours, so that it was dark when she reached the Osage, lying opposite another battery of the enemy, which she had been engaging during the day.

During that night the vessels still above were busy repairing damages and getting ready for the perils of the next day. Fearing the enemy might obstruct the channel by sinking the captured pump-boat across it, a shell was fired at her from time to time. The repairs were made before noon, but the Juliet being still crippled, the Hindman took her alongside, and so headed down for the batteries. Before going far the Juliet struck a snag, which made it necessary to go back and stop the leak. Then they started again, the remaining pump-boat following. When within five hundred yards the enemy opened a well-sustained fire, and a shot passed through the pilot-house of the Hindman, cutting the wheel-ropes. This made the vessel unmanageable, and the two falling off broadside to the stream drifted down under fire, striking now one shore and now the other but happily going clear. The guns under these circumstances could not

---

eighteen, as stated by Porter. Brent was not present, and Captain Cornay, commanding the battery, was killed. The pilot Maitland, who was captured the next day, states, in a separate report made two months later, that he heard among the enemy that the number was eighteen. Phelps, who, like the admiral, was hardened to fire, speaks of them as numerous. The reader must decide for himself the probability of four smooth-bore light pieces striking one small boat thirty-eight times in five minutes, besides badly disabling three others.

be used very effectively, and the pump-boat suffered the more from the enemy's fire. Maitland was still piloting her, and when nearly opposite the batteries he was wounded in both legs by a shell. He dropped on his knees, unable to handle the wheel, and the boat ran into the bank on the enemy's side. Another shell struck the pilot-house, wounding him again in several places, and a third cut away a bell-rope and the speaking-tube. Rallying a little, Maitland now got hold of and rang another bell and had the boat backed across the river. The crew attempted to escape, but were all taken prisoners, the captain and one other having been killed. In the two days encounters the Juliet was hit nearly as often as the Cricket and lost 15 killed and wounded; the Hindman, though repeatedly struck and much cut up, only 3 killed and 5 wounded. The fire of the enemy's sharpshooters was very annoying for some miles farther down, but twelve miles below the batteries they met the Neosho going up to their assistance.

The main interest of the retreat of the squadron centres in the Eastport and her plucky little consorts, but the other vessels had had their own troubles in getting down the river. The obstacles to be overcome are described as enough to appal the stoutest heart by the admiral, who certainly was not a man of faint heart. Guns had to be removed and the vessels jumped over sand-bars and logs, but the squadron arrived in time to prevent any attack on the reserve stores before the main body of the army came up.

At Alexandria the worst of their troubles awaited them, threatening to make all that had yet been done vain. The river, which ordinarily remains high till June, had not only failed to reach its usual height but had so fallen that they could not pass the rapids. General W. T. Sherman, who had lived at Alexandria before the war, thought twelve feet necessary before going up, a depth usually found from March to June. At the very least seven were needed by the gunboats to go down, and on the 30th of April of this year there were actually only three feet four inches. The danger was the greatest that had yet befallen the fleet, and seemingly hopeless. A year before, in the Yazoo bayous, the position had been most critical, but there the peril came from the hand of man and was met and repelled by other men. Here Nature herself had turned against them, forsaking her usual course to do them harm. Ten gunboats and two tugs were thus imprisoned in a country soon to pass into the enemy's hands by the retreat of the army.

Desperate as the case seemed, relief came. Lieutenant-Colonel Joseph Bailey, of the Fourth Wisconsin Volunteers, was at this time acting as Chief Engineer of the Nineteenth Army Corps, General Franklin's. He was a man who had had much experience on the watercourses of the Northwestern country, and had learned to use dams to overcome obstacles arising from shallow water in variable streams. The year before he had applied this knowledge to free two transport steamers, which had been taken when Port Hudson fell, from their confinement in Thompson's Creek, where the falling water had left them sunk in the sand. As the army fell back, and during its stay at Grand Ecore, he had heard rumors about the scant water at the Falls, and the thought had taken hold of his mind that he might now build a dam on a greater scale and to a more vital purpose than ever before.

His idea, first broached to General Franklin, was through him conveyed to Banks and Porter, and generally through the army. Franklin, himself an engineer, thought well of it, and so did some others; but most doubted, and many jeered. The enemy themselves, when they became aware of it, laughed, and their pickets and prisoners alike cried scoffingly, "How about that dam?" But Bailey had the faith that moves mountains, and he was moreover happy in finding at his hands the fittest tools for the work. Among the troops in the far Southwest were two or three regiments from Maine, the northeasternmost of all the States. These had been woodmen and lumbermen from their youth, among their native forests, and a regiment of them now turned trained and willing arms upon the great trees on the north shore of the Red River; and there were many others who, on a smaller scale and in different scenes, had experience in the kind of work now to be done. Time was pressing, and from two to three thousand men were at once set to work on the 1st of May. The Falls are about a mile in length, filled with rugged rocks which, at this low water, were bare or nearly so, the water rushing down around, or over, them with great swiftness. At the point below, where the dam was to be built, the river is 758 feet wide, and the current was then between nine and ten miles an hour. From the north bank was built what was called the "tree dam," formed of large trees laid with the current, the branches interlocking, the trunks down stream and cross-tied with heavy timber; upon this was thrown brush, brick, and stone, and the weight of water as it rose bound the fabric more closely down upon the bottom of the river. From the other bank, where the bottom was more stony and trees less plenty, great cribs were pushed out, sunk and filled with stone and brick —the stone brought down the river in flat-boats, the bricks obtained by pulling down deserted brick buildings. On this side, a mile away, was a large sugar-house; this was torn down and the whole building, machinery, and kettles went to ballast the dam. Between the cribs and the tree dam a length of 150 feet was filled by four large coal barges, loaded with brick and sunk. This great work was completed in eight working days, and even on the eighth, three of the lighter vessels, the Osage, Neosho, and Fort Hindman, were able to pass the upper falls and wait just above the dam for the chance to pass ; but the heavier vessels had yet to delay for a further rise. In the meantime the vessels were being lightened by their crews. Nearly all the guns, ammunition, provisions, chain cables, anchors, and everything that could affect the draught, were taken out and hauled round in wagons below the falls. The iron plating was taken off the Ozark, and the sides of our old friends the Eads gunboats, the four survivors of which were here, as ever where danger was. This iron, for want of wagons, could not be hauled round, so the boats ran up the river and dumped it overboard in a five-fathom hole, where the shifting sand would soon swallow it up. Iron plating was then too scarce and valuable to the Confederates to let it fall into their hands. Eleven old 32-pounders were also burst and sunk.

The dam was finished, the water rising, and three boats below, when, between 7 and 10 A.M. of the 9th, the pressure became so great as to sweep away two of the barges in mid-stream and the pent-up water poured through. Admiral Porter rode round to the upper falls and ordered the Lexington to pass them at once and try to go through the dam without a stop. Her steam was ready and she went ahead, passing scantly over the rapids, the water falling all the time ; then she steered straight for the opening, where the furious rushing of the waters seemed to threaten her with destruction. She entered the gap, which was but 66 feet wide, with a full head of steam, pitched down the roaring torrent, made two or three heavy rolls, hung for a moment on the rocks below, and then, sweeping into deep water with the current, rounded to at the bank, safe. One great cheer rose from the throats of the thousands looking on, who had before been hushed into painful silence, awaiting the issue with beating hearts. The Neosho followed, but stopping her engine as she drew near the opening, was carried helplessly through; for a moment her low hull disappeared in the water, but she escaped with a hole in her bottom, which was soon repaired. The Hindman and Osage came through without touching.

The work on the dam had been done almost wholly by the soldiers, who had worked both day and night, often up to their waists and even to their necks in the water, showing throughout the utmost cheerfulness and good humor. The partial success, that followed the first disappointment of the break, was enough to make such men again go to work with good will. Bailey decided not to try again, with his limited time and materials, to sustain the whole weight of water with one dam; and so, leaving the gap untouched, went on to build two wing-dams on the upper falls. These, extending from either shore toward the middle of the river and inclining slightly down stream, took part of the weight, causing a rise of 1 foot 2 inches, and shed the water from either side into the channel between them. Three days were needed to build these, one a crib- and the other a tree-dam, and a bracket-dam a little lower down to help guide the current. The rise due to the main dam when breached was 5 feet 4½ inches, so that the entire gain in depth by this admirable engineering work was 6 feet 6½ inches. On the 11th the Mound City, Carondelet, and Pittsburg came over the upper falls, but with trouble, the channel being very crooked and scarcely wide enough. The next day the remaining boats, Ozark, Louisville, and Chillicothe, with the two tugs, also came down to the upper dam, and during that and the following day they all passed through the gap, with

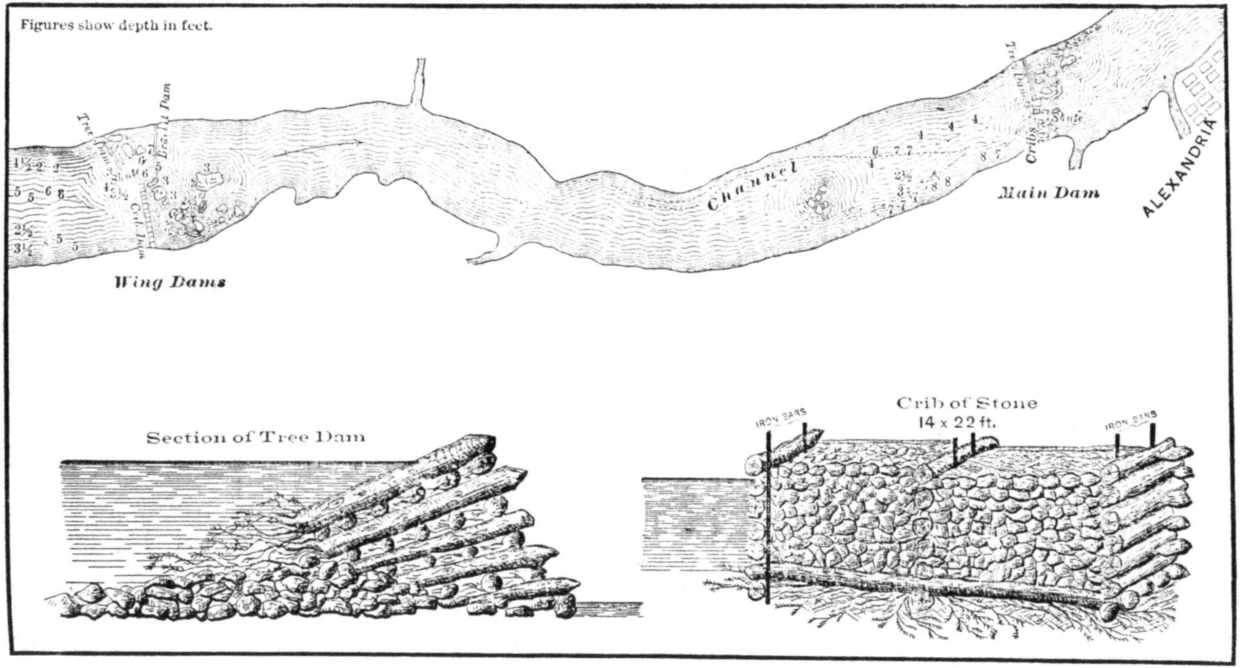
Figures show depth in feet.
Tree Dam
Bracket Dam
Crib Dam
Wing Dams
Channel
Tree Dam
Cribs
Shute
Main Dam
ALEXANDRIA
Section of Tree Dam
Crib of Stone
14 x 22 ft.
IRON BARS
IRON BARS

Red River Dam.

hatches closely nailed down and every precaution taken against accident. No mishap befell them beyond the unshipping of rudders, and the loss of one man swept from the deck of a tug. The two barges which had been carried out at the first break of the dam stuck just below and at right angles to it, and there staid throughout, affording an excellent cushion on the left side of the shoot. What had been a calamity proved thus a benefit. The boats having taken on board their guns and stores as fast as they came below, that work was completed, even by the last comers, on the 13th, and all then steamed down the river with the transports in company. The water had become very low in the lower part, but providentially a rise of the Mississippi sent up so much back-water that no stoppage happened.

For the valuable services rendered to the fleet in this hour of great danger, Lieutenant-Colonel Bailey was promoted to the rank of brigadier-general and received the thanks of Congress. The stone cribs of the dam have long since been swept away, but the tree-dam has remained until this day, doubtless acquiring new strength from year to year by the washing of the river. Its position has forced the channel over to the south shore, encroaching seriously upon the solid land, especially when the water is high. A very large part of the front of Alexandria, at the upper suburb, has thus been washed away, and the caving still continues.

While the fleet and army were at Alexandria, the enemy had passed round the city and appeared on the banks below, where they made the passage of light steamers very dangerous. Two light-draught gunboats, the Covington and Signal, were thus lost to the service They had gone down convoying a transport called the Warner. The Warner was put in advance, the gunboats following in line ahead. The enemy began with heavy musketry and two field pieces, by which the Warner's rudders were disabled; she continued on a short distance till a bend was reached, and here, being unable to make the turn, she went ashore, blocking also the channel to the two armed vessels. A heavy force of infantry with artillery now opened on the three, the gunboats replying for three hours, when the Warner hoisted a white flag. Lieutenant Lord of the Covington still kept up his fire and sent to burn the transport; but learning from the colonel in charge that there were nearly 125 killed and wounded on board he desisted. Soon after this the Signal was disabled. The Covington then rounded to and took the others in tow up stream, but her own rudders were disabled and the Signal went adrift. The latter then anchored, and the Covington running to the left bank tied up with her head up stream. In this position the action was continued with the enemy, reinforced now by the first battery which had been brought down, till the steam-drum was penetrated and a shot entering the boilers let out all the water; the ammunition gave out and several guns were disabled, one officer and several men being killed. Lord set the vessel on fire and escaped with the crew to the banks. On mustering, 9 officers and 23 men were found out of a crew of 76. Most of those who reached the banks escaped through the woods to Alexandria. The Covington was riddled, having received some fifty shots. The disabled Signal was fought with equal obstinacy by her commander, Lieutenant Morgan, but after the destruction of the Covington was surrendered, not burned; it being found impossible to remove the wounded under the fire of the enemy.

The army marched out of Alexandria on the 14th toward Simmesport, which they reached on the 16th. Having no regular pontoon train, the Atchafalaya, which is here about six hundred yards wide, was crossed by a bridge of transport steamers moored side by side; an idea of Colonel Bailey's. The crossing was made on the 20th, and on that same day General Banks was relieved by General Canby, who had been ordered to command the Department of the West Mississippi, with headquarters at New Orleans. A. J. Smith's corps embarked and went up the river, and the expedition was over. The disastrous ending and the lateness of the season made it impracticable to carry out Grant's previous plan of moving on Mobile with force sufficient to insure its capture.

After the Red River expedition little is left to say, in a work of this scope, of the operations of the Mississippi Squadron during the rest of the war. Admiral Porter was relieved during the summer, leaving Captain Pennock in temporary charge. Acting Rear-Admiral S. P. Lee took the command on the 1st of November. The task and actions of the squadron were of the same general character as those described in Chapter VI. Guerillas and light detached bodies of the enemy continued to hover on the banks of the Mississippi, White, Arkansas, Tennessee, and Cumberland Rivers. The Red River was simply blockaded, not occupied, and much of the Yazoo Valley, having no present importance, had been abandoned to the enemy. The gunboats scattered throughout these waters were constantly patrolling and convoying, and often in action. The main operations of the army being now far east of the Mississippi, the work and exposure of the boats became greater. Masked batteries of field pieces were frequently sprung upon them, or upon unarmed steamers passing up and down; in either case the nearest gunboat must hasten and engage it. Weak isolated posts were suddenly attacked; a gunboat, usually not far off, must go to the rescue. Reconnoissances into the enemy's country, as the Yazoo Valley, were to be made, or troops carried in transports from point to point; gunboats went along with their heavy yet manageable artillery, feeling doubtful places with their shells and clearing out batteries or sharpshooters when found. The service was not as easy as it sounds. It would be wrong to infer that their power was always and at once recognized. Often they were outnumbered in guns, and a chance shot in a boiler or awkward turn of a wheel, throwing the vessel aground, caused its loss. Even when victorious they were often hardly used. The limits of this book will permit the telling of but two or three stories.

In the latter part of June, 1864, General Steele, commanding the Union troops in Arkansas, wished to move some round in transports from Duval's Bluff on the White River to the Arkansas, hoping to reach Little Rock in this way. One attempt was made, but, the enemy being met in force on the Arkansas, the transports were turned back. Lieutenant Bache assured him that the trip could not be made, but as the General thought otherwise, he consented to try again and left the Bluff with a large convoy on the 24th, having with him of armed vessels the Tyler, his own, the Naumkeag and Fawn. The two latter were tinclads, the first an unarmored boat. When about twenty miles down, two men were picked up, part of the crew of the light-draught Queen City, which had been captured by the Confederates five hours before. It was then nine o'clock. Bache at once turned the transports back and went ahead fast himself to take or destroy the lost boat before her guns could be removed. Before reaching Clarendon two reports were heard, which came from the Queen City, blown up by the enemy when the others were known to be coming. The three boats formed line ahead, the Tyler leading, Naumkeag second, and Fawn third, their broadsides loaded with half-second shrapnel and canister. As they drew near, the enemy opened with seven field pieces and some two thousand infantry and put one of their first shots through the pilot-house of the Tyler, the vessels being then able to reply only with an occasional shell from their bow guns. As they came nearly abreast they slowed down and steamed by, firing their guns rapidly. When under the batteries the Fawn received a shot through her pilot-house, killing the pilot and carrying away the bell gear, at the same time ringing the engine-room bell, causing the engineers to stop the boat under fire. Some little delay ensued in fixing the bells, the paymaster took the wheel, and the Fawn, having another shot in the pilot-house, passed on. As soon as the Tyler and Naumkeag were below they turned and steamed up again, delivering a deliberate fire as they passed, in the midst of which the enemy ran off, leaving behind them most of their captures, including a light gun taken from the Queen City. The boats were struck twenty-five times, and lost 3 killed and 15 wounded. The Queen City had been taken by surprise, and her engines disabled at the first fire. She lost 2 killed and 8 wounded, including her commander; and, while many of her crew escaped to the opposite bank, many were taken prisoners.

The main course of the war in the West having now drifted away from the Mississippi Valley to the region south and southeast of Nashville, embracing Southern and Eastern Tennessee and the northern parts of Georgia, Alabama, and Mississippi, the convoy and gunboat service on the Tennessee and Cumberland assumed new importance. An eleventh division was formed on the upper waters of the Tennessee, above Muscle Shoals, under the command of Lieutenant Moreau Forrest; Lieutenant-Commander Shirk had the lower river, and Fitch still controlled the Cumberland. When Hood, after the fall of Atlanta, began his movement toward Tennessee in the latter part of October, General Forrest, the active Confederate cavalry leader, who had been stationed at Corinth with his outposts at Eastport and on the Tennessee River, moved north along the west bank, and with seventeen regiments of cavalry and nine pieces of artillery appeared on the 28th before Fort Heiman, an earthwork about seventy-five miles from Paducah. Here he captured two transports and a light-draught called the Undine. On the 2d of November he had established batteries on the west bank both above and below Johnsonville, one of the Union army's bases of supplies and a railway terminus, thus blockading the water approach and isolating there eight transports, with barges, and three light-draughts, the Key West, Elfin, and Tawah. Nevertheless, the three boats went down and engaged the lower battery, and though they found it too strong for them they retook one of the transports. Meantime Shirk had telegraphed the Admiral and Fitch, and the latter came to his assistance with three of the Cumberland River light-draughts. Going on up the Tennessee Fitch picked up three other light-draughts, and on the morning of the 4th approached the lower battery from below, Lieutenant King, the senior officer above, coming down at the same time. The enemy then set fire to the Undine, but the channel was so narrow and intricate that Fitch did not feel justified in attempting to take his boats up, and King was not able to run by. Fitch, whose judgment and courage were well proved, said that the three blocked gunboats were fought desperately and well handled, but that they could not meet successfully the heavy rifled batteries then opposed to them in such a channel. All three were repeatedly struck and had several of their guns disabled. They then retired to the fort, where the enemy opened on them in the afternoon with a battery on the opposite shore. After firing away nearly all their ammunition, and being further disabled, Lieutenant King, fearing that they might fall into the enemy's hands, burnt them with the transports. The place was relieved by General Schofield twenty-four hours later, so that if King had patiently held on a little longer his pluck and skill would have been rewarded by saving his vessels. At about the same time, October 28th, General Granger being closely pressed in Decatur, Alabama, above the Muscle Shoals, the light-draught General Thomas, of the Eleventh Division, under the command of Acting-Master Gilbert Morton, at great risk got up in time to render valuable service in repelling the attack.

The Union forces continued to fall back upon Nashville before the advance of Hood, who appeared before the city on the 2d of December, and by the 4th had established his lines round the south side. His left wing struck the river at a point four miles below by land, but eighteen by the stream, where they captured two steamers and established a battery. Fitch, receiving word of this at 9 P.M., at once went down with the Carondelet and four light-draughts to attack them. The boats moved quietly, showing no lights, the Carondelet and Fairplay being ordered to run below, giving the enemy grape and canister as they passed in front, and then to round to and continue the fight up stream, Fitch intending to remain above with the other boats. The Carondelet began firing when midway between the upper and lower batteries, and the enemy replied at once with heavy musketry along the whole line and with his field pieces. The river at this place is but eighty yards wide, but the enemy, though keeping up a hot fire, fortunately aimed high, and the boats escaped without loss in an action lasting eighty minutes. The two steamers were retaken and the enemy removed their batteries; but they were shortly reestablished. On the 6th Fitch again engaged them with the Neosho and Carondelet, desiring to pass a convoy below, but the position was so well chosen, behind spurs of hills and at a good height above the river, that only one boat could engage them at one time and then could not elevate her guns to reach the top without throwing over the enemy. The Neosho remained under a heavy fire, at thirty yards distance, for two and a half hours, being struck over a hundred times and having everything perishable on decks demolished ; but the enemy could not be driven away. The river being thus blockaded the only open communication for the city was the Louisville Railroad, and during the rest of the time the gunboats, patrolling the Cumberland above and below, prevented the enemy's cavalry from crossing and cutting it.

When Thomas made his attack of the 15th, which resulted in the entire defeat and disorganization of Hood's army, Fitch, at his wish, went down and engaged the attention of the batteries below until a force of cavalry detached for that special purpose came down upon their rear. These guns were taken and the flotilla then dropped down to the scene of its previous fights and engaged till dark such batteries as it could see. The routed and disorganized army of the enemy were pressed as closely as the roads allowed down to the Tennessee, where Lieutenant Forrest of the Eleventh District aided in cutting off stragglers. Admiral Lee, who was at once notified, pressed up the river with gunboats and supply steamers as far as the shoals ; but the low state of the river prevented his crossing them. The destruction of boats and flats along the river, however, did much to prevent stragglers from crossing and rejoining their army.

This was the last of the very important services of the Mississippi Squadron. Five months later, in June, 1865, its officers received the surrender of a small naval force still held by the Confederates in the Red River. Our old friend, the ram Webb, which had heretofore escaped capture, ran out of the Red River in April with a load of cotton and made a bold dash for the sea. She succeeded in getting by several vessels before suspected, and even passed New Orleans; but the telegraph was faster than she, and before reaching the forts she was headed off by the Richmond, run ashore, and burned. On the 14th of August, 1865, Admiral Lee was relieved and the Mississippi Squadron, as an organization, ceased to be. The vessels whose careers we have followed, and whose names have become familiar, were gradually sold, and, like most of their officers, returned to peaceful life.

CHAPTER VIII.

MOBILE.

ADMIRAL FARRAGUT resumed the command of his squadron on January 18th, 1864. His wish was to attack at once the defences of Mobile before the Confederates had finished the ironclads they were building; but troops were needed for the reduction of the forts, and the Red River expedition had diverted those that might have been available.

The city of Mobile is thirty miles from the Gulf, at the head of a great bay of the same name. The width of the bay varies from fifteen miles at the lower end to six at the upper; the depth throughout the greater part is from twelve to fourteen feet, shelving gently near the shores, but at the lower end there is a deep hole extending from the mouth north-northwest for six miles, with an average width of two and a half. In this the depth is from twenty to twenty-four feet. The principal entrance is from the Gulf direct, between Mobile Point, a long low projection from the mainland, on the east, and Dauphin Island on the west, the latter being one of the chain which bounds Mississippi Sound. The distance between these points is nearly three miles, but from Dauphin Island a bank of hard sand makes out under water both east and south, defining one side of the main ship channel, which closely skirts Mobile Point, and narrowing it to a little less than two thousand yards. Near the southeast point of this bank there rise two small islands, called Sand Islands, distant three miles from Mobile Point. The channel on the other side is bounded by a similar sand bank running seaward from the Point, the two approaching so that at Sand Islands they are not more than seven hundred and fifty yards apart. Vessels of very light draught could also enter the bay from Mississippi Sound, but it was not practicable for the fleet.

The entrance from the Gulf was guarded by two works, Fort Morgan on Mobile Point and Fort Gaines on Dauphin Island. The approach by Mississippi Sound was covered by Fort Powell, a small earthwork on Tower Island, commanding the channel which gave the most water, known as Grant's Pass. Gaines was too far distant from the main ship channel to count for much in the plans of the fleet. It was a pentagonal work mounting in barbette[1] three X-inch columbiads, five 32-, two 24-, and two 18-pounder smooth-bore guns, and four rifled 32-pounders; besides these it had eleven 24-pounder howitzers, siege and for flank defence. In Fort Powell there were[1] one X-inch, two VIII-inch and one 32-pounder smooth-bore and two VII-inch Brooke rifles; these bore on the sound and channels, but the rear of the fort toward the bay was yet unfinished and nearly unarmed. The third and principal work, Fort Morgan, was much more formidable. It was five sided, and built to carry guns both in barbette and casemates; but when seized by the Confederates the embrasures of the curtains facing the channel were masked and a heavy exterior water battery was thrown up before the northwest curtain. The armament at this time cannot be given with absolute certainty.[2] The official reports of the United States engineer and ordnance officers,

---

[1] Report of the United States Ordnance Officer of Department, dated October, 1864.

[2] See Appendix.

made after the surrender, differ materially, but from a comparison between them and other statements the following estimate has been made: Main fort seven X-inch, three VIII-inch and twenty-two 32-pounder smooth-bore guns,[1] and two VIII-inch, two 6.5-inch and four 5.82-inch rifles.[2] In the water battery there were four X-inch and one VIII-inch columbiads and two 6.5-inch rifles.[3] Of the above, ten X-inch, three VIII-inch, sixteen 32-pounders and all the rifles, except one of 5.82 calibre, bore upon the channel. There were also twenty flanking 24-pounder howitzers and two or three light rifles, which were useless against the fleet from their position.

Such were the shore defences. In the waters of the bay there was a little Confederate squadron under Admiral Franklin Buchanan, made up of the ram Tennessee and three small paddle-wheel gunboats, the Morgan, Gaines, and Selma, commanded respectively by Commander George W. Harrison, and Lieutenants J. W. Bennett and P. U. Murphy. They were unarmored, excepting around the boilers. The Selma was an open-deck river steamer with heavy hog frames; the two others had been built for the Confederate Government, but were poorly put together. The batteries were: Morgan, two VII-inch rifles and four 32-pounders; Gaines, one VIII-inch rifle and five 32-pounders; Selma, one VI-inch rifle, two IX-inch, and one VIII-inch smooth-bore shell-guns. Though these lightly built vessels played a

---

[1] Of these guns twelve 32-pounders were at the southwest angle of the covered way. This is believed by the writer to be the battery known to the fleet as the lighthouse battery.

[2] 24-pounder smooth-bore guns rifled.

[3] In a paper read in 1868, before the Essayons Club, at Willett's Point, N. Y., by Captain A. H. Burnham, U. S. Engineers, it is stated that there were three VII- and VIII-inch rifles in this battery. If this is correct, they had probably been moved from the barbette of the main work.

very important part for some minutes, and from a favorable position did much harm to the Union fleet in the subsequent engagement, they counted for nothing in the calculations of Farragut. There were besides these a few other so-called ironclads near the city; but they took no part in the fight in the bay, and little, if any, in the operations before the fall of Mobile itself in the spring of 1865.

The Tennessee was different. This was the most powerful ironclad built, from the keel up, by the Confederacy, and both the energy shown in overcoming difficulties and the workmanship put upon her were most creditable to her builders. The work was begun at Selma, on the Alabama River, one hundred and fifty miles from Mobile, in the spring of 1863, when the timber was yet standing in the forests, and much of what was to be her plating was still ore in the mines. The hull was launched the following winter and towed to Mobile, where the plating had already been sent from the rolling mills of Atlanta.

Her length on deck was 209 feet, beam 48 feet, and when loaded, with her guns on board, she drew 14 feet. The battery was carried in a casemate, equidistant from the bow and stern, whose inside dimensions were 79 feet in length by 29 feet in width. The framing was of yellow pine beams, 13 inches thick, placed close together vertically and planked on the outside, first with 5½ inches of yellow pine, laid horizontally, and then 4 inches of oak laid up and down. Both sides and ends were inclined at an angle of forty-five degrees, and over the outside planking was placed the armor, 6 inches thick, in thin plates of 2 inches each, on the forward end, and elsewhere 5 inches thick. Within, the yellow pine frames were sheathed with 2½ inches of oak. The plating throughout was fastened with bolts 1¼ inch in diameter, going entirely through and set up with nuts and washers inside. Her gunners were thus sheltered by a thickness of five or six inches of iron, backed by twenty-five inches of wood. The outside deck was plated with two-inch iron. The sides of the casemate, or, as the Confederates called it, the shield, were carried down to two feet below the water-line and then reversed at the same angle, so as to meet the hull again six to seven feet below water. The knuckle thus formed, projecting ten feet beyond the base of the casemate, and apparently filled in solid, afforded a substantial protection from an enemy's prow to the hull, which was not less than eight feet within it. It was covered with four inches of iron, and being continued round the bows, became there a beak or ram. The pilot-house was made by carrying part of the forward end of the shield up three feet higher than the rest. The casemate was covered with heavy iron gratings, through whose holes the smoke could rise freely, and it was pierced with ten ports, three in each end and two on each side. The vessel carried, however, only six guns; one VII½-inch rifle at each end and two VI-inch rifles on each broadside. These were Brooke guns, made in the Confederacy; they threw 110-pound and 90-pound solid shot. The ports were closed with iron sliding shutters, five inches thick; a bad arrangement, as it turned out.

Though thus powerfully built, armored, and armed, the Tennessee must have been a very exasperating vessel to her commander. She had two grave defects; the first, perhaps unavoidable from the slender resources of the Confederacy, was lack of speed. Her engines were not built for her, but taken from a high-pressure river steamboat, and though on her trial trip she realized about eight knots, six seems to be all that could usually be got from her. She was driven by a screw, the shaft being connected by gearing with the engines. The other defect was an oversight, yet a culpable one ; her steering chains, instead of being led under her armored deck, were over it, exposed to an enemy's fire. She was therefore a ram that could only by a favorable chance overtake her prey, and was likely at any moment to lose the power of directing her thrust.

Such as she was the Tennessee was ready for service early in March, 1864, when Commander J. D. Johnston was ordered as her captain. She was taken from the city, through one of the arms of the Alabama, to the mud flats which reach to a point twenty miles down the bay, and are called Dog River Bar. The least depth of water to be traversed was nine feet, but throughout the whole distance the fourteen feet necessary to float the vessel could not be counted upon. She was carried over on camels, which are large floats made to fit the hull below the water line, and fastened to it, on either side, by heavy chains passing around them and under the keel, while the camels are filled with water. When the water was pumped out the buoyancy of the camels lifted the ram five feet, reducing her draught enough to let her go over the bar. Two months were taken up in building and placing the camels, during all which time Farragut was begging either for ironclads or for co-operation by the land forces, in reducing the forts. In either case he was willing to enter the bay, but he did not like to run the risk of getting inside with his wooden ships crippled, the forts intact in his rear, and the enemy's ironclads to contend with as well. Neither assistance was given, and he was therefore compelled to look on while the Tennessee was moved from a position in which she could do no harm to one in which she became the principal menace to the attacking fleet. On the 18th of May she was finally towed across and anchored in the lower bay six miles from the entrance. That night the camels were removed, steam raised, and everything made ready to cross the outer bar and attack the fleet; but when the anchor was weighed the ship was found to be hard aground. The intended attack was given up, and when the tide rose enough to float her, she was moved down to Fort Morgan, near which she remained from that time.

The preparations for defence of the enemy were not confined to the forts and the ships. From the point of Dauphin Island a line of pile obstructions extended across the sand bank, in the direction of Fort Morgan, blocking the passage of any light vessels that might try to pass that way. Where the piles ended, near the edge of the bank, a triple line of torpedoes in échelon began, extending across the main ship channel to a red buoy, distant two hundred and twenty-six yards from the water battery under Fort Morgan. This narrow passage, not much exceeding one hundred yards from the beach, was left open for blockade-runners, and through it the admiral intended his fleet to pass; for the reports of refugees and the examinations made by officers of the fleet who dared at night to push their search thus close under the enemy's guns, alike affirmed that there at least no torpedoes were.

The torpedoes planted in this part of the defences of Mobile were principally of two kinds, both of the class known as floating torpedoes. One was made of an ordinary barrel, lager-beer kegs being preferred, pitched inside and out and with wooden cones secured to the two ends to keep it from tumbling over. The barrel was filled with powder and furnished with several, generally five, sensitive primers, placed near together in that part of the bilge which was to float uppermost. The primers were exploded by a vessel striking them and communicated their flame to the charge. The other torpedo was made of tin, in the form of a truncated cone, the upper diameter being the greater. It was divided into two parts, the upper being an air-chamber and the lower containing the charge. On top was a cast-iron cap so secured that a slight blow, like that from a passing vessel, would knock it off. The cap was fast to a trigger, and as it fell, its weight pulled the trigger and exploded the charge. In July, 1864, there were planted forty-six of the former and one hundred and thirty-four of the latter kind. Besides these which exploded on contact there are said to have been several electrical torpedoes.

The first six months of 1864 wore away in the monotonous routine of the blockade, broken only by an attack upon Fort Powell, made from Mississippi Sound by the admiral with the light-draught vessels. These could not get nearer than four thousand yards, but at the time, February 28th, Sherman was on his raid into Mississippi and the attack was believed to be of service as a diversion. During this half of the year none but wooden vessels lay before Mobile. Toward the end of July the co-operation of Canby's forces was assured and the monitor ironclads began to arrive.

The root idea from which the monitor type of ironclads grew was a raft carrying a fort; their hulls, therefore, floated low in the water, the deck being but a foot or two above it. Upon the deck were one or more circular turrets, made of one-inch rolled wrought-iron plates, the whole thickness depending upon the number of these thin plates bolted together. The decks, and the hulls to some distance below the water-line, were also armored, but less heavily. In the turret two guns were mounted, of a size varying with the size of the vessel. They could be moved in and out, but the aim from side to side was changed by turning the whole turret, which revolved on a central spindle. After firing, the ports were turned away from the enemy and the unbroken iron toward him, until the guns were reloaded. Above and concentric with the turret was another circular structure, of much less diameter and similarly armored. This, called the pilot-house, contained the steering-wheel, and was thè station in battle of the captain, helmsman, and pilot if there were one. It was stationary, not sharing the revolving motion of the gun-turret, and could be entered only by a hole opening down into the latter, the top being closed by iron plates, which had been given greater thickness since a shot in one instance had struck and broken them, killing the captain of the vessel. Narrow horizontal slits were cut in the armor of the pilot-house, through which the captain peered, as through the bars of a helmet, to see his enemy and direct the course of his ship. The gun-turret could be entered or left by the hull below, which contained the living rooms of the officers and crew and all the usual and necessary arrangements of a ship of war, or by the gun-ports, which were large enough for a man to pass through. In action the hatches were down, and ordinarily the only exit from the hull below was through the turret and its ports. Four of these vessels were sen to Farragut after many askings and months of delay; two from the Atlantic coast, the Tecumseh and Manhattan, having ten-inch armor on their turrets, and two from the Mississippi River, the Chickasaw and Winnebago, with eight-and-a-half-inch armor. The former carried two XV-inch guns in one turret; the latter four XI-inch guns in two turrets. They were all screw ships, but the exigencies of the Mississippi service calling for light draught, those built for it had four screws of small diameter, two on each quarter. The speed of the monitors was poor and, as they had iron hulls, varied much as their bottoms were clean or foul. From a comparison of differing statements it may be taken at from five to seven knots.

During these six months, though the admiral paid frequent

visits to the fleet off Mobile, the immediate direction of affairs was left to the divisional commander, Captain Thornton A. Jenkins, of the Richmond. In the last week of July, however, Farragut took charge in person, and sent the Richmond, and others of the blockading force that were to attempt the entry of the bay, to Pensacola to complete their preparations. The Manhattan had arrived on the 20th and the Chickasaw came in from New Orleans on the 1st of August. These, with the Winnebago, were anchored under the lee of Sand Island; but the Tecumseh did not get down until the Richmond, with the others, returned on the night of the 4th; and it was only by the untiring efforts of her commander and Captain Jenkins that she was ready even then. With her, and the return of the blockaders, the admiral's force was complete.

The understanding with General Granger, in immediate command of the troops, was that he should land on the 4th on Dauphin Island and invest Gaines, as he had not men enough to attack both forts at once. The admiral was to pass Morgan and enter the bay the same morning. Granger landed, but Farragut could not fulfil his part of the bargain, because so many of his ships were still away. The delay, though he chafed under it, was in the end an advantage, as the enemy used that last day of his control of the water to throw more troops into Gaines, who were all taken two days later.

In forming his plan of attack the admiral wanted two favors from nature; a westerly wind to blow the smoke from the fleet and toward Morgan, and a flood-tide. In regular summer weather the wind from sunrise till eight o'clock is light from the southward and then hauls gradually round to the west and northwest, growing in strength as it does so. The tide was a matter of calculation, if no exceptional wind modified its direction. The admiral wished it flood for two reasons: first, because, as he intended to go in at any cost, it would help a crippled ship into the harbor; and secondly, he had noticed that the primers of the barrel-torpedoes were close together on top, and thought it likely that when the flood-tide straightened out their mooring-lines the tops would be turned away from the approaching ships.

As at New Orleans, the preparations were left very much to the commanders of ships. A general order directed spare spars and boats to be landed, the machinery protected, and splinter-nettings placed. As the fleet was to pass between the eastern buoy and the beach, or two hundred yards from Morgan, little was feared from Gaines, which would be over two miles away; the preparations[1] were therefore made mainly on the starboard side, and port guns were shifted over till all the ports were full. The boats were lowered and towed on the port side. The admiral himself and the captain of the Brooklyn preferred to go in with their topsail yards across; but the Richmond and Lackawanna sent down their topmasts, and the other vessels seem to have done the same.

In the order of battle the wooden ships, as at Port Hudson, were to be lashed in couples, the lighter vessels on the off hand; the four monitors in a column inshore and abreast of the leading ships, the Tecumseh, which led, slightly in advance of the van of the other column. The admiral had intended to lead the latter himself in the Hartford, but the representations of many officers led him to yield his own judgment so far as to let the Brooklyn, whose captain ear-

[1] The Richmond, while at Pensacola, built a regular barricade of sand-bags, extending from the port bow round the starboard side to the port quarter, and from the berth to the spar-deck. Three thousand bags of sand were used for this defence, which was in places several feet thick.

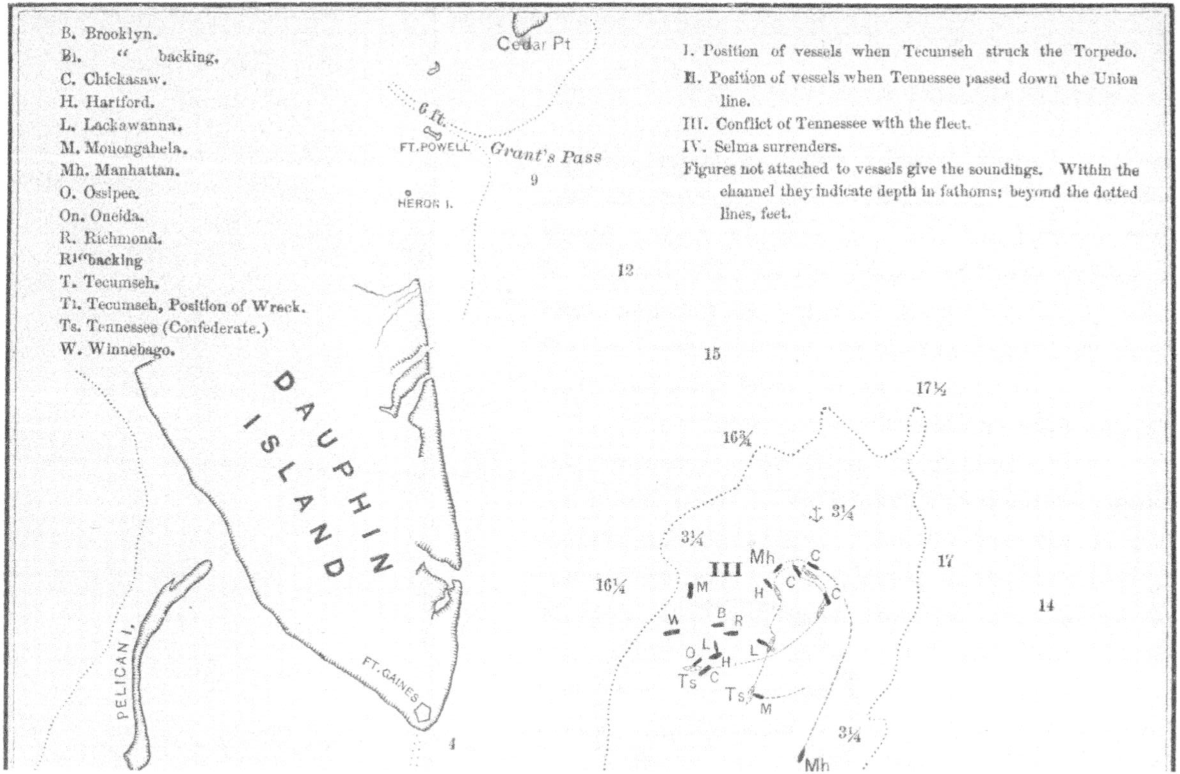
B. Brooklyn.
B1. " backing.
C. Chickasaw.
H. Hartford.
L. Lackawanna.
M. Monongahela.
Mh. Manhattan.
O. Ossipee.
On. Oneida.
R. Richmond.
R1 " backing
T. Tecumseh.
T1. Tecumseh, Position of Wreck.
Ts. Tennessee (Confederate.)
W. Winnebago.
I. Position of vessels when Tecumseh struck the Torpedo.
II. Position of vessels when Tennessee passed down the Union line.
III. Conflict of Tennessee with the fleet.
IV. Selma surrenders.
Figures not attached to vessels give the soundings. Within the channel they indicate depth in fathoms; beyond the dotted lines, feet.
Cedar Pt
6 Ft.
FT. POWELL
Grant's Pass
HERON I.
DAUPHIN ISLAND
FT. GAINES
PELICAN I.
III

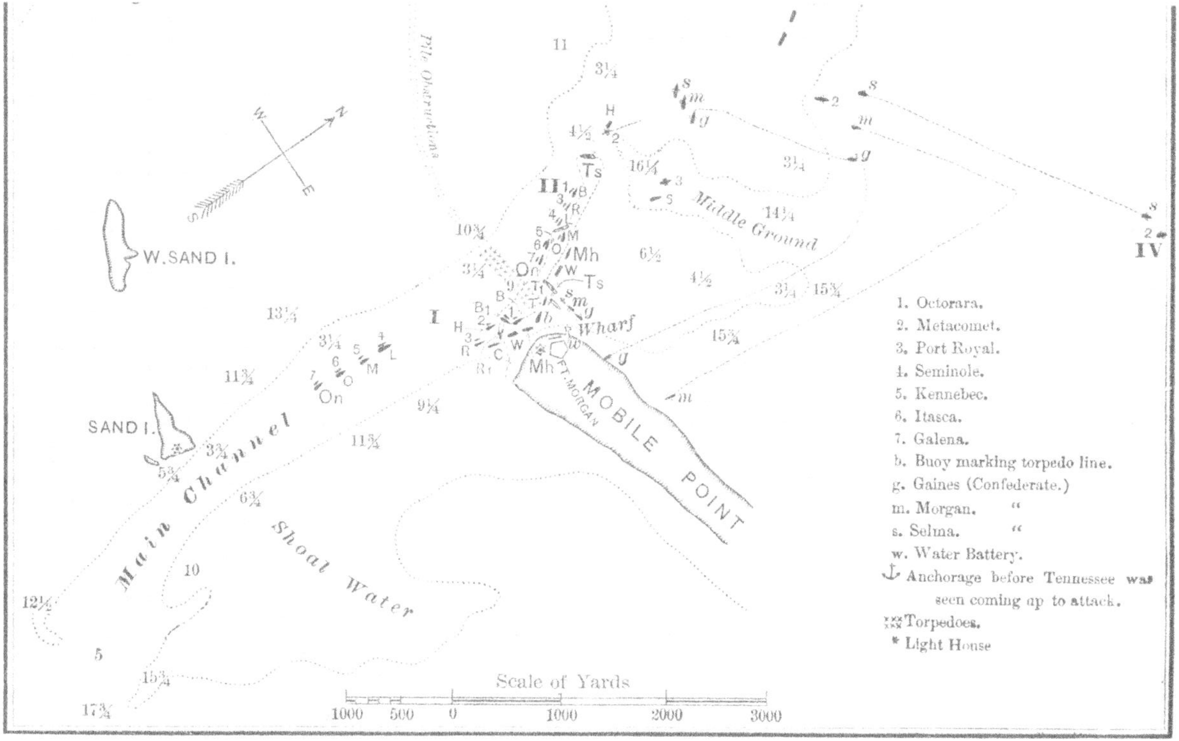
Pile Obstructions
W. SAND I.
SAND I.
Middle Ground
Wharf
FT. MORGAN
MOBILE POINT
Main Channel
Shoal Water
1. Octorara.
2. Metacomet.
3. Port Royal.
4. Seminole.
5. Kennebec.
6. Itasca.
7. Galena.
b. Buoy marking torpedo line.
g. Gaines (Confederate.)
m. Morgan. "
s. Selma. "
w. Water Battery.
Anchorage before Tennessee was seen coming up to attack.
Torpedoes.
* Light House
Scale of Yards
1000 500 0 1000 2000 3000

BATTLE OF MOBILE BAY.

nestly wished it, go ahead of him. The order of attack, as it stood at last, was as follows:

MONITORS—STARBOARD COLUMN.

Tecumseh......	1,034 tons,	2[1] guns,	Commander	T. A. M. Craven.
Manhattan.....	1,034 "	2 "	"	J. W. A. Nicholson.
Winnebago.....	970 "	4 "	"	Thomas H. Stevens.
Chickasaw.....	970 "	4 "	Lieut.-Com'r	George H. Perkins.

WOODEN SHIPS—PORT COLUMN.

Brooklyn	2,070 tons,	24 guns,	Captain James Alden.
Octorara......	829 "	6 "	Lieut.-Com'r Chas. H. Greene.
Hartford	1,900 "	21 "	Rear-Admiral David G. Farragut. Captain Percival Drayton.
Metacomet....	974 "	6 "	Lieut.-Com'r Jas. E. Jouett.
Richmond	1,929 "	20 "	Captain Thornton A. Jenkins.
Port Royal....	805 "	6 "	Lieut.-Com'r Bancroft Gherardi.
Lackawanna ..	1,533 "	8 "	Captain John B. Marchand.
Seminole......	801 "	8 "	Commander Edward Donaldson.
Monongahela..	1,378 "	8 "	Commander James H. Strong.
Kennebec.....	507 "	5 "	Lieut.-Com'r Wm. P. McCann.
Ossipee.......	1,240 "	11 "	Commander William E. Le Roy.
Itasca	507 "	5 "	Lieut.-Com'r George Brown.
Oneida	1,032 "	9 "	Commander J. R. M. Mullany.
Galena........	738 "	10 "	Lieut.-Com'r Clark H. Wells.

The Octorara, Metacomet, and Port Royal were side-wheel double-enders; the others were screw ships. All had been built for the naval service.

The evening before the action it was raining hard, but toward midnight stopped and became clear, hot, and calm. The preparations were all made and the vessels lay quietly at their anchors; the wooden ships outside, the monitors behind Sand Island. Later a light air sprung up from the

[1] For particulars of batteries, see Appendix.

southwest, thus fulfilling the admiral's wish. He was not well, sleeping restlessly, and about three in the morning sent his steward to find out how the wind was. When he learned it was southwest, he said: "Then we will go in this morning." Soon after, the hands were turned up and hammocks stowed. Between 4 and 5 o'clock the lighter vessels came alongside and were lashed to their consorts. At 5.30 the signal was made to get under way and the Brooklyn weighed at once, the other vessels following in order, the monitors at the same time standing out from their anchorage. The fleet steamed slowly in to the bar, to allow its members to take and keep their stations, the crews in the meantime going to quarters and clearing for action. At 6.10 the bar was crossed by the flag-ship, and by 6.30 the order for battle was fairly formed and the monitors taking their stations; in doing which a slight delay occurred. At this time all the ships hoisted the United States flag at the peak and the three mastheads, and the Tecumseh fired the first two shots at the fort. At five minutes before seven the fleet went ahead again, and at five minutes past the fort opened upon the Brooklyn, the leading ship, which answered at once with her bow rifle, and immediately afterward the action became general along the line between the fort, the monitors (except the Tecumseh), and the bow guns of the fleet; at the same time the enemy's gunboats moved out from behind Morgan and formed in line ahead, east and west, across the channel just inside the lines of torpedoes. From this position they had a raking fire upon the fleet, which was confined to a nearly north course (north by east), until it had passed the fort and the buoy. At half-past seven the leading ships had their broadsides bearing fairly on the works, and while they maintained that position their heavy fire so kept down the enemy's that the latter did little harm.

The Tecumseh, after firing the two first guns, as stated above, had turned her turret from the enemy and loaded again with steel shot and the heaviest charge[1] of powder. Intent only upon the Tennessee, she steamed quietly on, regardless of the fort, a little ahead of the Brooklyn, the other monitors following her closely. As they drew near the buoy, Craven from the pilot-house of his ship saw it so nearly in line with the beach that he turned to his pilot and said, "It is impossible that the admiral means us to go inside that buoy; I cannot turn my ship." At the same moment the Tennessee, which till that time had lain to the eastward of the buoy, went ahead to the westward of it, and Craven, either fearing she would get away from him or moved by the seeming narrowness of the open way, gave the order "Starboard" and pushed the Tecumseh straight at the enemy. She had gone but a few yards and the lockstring was already taut in the hands of an officer of the enemy's ship, Lieutenant Wharton, waiting to fire as they touched, when one or more torpedoes exploded under her. She lurched from side to side, careened violently over, and went down head foremost, her screw plainly visible in the air for a moment to the enemy, that waited for her, not two hundred yards off, on the other side of the fatal line. It was then that Craven did one of those deeds that should be always linked with the doer's name, as Sidney's is with the cup of cold water. The pilot and he instinctively made for the narrow opening leading to the turret below. Craven drew back: "After you, pilot," he said. There was no afterward for him; the pilot was saved, but he went down with his ship.

When the Tecumseh sank, the Brooklyn was about three hundred yards astern of her and a little outside; the Hart-

[1] Sixty pounds; one hundred pounds have since been used in these guns.

ford between one and two hundred yards from the Brooklyn, on her port quarter; the Richmond about the same distance from the Hartford and in the Brooklyn's wake. The Winnebago, the second astern of the Tecumseh, was five hundred yards from her, and the Manhattan in her station, two hundred yards ahead of the Winnebago; both, however, skirting the beach and steering to pass inside of the buoy, as they had been ordered. The sunken vessel was therefore well on their port bow. Unmoved by the fate of their leader, the three remaining ironclads steamed on in line ahead, steadily but very slowly, being specially directed to occupy the attention of the guns ashore, that were raking the approaching ships. As they passed, the admiration of the officers of the flag-ship and Metacomet was aroused by the sight of Commander Stevens, of the Winnebago, walking quietly, giving his orders, from turret to turret of his unwieldy vessel, directly under the enemy's guns. Five minutes later were seen from the Brooklyn certain objects in the water ahead, which were taken at the moment for buoys to torpedoes. The ship and her consort were stopped and then began to back, coming down upon the next astern; at the same time their bows fell off toward the fort and they soon lay nearly athwart the channel. The Hartford's engines were at once stopped, but, as she held her way and drifted on with the flood-tide, her bow approached dangerously near the Brooklyn's stern and the Richmond was close behind; fortunately the rest of the fleet had opened out somewhat. While the vessels were thus close the admiral hailed to know what was the matter. "Torpedoes ahead," was the reply. Farragut, who did not go heedlessly into action, had reckoned on torpedoes and counted the cost. Without any seeming hesitation, though in the story of his life it appears that for a moment he felt overcome till he could throw himself on a

Power greater than his own, he ordered his own ship and his consort ahead, at the same time making the signal "Close order." From the position of the Brooklyn it was no longer possible to pass inside, and accordingly, backing the Metacomet and going ahead with the flagship, their heads were turned to the westward and they passed outside of the fatal buoy, about five hundred yards from the fort. As they went over the line the torpedo cases were heard knocking against the bottom of the ship and the primers snapping,[1] but none of the torpedoes themselves exploded and the Hartford went safely through.

Yet, in the midst of Farragut's grave anxieties about the great issues touching his fleet, the drowning men on board the Tecumseh had not been forgotten, and, while still fettered by the Brooklyn's action, he hailed Captain Jouett, of the Metacomet,[2] to know if he had not a boat that he could send to save them. Jouett, having seen the disaster, and not having the other cares on his mind, had by a few instants forestalled the admiral, and the boat was about leaving the port quarter of the Metacomet, in charge of Ensign H. C. Nields, an officer of the Volunteer Navy. She pulled round under the Hartford's stern and broadside, across the bows of the Brooklyn, toward the wreck, where she saved the pilot, John Collins, and nine of the ship's company. While on his way Nields, who was but a lad, did one of those acts, simple in intention, which appeal strongly to

[1] The evidence for this singular and striking incident is, both in quality and quantity, such as puts the fact beyond doubt. The same sounds were heard on board the Richmond. The tin torpedoes were poorly lacquered and corroded rapidly under the sea-water. There is good reason to believe that those which sunk the Tecumseh had been planted but two or three days before. A story recently current in the South, that she was sunk by a torpedo carried at her own bow, is wholly without foundation.

[2] Farragut was in the port main rigging of the Hartford, Jouett on the starboard wheel-house of his ship, so that there were but a few feet between them.

the feelings and imagination and indicate the calm self-possession of the doer. He was steering the boat himself, and his captain, who was watching, saw him, after pulling some fifty yards, look up and back to see if the flag was flying; missing it, he stooped down, took it out of the cover in which it is habitually kept and shipped it, unfurled, in its place in the boat before the eyes of friends and foes. His heroic and merciful errand was not accomplished without the greatest risk, greater than he himself knew; for not only did he pass under the continued and furious fire of the fort and the fleet, but the ensign of the forecastle division of the Hartford, seeing the boat without a flag and knowing nothing of its object, but having torpedoes uppermost in his mind, connected its presence with them, trained one of his hundred-pounders upon it,[1] and was about to pull the lock-string when one of the ship's company caught his arm, saying: "For God's sake, don't fire! it is one of our own boats!" The Hartford had passed on when Nields had picked up the survivors, and, after putting them aboard the Winnebago, he pulled down to the Oneida, where he served during the rest of the action. Two officers and five men had also escaped in one of the Tecumseh's boats, which was towing alongside, and four swam to the fort, where they were made prisoners; so that twenty-one were saved out of a complement of over one hundred souls.

Meanwhile the Brooklyn was lying bows on to the fort, undergoing a raking fire and backing down upon the starboard bow of the Richmond, whose engines were stopped, but the vessel drifting up with the young flood-tide. Her captain, seeing a collision in such critical circumstances imminent, gave the order to back hard both his own ship and her consort;

[1] This was told the writer by the officer himself.

fearing that, if the four became entangled, not only would they suffer damage themselves, but, if sunk by the fire of the fort, would block the channel to the rest of the squadron. As she backed, the Richmond's bow fell off to port, bringing her starboard broadside fairly toward the fort and batteries, on which she kept up a steady and rapid fire, at a distance of from three hundred to one hundred and fifty yards, driving the enemy out of the water-battery and silencing it; being at the same time wrapped in a cloud of smoke which hid her hull and rose above her lower mast-heads.

As her topmasts were down, the ship was thus so completely hidden that Buchanan, the Confederate admiral, who had had her captain under him as a midshipman in days long gone by, and again as first lieutenant of a corvette during the war with Mexico, asked after the surrender: "What became of Jenkins? I saw his vessel go handsomely into action and then lost sight of her entirely." While thus backing and fighting the ship was in great danger of getting aground, having at times less than a foot of water under her keel; but her commander thought the situation so critical as to necessitate the risk. During the same time the Brooklyn, from her unfortunate position, was unable to use any but her bow guns, and, even when her hull was obscured by the smoke of the battle, her position was shown to the gunners of the fort by her tall spars towering above. These moments of anxiety were ended when she brought her head once more in the right direction and steamed on; the Richmond followed with the other ships of the port column, which had closed up and joined in the action during the delay. Their fire, with the monitors', kept down that of the fort until the bulk of the fleet had gone by, but when the heavier ships were out of range the enemy returned to their guns and severely punished the rear of the line; the last ship, the Oneida, receiving a VII-inch rifle shell, which passed through her chain armor and into the starboard boiler, where it burst, the larger part of the watch of firemen being scalded by the escaping steam. About the same moment a similar projectile burst in the cabin, cutting both wheel-ropes, while her forward XI-inch gun and one of the VIII-inch were disabled. In this condition the Oneida was pulled past the forts by her consort, the Galena.

As the Hartford advanced over the line of torpedoes the three smaller gunboats of the enemy took their position on her starboard bow and ahead, whence they kept up a raking and most galling fire, to which the Hartford, confined to the direction of the channel, could only reply with her bow guns, one of which was speedily disabled by a shell bursting under it. As the flag-ship advanced they retreated, keeping their distance and range about the same, from one thousand to seven hundred yards, and fighting mainly the stern guns. At no period of the action did she suffer as now, and the quarters of her forward division became a slaughter-pen; a single shot killing ten and wounding five men, while the splinters and shreds of bodies were hurled aft and on to the decks of her consort. The greater part of the ship's company had never been in action, but so admirable was their spirit and discipline that no wavering was seen, nor was there any confusion even in reorganizing the more than decimated crews of the guns. The Tennessee meantime waited for her, Buchanan having set his heart on sinking the enemy's admiral, but as the ram stood down the Hartford put her helm to starboard and, having the greater speed, avoided the thrust without difficulty. Two shots were fired by the ram at the same moment at such short range that it seemed wonderful they missed. The Tennessee then followed up the bay till her opponent was about a mile from his own fleet, when for some reason she gave up the pursuit and turned to meet the other wooden ships, which were advancing in close order, the Brooklyn still leading. The Tennessee stood for the latter vessel, as though intending to ram, but sheered off and went by on her starboard side, at less than one hundred yards, firing two shots, which struck and went through and through, and receiving the contents of the Brooklyn's guns in return. She passed on down the line to the Richmond, which was ready with her broadside and a party of musketeers, who kept up a brisk fire into the ram's ports. Whether the aim was thus disordered or there was not time to lay the guns properly after reloading, the two shots flew high and no harm was done. The Tennessee passed the next ship, the Lackawanna, also on the starboard side, but then made a determined sheer toward the line as though certainly intending tc ram. Captain Strong of the Monongahela seeing this, headed for her, putting his helm to port and then shifting it so as to strike at right angles, but the Monongahela could not get her full speed, from having the gunboat Kennebec in tow alongside; she therefore struck the ram somewhat glancing and on her port quarter. The blow threw the Tennessee's stern around and she passed close along the port side of the Kennebec, injuring the planking on the latter's bow and leaving one of her boats and its iron davit with the gunboat as a memento of the collision. As she went by she fired a shell which entered the berth-deck and exploded, seriously wounding an officer and four men. The Ossipee, which was on the port quarter of the Monongahela when the collision took place, seeing how the ram was heading, also put her helm to port following the Monongahela's motion; but when the ram swung round under the blow she righted it and the Tennessee passed between the two, giving the Ossipee two shots, which entered nearly together below the spar-deck abreast the forward pivot gun. The ram then passed on the starboard side of the crippled Oneida, about a hundred yards off, and tried to fire her broadside; but the primers snapped several times, and she only succeeded in getting off one gun, the shot from which hit the after XI-inch pivot, which had just been fired at and struck her. She then passed under the Oneida's stern, delivering a raking fire, and severely wounding Commander Mullany, who lost an arm. At this moment the Union iron-clads which, in obedience to their orders, had delayed before the fort, occupying its guns until the fleet had passed, drew near the rear wooden ships and opened their fire on the Tennessee. As the enemy passed under the stern of the Oneida the Winnebago came up and took position between the two, upon which the crew of the crippled ship, who were expecting to be rammed, leaped upon the rail and cheered Commander Stevens, lately their own captain,[1] he having left them but a few days before.

About the time that the Tennessee gave up her pursuit of the Hartford, the flag ship reached the point where she was able to keep away a little to the westward. As she did so her starboard broadside came to bear and the Confederate gunboats edged off, though still keeping up a hot fire from their stern guns. A shot soon struck the Gaines under the port counter below water, and a shell striking soon after near the same place on the starboard side exploded, also below water, and started a heavy leak in the magazine. At this time the admiral directed the Metacomet to cast off and chase the gunboats, specially cautioning her commander to let none of them escape to Mobile; and a signal to the same effect was

[1] Commander Stevens had given up the command of the Oneida at the request and in favor of Commander Mullany, whose own ship was not fitted for such an engagement, and who had heretofore been less fortunate than his friend in having opportunities for distinction thrown in his way by the war. Stevens, being an old iron-clad captain, took the command of the Winnebago, which was vacant.

made to the lighter vessels in the rear. Jouett, who had been impatiently waiting, cut his fasts, backed clear, and pressed hard after the three, who retreated up the bay. The Gaines had to haul off toward Morgan at 8.30, the leak increasing rapidly, but the other two kept on still. The Metacomet, not being able to fire straight ahead, yawed once or twice to discharge her bow gun; but finding she lost too much ground by this discontinued it, though the enemy were still keeping up a harassing fire. The chase led her into shoal water, the leadsman in the chains reporting a foot less than the ship drew. The executive officer, having verified the sounding, reported it to the captain, who, intent simply upon carrying out his orders, and seeing that the bottom was a soft ooze, replied: "Call the man in; he is only intimidating me with his soundings." Soon after this a heavy squall accompanied by rain and dense mist came up, and during it the Morgan, which was on the starboard bow of the Metacomet, first got aground, and then getting off ran down to the southeastward toward Fort Morgan. The Selma kept straight on, as did the Metacomet; and when the squall lifted the latter found herself ahead and on the starboard bow of her chase. One shot was fired, killing the executive officer and some of the crew of the Selma, and then the latter hauled down her flag, having lost five killed and ten wounded. The other Union gunboats being far in the rear and embarrassed by the mist did not succeed in cutting off the others—both of which escaped under Fort Morgan. The Gaines being wholly disabled was burnt; the Morgan made good her escape to Mobile the same night.

After passing down the Union line, Buchanan said to his flag-captain, it being then about half-past eight: "Follow them up, Johnston, we can't let them off that way." Five minutes later the Hartford anchored four miles from

Morgan, and the crew were sent to breakfast. Captain Drayton went up on the poop and said to the admiral: "What we have done has been well done, sir; but it all counts for nothing so long as the Tennessee is there under the guns of Morgan." "I know it," said the admiral, "and as soon as the people have had their breakfasts I am going for her."[1] Buchanan by his move thus played directly into Farragut's hands. From some difficulty in the ground it was found necessary to bring the head of the Tennessee round toward Morgan, and this, with the length of time occupied in the manœuvre and the improbability of her attacking the whole fleet by daylight, caused the admiral to think that she had retired under the guns of the fort. He was soon undeceived. At ten minutes before nine, when the crew had hardly got seated at their breakfast, the Tennessee was reported approaching. The mess-gear was hustled aside, and the flagship at once got under way, as did the other vessels that had anchored, and signal was made to the monitors to destroy the ram and to the Monongahela, Lackawanna, and Ossipee to ram the enemy's principal vessel. These ships took ground to carry out their orders, and when the Tennessee was about four hundred yards from the fleet the Monongahela struck her fairly amidships on the starboard side. Just before the blow the ram fired two shells, which passed through her enemy's berth-deck, one exploding and wounding an officer and two men. She then passed on the starboard side of the Monongahela and received a broadside at the distance of ten yards, but without harm. The Lacka-

---

[1] This was said in the hearing of Lieutenant-Commander (now Captain) Kimberley, the executive officer of the Hartford. Commodore Foxhall A. Parker (Battle of Mobile Bay) mentions that Farragut had written in a note-book after the engagement: "Had Buchanan remained under the fort, I should have attacked him *as soon as it became dark* with the three monitors." The statements are easily reconciled, the latter representing the second thought.

wanna followed, striking a square blow on the port side at the after end of the casemate. The Tennessee listed over heavily and swung round, so that the two vessels lay alongside head and stern, the port sides touching; but as the Lackawanna's battery had been mostly shifted to the starboard side to engage the fort she had only one IX-inch gun available, the shot from which struck one of the enemy's port shutters driving fragments into the casemates. The Lackawanna then kept away, making a circuit to ram again. She had her stem cut and crushed from three feet above the water-line to five below, causing some leakage, and the Monongahela had her iron prow carried away and the butt ends of the planking started on both bows; but the only damage caused to the Tennessee, protected by her sponsons, was a leak at the rate of about six inches an hour. The flag-ship now approached to ram, also on the port side; but the Tennessee turned toward her so that the bluff of the port bow in each ship took the blow. The Hartford's anchor was hanging from the hawse-pipe, there not having been time to cat it, and acted as a fender, being doubled up under the blow, and the two vessels rasped by, the port sides touching. Most of the Hartford's battery was also on the starboard side, but there were still seven IX-inch guns which sent out their solid shot with their heaviest charge of powder; yet at a distance of ten feet they did the Tennessee no harm. The primers of the latter again failed her, being heard by the flagship's people to snap unsuccessfully several times; one gun finally went off, and the shell exploding on the berth-deck killed and wounded an officer and several men. This was the last shot fired by the Tennessee. The Hartford put her helm to starboard and made a circle to ram again, but in mid career the Lackawanna ran into her, striking near the person of the admiral, who had a narrow escape from being killed, and cutting the flag-ship down to within two feet of the water.

Meanwhile the monitors had come up. The Manhattan had lost the use of one of her XV-inch guns early in the day by a fragment of iron which dropped into the vent and could not be got out; she was therefore able to fire only six of her heavy shot, one of which broke through the port side of the casemate leaving on the inside an undetached mass of oak and pine splinters. The Winnebago's turrets could not be turned, so the guns could only be trained by moving the helm and her fire was necessarily slow. The Chickasaw was more fortunate; her smoke-stack had been pierced several times by the fort, so that her speed had run down and she had not yet reached the anchorage when the Tennessee came up, but by heaping tallow and coal-tar on the furnaces steam was raised rapidly and she closed with the enemy immediately after the Hartford rammed and fired. Passing by her port side and firing as she did so, she took position under her stern, dogging her steadily during the remainder of the fight, never over fifty yards distant, and at times almost touching, keeping up an unremitting fire with her four XI-inch guns.[1]

The bow and stern port shutters of the Tennessee were now jammed, so that those guns could not be used. Soon

[1] Lieutenant-Commander Perkins and the executive officer of the Chickasaw, Volunteer Lieutenant William Hamilton, were going North from other ships on leave of absence, the latter on sick leave, but had offered their services for the battle. The fire of the Chickasaw was the most damaging to the Tennessee. In her engagement with the ram she fired fifty-two XI-inch solid shot, almost all into the stern, where the greatest injury was done. The Metacomet went to Pensacola that night under a flag of truce with the wounded from the fleet and the Tennessee, and was taken out by the pilot of the latter. He asked Captain Jouett who commanded the monitor that got under the ram's stern, adding: "D—n him! he stuck to us like a leech; we could not get away from him. It was he who cut away the steering gear, jammed the stern port shutters, and wounded Admiral Buchanan."

her smoke-stack came down and the smoke rising from its stump poured through the gratings on to the gun-deck, where the thermometer now stood at 120°. At about the same time the tiller-chains were shot away from their exposed position over the after-deck. Losing thus the power of directing her movements, the Tennessee headed aimlessly down the bay, followed always by the unrelenting Chickasaw, under the pounding of whose heavy guns the after-end of the shield was now seen, by those within, to be perceptibly vibrating. The Manhattan and Winnebago were also at work, and the Hartford, Ossipee, and other vessels were seeking their chance to ram again. During this time Buchanan, who was superintending in person the working of the battery, sent for a machinist to back out the pin of a jammed port shutter; while the man was at work a shot struck just outside where he was sitting, the concussion crushing him so that the remains had to be shovelled into buckets. At the same moment the admiral received a wound from an iron splinter, breaking his leg. The command then fell upon Captain Johnston, who endured the hammering, powerless to reply, for twenty minutes longer; then, after consultation with the admiral, he hauled down the flag which was hoisted on a boat-hook thrust through the grating. As it had before been shot away the fire of the fleet did not stop, and Johnston accordingly went on the roof and showed a white flag. As he stood there the Ossipee was approaching at full speed to ram on the starboard side, passing the sluggish Winnebago, whose captain, still outside his turret, exchanged greetings with his more fortunate competitor. Her helm was put over and engines backed at once, but it was too late to avoid the collision. As they came together her captain appeared on the forecastle and, along with the blow, Johnston received a genial greeting from the most genial of men: "Hallo, Johnston, old fellow! how are you? This is the United States Steamer Ossipee. I'll send a boat alongside for you. Le Roy, don't you know me?" The boat was sent and the United States flag hoisted on board the Tennessee at ten o'clock.[1]

The fight had lasted a little over an hour. The loss of the Tennessee was 2 killed and 10 wounded, that of the Union fleet, from the forts and the enemy's squadron, 52 killed and 170 wounded.[2] Besides the loss of the smoke-stack and

---

[1] It is not easy to fix the exact times of particular occurrences from the notes taken in the heat of action by different observers, with watches not necessarily running together; yet a certain measure of duration of the exciting events between 7 and 10 A.M. in this battle seems desirable. From a careful comparison of the logs and reports the following table of times has been compiled:

Fort Morgan opened	7.07 A.M.
Brooklyn opened with bow guns	7.10 A.M.
Fleet generally with bow guns	7.15 A.M.
Fleet generally with broadside guns	7.30–7.50 A.M.
Tecumseh sunk	7.45 A.M.
Hartford took the lead	7.52 A.M.
Hartford casts off Metacomet	8.05 A.M.

At this time the rest of the fleet were about a mile astern of the flag-ship, crossing the lines of torpedoes, and the Tennessee turned to attack them.

Tennessee passed rear ship (Oneida)	8.20 A.M.
Hartford anchored	8.35 A.M.
Tennessee sighted coming up	8.50 A.M.
Monongahela rammed	9.25 A.M.
Lackawanna rammed	9.30 A.M.
Hartford	9.35 A.M.
Tennessee surrendered	10.00 A.M.

[2]	Killed.	Wounded.
Hartford	25	28
Brooklyn	11	43
Lackawanna	4	35
Oneida	8	30
Monongahela	0	6
Metacomet	1	2
Ossipee	1	7
Richmond	0	2
Galena	0	1
Octorara	1	10
Kennebec	1	6

steering-gear, the injuries to the casemate of the ram were very severe. On the after-side nearly all the plating was found to be started, the after gun-carriage was disabled and there were distinct marks of nine XI-inch solid shot having struck within a few square feet of that port. The only shot that penetrated the casing was the one XV-inch from the Manhattan. Three port shutters were so damaged as to stop the firing of the guns.

The Chickasaw, which had so persistently stuck to the ram, now took her in tow and anchored her near the flag-ship. At half-past two of the same afternoon the Chickasaw again got under way and stood down to Fort Powell, engaging it for an hour at a distance of three hundred and fifty yards. The fort had been built to resist an attack from the sound and was not yet ready to meet one coming like this from the rear. That same night it was evacuated and blown up.

On the 6th the Chickasaw went down and shelled Fort Gaines, and the following day it was surrendered. Fort Morgan still held out. The army under General Granger was transferred from Dauphin Island to Mobile Point and a siege train, sent from New Orleans, was landed three miles in rear of the fort on the 17th. In the meantime batteries had been constructed; and thirty-four guns had been put in position, with everything ready for opening, on the evening of Saturday the 20th. On Monday the 22d, at daylight, the bombardment began from the batteries, the three monitors, and the ships outside as well as inside the bar. On the 23d the fort surrendered.

Mobile as a port for blockade-running was thus sealed by the fleet holding the bay; but the gigantic struggle going on in Virginia, Tennessee, and Georgia hindered for the time any attempt to reduce the city. That would have withdrawn from more important fields a large force for a secondary object, which was put off till the following spring. In the meantime Admiral Farragut went north in December, leaving Commodore Palmer in command of the squadron till the following February, when he was relieved by Acting Rear-Admiral H. K. Thatcher. Palmer, however, stayed by his own wish until the city fell.

Several streams having a common origin and communicating with one another enter the head of the bay. Of these the chief and most western is the Mobile River, formed by the junction of the Alabama and Tombigbee. It empties by two principal branches, of which the western keeps the name Mobile, the eastern one being called Spanish River; the city of Mobile is on the west bank of the former. On the east side of the bay the Tensaw[1] enters, also by two mouths, of which the western keeps the name and the eastern is called the Blakely River. The Tensaw and Spanish Rivers have a common mouth about a mile from the city. It is therefore practicable to go from the Mobile to Spanish River, and thence to the Tensaw and Blakely without entering the bay.

The works around the city inland were very strong, but it was not approached from that side. General Canby, commanding the Army of the West Mississippi, began to move against it in March 1865. One corps marched from Fort Morgan up the east side of the bay to a small stream called Fish River, where a landing was secured; the remainder of the army were then brought to this point in transports. At the same time a column under General Steele left Pensacola, directing its march upon Blakely, a point near the mouth of the Blakely River on the east bank. A short distance below

[1] The Tensaw branches off from the Alabama thirty miles up, and the whole really forms a bayou, or delta, system.

Blakely was Spanish Fort, upon the defence of which the fate of the city turned.

The gunboats had not hitherto crossed Dog River Bar, partly on account of the low water and partly because of the torpedoes, which were known to be thickly sowed thereabouts. It now became necessary for the navy to cut off the communication of the fort with Mobile by water, while the army invested it by land. On the 27th of March the fleet moved up and the bar was safely crossed by the double-ender Octorara, Lieutenant Commander W. W. Low; and the ironclads, Kickapoo, Lieutenant-Commander M. P. Jones; Osage, Lieutenant-Commander William M. Gamble; Milwaukee, Lieutenant-Commander James H. Gillis; Winnebago, Lieutenant-Commander W. A. Kirkland; and Chickasaw, Lieutenant-Commander George H. Perkins. They opened that day on the enemy's works, which were invested by the army the same night.

Before and after crossing, the bay had been thoroughly swept for torpedoes, and it was hoped that all had been found; but, unfortunately, they had not. On the 28th the Winnebago and Milwaukee moved up toward Spanish Fort, shelling a transport lying there from a distance of two miles. As the enemy's works were throwing far over, they were ordered to return to the rest of the fleet when the transport moved off. The Milwaukee dropped down with the current, keeping her head up stream, and had come within two hundred yards of the fleet when she struck a torpedo, on her port side forty feet from the stern. She sank abaft in three minutes, but her bow did not fill for nearly an hour. No one was hurt or drowned by this accident. The next day, the Winnebago having dragged in a fresh breeze too near the Osage, the latter weighed and moved a short distance ahead. Just as she was about to drop her anchor, a torpedo exploded under the bow and she began to sink, filling almost immediately. Of her crew 5 were killed and 11 wounded by the explosion, but none were drowned. The place where this happened had been thoroughly swept and the torpedo was thought to be one that had gone, or been sent, adrift from above. The two vessels were in twelve feet water, so that the tops of the turrets remained in sight. Lieutenant-Commander Gillis, after the loss of his vessel, took command of a naval battery in the siege and did good service.

On the 1st of April the light-draught steamer Rodolph, having on board apparatus for raising the Milwaukee, was coming near the fleet when she too struck a torpedo, which exploded thirty feet abaft her stem and caused her to sink rapidly, killing 4 and wounding 11 of the crew.

The siege lasted until the evening of the 8th of April, when Spanish Fort surrendered. Up to the last the enemy sent down torpedoes, and that night eighteen were taken from Blakely River. Commander Pierce Crosby, of the Metacomet, at once began sweeping above, and so successfully that on the 10th the Octorara and ironclads were able to move abreast Spanish Fort and shell two earthworks, called Huger and Tracy, some distance above. These were abandoned on the evening of the 11th, when the fleet took possession. Commander Crosby again went on with the work of lifting torpedoes, removing in all over one hundred and fifty. The way being thus cleared, on the 12th Commander Palmer with the Octorara and ironclads moved up the Blakely to the point where it branches off from the Tensaw, and down the latter stream, coming out about a mile from Mobile, within easy shelling distance. At the same time Admiral Thatcher, with the gunboats and 8,000 troops under General Granger, crossed the head of the bay to attack the city, which was immediately given up ; the Confederate troops having already withdrawn. The vessels of the enemy, which had taken little part in the defence, had gone up the Tombigbee.

The navy at once began to remove the obstructions in the main ship channel and lift the torpedoes, which were numerous. While doing the latter duty, two tugs, the Ida and Althea, and a launch of the ironclad Cincinnati were blown up. By these accidents 8 were killed and 5 wounded. The gunboat Sciota was also sunk in the same manner on the 14th of April, the explosion breaking the spar deck beams and doing much other damage. Her loss was 6 killed and 5 wounded.

The rebellion was now breaking up. Lee had laid down his arms on the 9th, and Johnston on the 24th of April. On the 4th of May General Richard Taylor surrendered the army in the Department of Alabama and Mississippi to General Canby; and the same day Commodore Farrand delivered the vessels under his command in the waters of Alabama to Admiral Thatcher, the officers and crews being paroled. Sabine Pass and Galveston, which had never been retaken after their loss early in 1863, were given up on the 25th of May and the 2d of June.

In July, 1865, the East and West Gulf Squadrons were merged into one under Admiral Thatcher. Reasons of public policy caused this arrangement to continue until May, 1867, when the attempt of the French emperor to establish an imperial government in Mexico having been given up, the Gulf Squadron as a distinct organization ceased to be. Thus ended the last of the separate fleets which the Civil War had called into existence. The old cruising ground of the Home Squadron again became a single command under the name, which it still retains, of the North Atlantic Squadron.

APPENDIX.

BATTERIES (EXCEPT HOWITZERS) OF VESSELS AT NEW ORLEANS, APRIL, 1862.

NAMES.	XI-in. sm.-bore.	X-in. sm.-bore.	IX-in. sm.-bore.	VIII-in. sm.-bore.	32-pdr. sm.-bore.	100-pdr. rifled.	80-pdr. rifled.	50-pdr. rifled.	30-pdr. rifled.	20-pdr. rifled.
Hartford	..	..	22	..	..	..	..	..	..	2
Brooklyn	..	..	20	..	..	..	1	..	1	..
Richmond	..	..	22	..	..	..	1	..	1	..
Pensacola	1	..	20	..	..	1	1	..	..	..
Mississippi	..	1	..	15	..	..	..	..	..	1
Oneida	2	..	..	..	4	..	..	..	3	..
Iroquois	2	..	..	..	4	..	..	1	..	..
Varuna	..	..	..	8	..	..	..	..	2	..
Cayuga [1]	1	..	..	..	..	..	..	..	1	..
Clifton	..	..	2	..	4	..	..	..	1	..
Jackson [2]	..	1	1	..	4	..	..	..	..	..
Westfield	..	..	1	4	..	1	..	..	..	..
Harriet Lane	..	..	3	..	..	..	..	..	..	..
Miami	..	..	2	..	..	1	1	..	1	..

BATTERIES (EXCEPT HOWITZERS) OF VESSELS[3] AT PORT HUDSON, MARCH, 1863.

NAMES.	XI-in. smooth-bore.	X-in. smooth-bore.	IX-in. smooth-bore.	32-pdr. smooth-bore.	150-pdr. rifled.	100-pdr. rifled.	30-pdr. rifled.
Monongahela	2	..	..	5	1	..	..
Genesee	..	1	4	..	..	2	..
Albatross	..	..	..	4	..	..	1

[1] Batteries of Katahdin, Kennebec, Kineo, Owasco, Pinola, Sciota, Winona, and Wissahickon were the same as of Cayuga. The Itasca had a X-inch instead of XI-inch.

[2] The Jackson carried also one VI-inch Sawyer rifle.

[3] The other vessels not having been North are assumed to have had the same batteries as in the preceding April.

BATTERIES (EXCEPT HOWITZERS) OF VESSELS AT MOBILE, AUGUST, 1864.

NAMES.	XV-in. sm.-bore.	XI-in. sm.-bore.	X-in. sm.-bore.	IX-in. sm.-bore.	32-pdr. sm.-bore.	150-pdr. rifled.	100-pdr. rifled.	60-pdr. rifled.	50-pdr. rifled.	30-pdr. rifled.	20-pdr. rifled.
Tecumseh	2	..	..	..	..	..	..	..	..	..	..
Manhattan	2	..	..	..	..	..	..	..	..	..	..
Winnebago	..	4	..	..	..	..	..	..	..	..	..
Chickasaw	..	4	..	..	..	..	..	..	..	..	..
Hartford	..	..	..	18	..	..	2	..	..	1	..
Brooklyn	..	..	..	20	..	..	2	2	..	..	..
Richmond	..	..	..	18	..	..	1	..	..	1	..
Lackawanna	..	2	..	4	..	1	..	..	1	..	..
Monongahela	..	2	..	..	5	1	..	..	..	..	..
Ossipee	..	1	..	..	6	..	1	..	..	3	..
Oneida	..	2	..	..	4	..	..	..	..	3	..
Galena	..	..	..	8	..	..	1	..	..	1	..
Seminole	..	1	..	..	6	..	..	..	..	1	..
Port Royal	..	..	1	2	..	..	1	..	2	..	..
Metacomet	..	..	..	4	..	..	2	..	..	..	..
Octorara	..	..	..	3	2	..	1	..	..	..	..
Itasca	..	1	..	..	2	..	..	..	..	..	2
Kennebec	..	1	..	..	2	..	..	..	..	..	2

BATTERIES (EXCEPT HOWITZERS) OF MISSISSIPPI SQUADRON, AUGUST,[1] 1862.

NAMES.	X-in. smooth-bore.	IX-in. smooth-bore.	VIII-in. smooth-bore.	32-pdr. smooth-bore.	Army 42's 70-pdr. rifled.	50-pdr. rifled.	30-pdr. rifled.
Benton	..	2	..	8	4	2	..
Cairo	..	..	3	6	3	..	1
Carondelet	..	..	4	6	1	1	1
Cincinnati	..	..	3	6	2	..	2
Louisville	..	..	3	6	2	..	2
Mound City	..	..	3	6	2	1	1
Pittsburg	..	..	3	6	2	..	2
St. Louis	..	..	3	6	2	..	2
Essex [2]	1	3	..	1	..	2	..
Conestoga	..	..	..	4	..	..	..
Lexington	..	..	4	1	..	..	2
Tyler	..	..	6	..	..	..	3
Eastport [2]	..	..	..	4	..	2	2
Gen. Bragg [2]	..	..	..	1	..	..	1
Sumter [2]	..	..	..	2	..	..	..
Price [2]	..	..	..	..	..	..	..
Little Rebel	..	..	..	..	..	..	1

[1] The batteries in January, 1862, are given in the text, pp. 16–17. [2] Rams.

Batteries (except Howitzers) of Mississippi Squadron, January, 1863.

Names.	XI-in. sm.-bore.	IX-in. sm.-bore.	VIII-in. sm.-bore.	42-pdr. rifled.	32-pdr. sm.-bore.	100-pdr. rifled.	80-pdr. rifled.	50-pdr. rifled.	30-pdr. rifled.	20-pdr. rifled.
Benton	..	8	..	..	4	2	..	2	..	..
Cairo	..	..	3	1	6	..	..	..	1	..
Carondelet	..	3	4	1	1	..	..	1	1	..
Cincinnati	..	3	2	..	6	..	..	..	2	..
DeKalb [1]	..	..	4	..	12	..	..	..	..	2
Louisville	..	2	2	..	6	..	..	..	2	..
Mound City	..	3	3	..	3	..	2	..	3	..
Pittsburg	..	2	3	..	6	..	..	..	2	..
Tuscumbia	3	..	..	..	..	2	..	..	..	..
Indianola	2	2	..	..	..	..	..	..	..	..
Choctaw	..	3	..	..	..	1	..	..	2	..
Lafayette	2	4	..	..	..	2	..	..	..	..
Chillicothe	2	..	.	..	..	..	..	..	..	..
Black Hawk		..	..	..	4	..	..	..	2	..

Returns of the Armament of Fort Morgan, Mobile Harbor.

	January, 1863.	January, 1864.	Confederate return, January, 1864.	Report of U. S. Ordnance Officer, October, 1864.
X-inch Columbiad	5	7	5	7
VIII-inch Columbiad	5	1	1	3 [2]
32-pounder smooth-bore	30	18	16	11
24-pounder smooth-bore	4	..	4	..
VIII-inch rifle	..	2	2	2
VII inch rifle	1	..	..	2
6.5-inch rifle	3	4	7	7
5.82-inch rifle	..	4	3	..
30-pounder rifle, R. P. P.	1	..	..	1
24-pounder rifle (Dahlgren)	..	..	..	1
Whitworth (calibre 2.71)	1	..	..	1
— Rifles (calibre not given)	2	..	..	..
Water Battery.				
X-inch	4	Not given.	Not separately given.	Not mentioned.
VIII-inch	1			
6.5-inch rifle	2			

The return for January, 1863, is taken from a captured Confederate plan showing position of the guns at that date, concerning which Captain M. D. McAlester, U. S. Engineers, says that he found some changes, but not material, when he inspected the works within a week after the surrender, and while nothing had yet been disturbed. January, 1864, is from reports of deserters to officers of United States fleet, verified by reconnoissances from tugs on clear days and by reports of spies. The indications seem to be that the lighter guns were partially withdrawn, perhaps for the landward defences of Mobile, and their place supplied by heavier and rifled guns. The estimate in the text gives for all the forts one hundred cannon, including flank howitzers. General Grant's report as Commander-in-Chief, December, 1864, says one hundred and four pieces of artillery were taken; there were a few field pieces.

[1] The DeKalb's battery was changed before the end of the month. See p. 122.

[2] Two of these are inventoried as "smooth-bore Brooke, double-banded," which seems unlikely.

INDEX.

ALABAMA, the, 108
Albatross, the, 134 et seq., 152, 165 et seq.
Alden, Commander James, 54, 134, 136, 229
Alexandria, dam built at, 203 et seq.
Alice Vivian, the, U. S. transport, 197
Althea, the, 249
Apalachicola, Fla., 3
Arkansas Post (Fort Hindman), 120, 161
Arkansas, the, Confederate ram, 98 et seq.; destruction of, 105, 119
Arizona, the, 164, 166 et seq., 187
Augur, General, 167
Averett, Lieutenant, 35

BACHE, Lieutenant George M., 121, 147, 170, 178, 191, 197, 212
Bacon, Lieutenant George B., 68
Bailey, Captain Theodorus, 53, 72, 82, 86 et seq.
Bailey, Lieutenant-Colonel Joseph, builds a dam at Alexandria, 204 et seq., 207; promoted to Brigadier-General, 209, 211
Baldwin, Lieutenant Charles H., 56
Banks, General, succeeds Butler in Gulf Department, 109, 139, 153; toward Alexandria, 164 et seq., 176, 183; sent to Texas, 185 et seq., 194 et seq.; on the Red River, 198 et seq., 204; relieved by Canby, 211
Baron de Kalb, the, see De Kalb.
Batey, the, Confederate steamer, 129, 131
Baton Rouge, La., surrender of, 90, 104 et seq., 109
Batteries: Chalmette, the, 60, 83, 85; McGehee, the, 60, 85
Beauregard's evacuation of Memphis, 47
Bell, Captain H. H., 54, 66, 77, 187
Belmont, Mo., Union victory at, 19, 21
Bennett, Lieutenant J. W., 220
Benton, the, Union gunboat, 15; before Island No. 10, 31, 42, 44 et seq., 47 et seq., 51, 103, 107, 116, 123, 155 et seq., 160 et seq., 166, 169 et seq., 191
Black Hawk, the, U. S. steamer, 114, 121, 123, 191
Blake, Lieutenant, 5

Blockade, purpose of, 3 et seq.
Blodgett, Lieutenant, of the Conestoga, 50
Blue Wing, the, U. S. transport, 120, 122
Boggs, Commander Charles S., 54, 82
Bois, Frank, 170
Bowling Green, Ky., 21
Brand, Lieutenant-Colonel, 129, 131
Breckenridge, General, commands an attack on Baton Rouge, 105 et seq.
Breese, Lieutenant-Commander K. R., 163, 168, 191
Brent, Major J. L. (afterward Colonel), 129, 131, 201 (note) et seq.
Brooklyn, U. S. sloop, 53 et seq., 76 et seq., 83, 85, 90, 94 et seq., 104, 228 et seq., 237, 244 (note)
Brown, Commander Isaac N., 99 et seq.
Brown, Lieutenant-Commander George, of the Indianola, 126, 128 et seq., 229
Browne, Lieutenant G. W., 191
Bryant, Lieutenant N. C., of the Cairo, 42
Buchanan, Admiral Franklin, 220, 235 et seq., 239 et seq.; wounded, 242 et seq.
Buchanan, Lieutenant-Commander, 109
Buell, Major-General, 37 et seq.
Burnham, Captain A. H., 220 (note)
Burnside, General, 183
Butler, General B. F., at New Orleans, 85, 87; succeeded by General Banks in Department of Gulf, 109
CAIRO, Ill., 9 et seq.
Cairo, the, Union gunboat, 14, 42, 48, 117
Caldwell, Lieutenant C. H. B., 54, 66 et seq.; before New Orleans, 72 et seq., 133, 168
Calhoun, the, Confederate gunboat, 40, 109, 164
Canal, cut by Pope, 31; around Vicksburg, 141
Canby, General, commands Department of West Mississippi, 211, 225, 246, 249
Carondelet, the, Union gunboat, 14, 21, 24; before Donelson, 26 et seq.; her passage to New Madrid in thunder-storm, 32 et seq., 36, 42, 44 et seq., 48, 51; fights with the Arkansas, 99 et seq.; losses on, 102, 123, 147, 154 et seq., 157, 160, 168, 170, 191, 194, 207, 215 et seq.
Cayuga, U. S. gunboat, 53 et seq., 72 et seq., 80, 82 et seq., 85, 105
Chickasaw, the, 226 et seq., 229, 242 et seq., 245, 247
Chillicothe, the U. S. vessel, 111 et seq., 123, 142 et seq., 145 et seq., 191, 194 et seq., 207
Choctaw, the, U. S. vessel, 111, 113, 163, 172, 177, 192
Churchill, General, surrenders to McClernand, 122
Cincinnati, the, Union gunboat, 14, 21 et seq., 42 et seq., 103, 120 et seq., 147; loss of, 170, 172, 177 et seq., 249
Clifton, the, U. S. gunboat, 55 et seq., 95 et seq., 164, 187
Collins, John, 233
Colorado, flag-ship, 5, 53, 57
Columbus, Ky., fortified by Con-

federates, 11, 18, 21; fall of, 28 et seq.
Conestoga, the, Union gunboat, 12, 18, 21, 27, 50
Confederate navy, commanded by Hollins, 40; fourteen river steamboats seized for, 41 et seq.; spirited attack by, 43 et seq.; ten vessels before New Orleans, 60 et seq.; condemnation of, 84 et seq.
Cooke, Commander A. P., 164
Cornay, Captain, 202 (note)
Cornyn, Colonel, 182
Corpus Christi, Texas, 108
Cotton, the, Confederate steamer, 109
Couthony, Lieutenant S. P., 191
Covington, the, 182, 209 et seq.
Cox, General, 183
Craven, Captain Thomas T., 54; commands a fleet from New Orleans, 90, 96
Craven, Commander T. A. M., 229; heroic death of, 231
Cricket, the, 178, 191 et seq., 195, 199 et seq.
Crocker, Lieutenant Frederick, 187
Crosby, Lieutenant Pierce, 54, 66, 248
Cummings, A. Boyd, 136
Curtis, General, 49, 107

DAHLGREN, Acting-Master C. B., 172
Dana, General, 188
Davis, Captain Charles H., 40, 47, 49; made flag-officer, 51; in the Yazoo, 97 et seq.; follows the Arkansas, 102 et seq.; arranges an expedition, 107; relieved in command, 110
Davis, Jefferson, 131
De Camp, Commander John, 54, 89
Defiance, the, Confederate vessel, 85
DeKalb, the, U. S. ironclad, 118, 120 et seq., 142, 145 et seq., 169, 171, 177. See the St. Louis.
De Soto, the, 126 et seq.
Donaldson, Lieutenant Edward, 54, 229
Donelson, Fort, see Fort Donelson.
Doubloon, the, Confederate steamer, 81
Dove, Commander, of the Louisville, 27
Drayton, Captain Percival, 229 240
Duncan, General, 60, 88
Dunnington, Colonel, surrenders to Admiral Porter, 122

EADS, JAMES B., 12
Eastport, the, Confederate gunboat, 24 et seq., 191 et seq., 198 et seq., 203
Elfin, the, 214
Ellet, Colonel Charles, jr., 46 et seq., 119 (note)
Ellet, Colonel Charles Rivers, 119, 124 et seq.; rashness of, 127 et seq., 140
Ellet, Lieutenant-Colonel A. W., of the Monarch, 48, 97, 103, 122; reckless daring of, 140
Ellet, Lieutenant-Colonel John A., 140
Emory, General, 195
Enoch Train, the, Confederate ram, 5 et seq.
Era No. 5, the, 127 et seq.
Erben, Lieutenant Henry, 42

Essex, the, 15, 21; disaster to, 23 et seq., 103, 105, 133, 135, 167 et seq., 190
Estrella, the, 109, 164 et seq., 188

FAIRPLAY, the, 215
Farragut, Flag-Officer David G., commands the Western Gulf Blockading Squadron, 8, 35 et seq.; before New Orleans, 40, 42; at Vicksburg, 51 et seq., 54, 62; prompt action of, 86, 90 et seq.; in the Yazoo, 97 et seq., 101 et seq.; on the Gulf, 107 et seq., 124, 126; moves up the river, 133 et seq.; his advice respecting the Ellet family, 139 et seq., 144; Porter communicates with, 151 et seq., 158; in the Red River, 164 et seq.; returns to Gulf, 174, 183, 187; resumes command, 218, 221; begs for co-operation, 223, 226 et seq.; in action, 232 et seq.; his attack on the Tennessee, 240 et seq.; goes North, 246
Fawn, the, 212 et seq.
Featherstone, brigade of, 149
Ferguson, Colonel, 148 et seq.
Fitch, Colonel, 50
Fitch, Lieutenant-Commander Le Roy, 180 et seq., 213 et seq.
Foote, Flag-Officer A. H., 15 et seq.; his views on manning ships, 17 et seq.; promotion of, 20 et seq.; returns to Cairo, 24 et seq.; wounded, 28, 31, 35 et seq.; at Fort Pillow, 39 et seq.
Forest Queen, the, 155, 157
Forest Rose, the, 123, 141 et seq., 171
Forrest, General, 181, 214
Forrest, Lieutenant Moreau, 213, 216
Fort Donelson, Ky., 23; plan of attack on, 25 et seq., 90, 161, 180
Fort Henry, Ky., expedition against, 21 et seq., 161, 180
Fort Hindman, see Arkansas Post.
Fort Hindman, the, 191 et seq., 194 et seq., 199 et seq., 206 et seq.
Fort Jackson, 58 et seq., 63, 66, 69 et seq., 76, 78 et seq., 87, 89
Fort McRae, 8
Fort Pickens, 8
Fort Pillow, 31, 39 et seq.; force at, 42 et seq., 45
Fort St. Philip, 58, 60, 62 et seq., 69, 72, 75 et seq., 78 et seq., 87 et seq.
Fort Sumter, 144
Foster, Lieutenant-Commander Joseph P., 142, 191
Franklin, General, 187, 190, 194 et seq., 204
Fremont, General, 17 et seq.
Fry, Captain Joseph, 50
Fulton, the, U. S. ram, 143

GABAUDAU, Mr., 153
Gaines, the, Confederate gunboat, 220, 239
Galena, the, 229, 236 244 (note)
Galveston, Tex., 3, 8; disaster at, 108 et seq., 188, 249
Gamble, Lieutenant-Commander William M., 247
Gazelle, the, 191

General Beauregard, the, Confederate ram, 47 et seq.
General Bragg, the, Confederate ram, 43, 47; capture of, 49, 101, 107, 116
General Lovell, the, Confederate ram, 47 et seq.
General Price, the, Confederate ram, 44, 47 et seq., 155 et seq., 166, 170
General Quitman, the, Confederate vessel, 61, 84
General Rusk, Confederate steamer, 8
General Sumter, the, Confederate ram, 44, 47; capture of, 49, 102, 105
General Thompson, the, Confederate ram, 47; destruction of, 49
General Van Dorn, the, Confederate ram, 44, 47, 49
Genesee, the, 134 et seq.
Gherardi, Lieutenant-Commander Bancroft, 229
Gillis, Lieutenant - Commander James H., 247
Gilmore, Theodore, 33
Glide, the, 122 et seq.
Gorman, General, 122
Gorringe, Master H. H., 191, 200
Governor Moore, the, Confederate vessel, 61, 81 et seq.
Grand Era, the, Confederate tender, 129
Grand Gulf, 11, 163 et seq.
Granger, General, 34, 215, 227, 245, 248
Granite City, the, 187 et seq.
Grant, Captain of the General Quitman, 61, 84 (note)
Grant, General U. S., commands military district about Cairo, 18 et seq.; at Fort Donelson, 25 et seq.; at Pittsburg Landing, 36 et seq.; at Vicksburg, 123 et seq., 139; orders the levee cut, 141, 153, 157, 161; at Grand Gulf, 163, 168 et seq., 172, 176, 178; directions to Steele, 190, 211
Greene, Lieutenant-Commander Charles H., 229
Greene, General Thomas, 197
Greer, Lieutenant - Commander James A., 155, 191
Gregory, Acting-Master, 43
Guest, Lieutenant John, 56
Gunboats, contract for seven, given to Eads, 12 et seq.; delay in equipping for lack of money, 15
Gwin, Lieutenant, of the Tyler, 21; invaluable service at Pittsburg Landing, 28 et seq.; 37 et seq.; in the Yazoo, 99; mortally wounded, 118 et seq.

HAINES's Bluff, 119, 148
Halleck, General, his orders unsatisfactory to Captain Foote, 16 et seq., 25; orders to Foote, 28; withdraws Pope's forces from Fort Pillow, 40, 49, 91, 186, 189
Hamilton, Lieutenant William, 242 (note)
Harding, Colonel, 180
Hart, Lieutenant-Commander, John E., 134, 165 et seq.
Harrell, Lieutenant A. D., 56
Harriet Lane, the, U. S. gunboat, 55 et seq., 88, 94 et seq., 108
Harrison, cavalry of, 197

Harrison, Commander George W., 220
Harrison, Lieutenant Napoleon B., 54
Hartford, the, U. S. flag-ship, 52 et seq., 68, 72, 77, 85, 90, 134 et seq., 139, 151 et seq., 165, 228 et seq., 231 et seq., 236, 238 et seq.
Hastings, the, U. S. transport, 197
Hatteras, the, 108
Helena, Ark., 49 et seq., 110, 116
Henry Clay, the, 155, 157
Henry, Fort, see Fort Henry.
Herron, General, 177
Hickman, Ky., fortified by Confederates, 11, 18, 29 et seq.
Higgins, Colonel, 60, 65; condemns Mitchell's course, 70 et seq., 87, 155 (note)
Hill, plantation of, 148, 150 et seq.
Hoel, Lieutenant William R., 33 147, 155, 160, 191
Hollins, Commodore George N., 7, 35; commands Confederate navy, 40 et seq.
Hood, General, 213, 215 et seq.
Hospital fleet, at Pilot Town, 57
Howard, Lieutenant Samuel, 191
Huger, Thomas B., mortally wounded, 83
Hurlburt, General, 37; report of, 39

Ida, the, 249
Illinois, her devotion to the Union, 9
Illinois, regiment of: Forty-second, 32
Imperial, the, 173
Indianola, the, U. S. vessel, 111 et seq., 123, 126, 128 et seq., 152, 165
Iowa, regiment of: Twenty-third, 176
Iroquois, the, U. S. corvette, 54, 77 et seq., 83, 89, 94 et seq.
Island No. 10, 28 et seq., 31 et seq.; surrender of, 34; disappearance of, 36, 39 et seq., 124
Itasca, the, U. S. gunboat, 54, 66 et seq., 71 et seq., 77, 79, et seq., 90, 229
Ivy, the, Confederate gunboat, 40, 166

Jackson, Fort, see Fort Jackson.
Jackson, the, Confederate gunboat, 40, 61, 81
Jackson, the, U. S. gunboat, 55 et seq., 95
Jenkins, Captain Thornton A., 184, 227, 229, 235
Johnson, Acting-Master Amos, 67
Johnson, Master J. V., 32
Johnston, Commander J. D., 223, 239; surrenders, 243 et seq., 249
Jones, Acting-Master Edmund, 67, 72 et seq.
Jones, Lieutenant-Commander M. P., 247
Jouett, Lieutenant James E., burns schooner Royal Yacht, 8, 229, 233, 239, 242 (note)
Juliet, the, 123, 199, 201 et seq.

Katahdin, the, U. S. gunboat, 54, 73, 95, 105
Kennebec, U. S. gunboat, 54, 77, 80, 95, 229, 237, 244 (note)

Kennon, Beverley, of the Governor Moore, 61 ; encounter with the Varuna, 81 et seq.
Kentucky, neutrality of, 17
Key West, description of, 1
Key West, the, 214
Kickapoo, the, 247
Kilby, Commander A. H., 42, 50
Kimberley, Captain, 240 (note)
Kineo, U. S. gunboat, 54, 73, 76 et seq., 85, 105, 134 et seq., 183
King, Lieutenant, 214 et seq.
Kinsman, the, 109
Kirkland, Lieutenant-Commander W. A., 247

Lackawanna, the, 228 et seq., 237, 240 et seq., 244 (note)
Lafayette, the, U. S. vessel, 111, 113, 155 et seq., 160 et seq., 166, 191 et seq.
Lancaster, the, 102, 140
Langthorne, Lieutenant A. R., 191
Lee, Admiral S. Phillips, 54, 82, 90, 211, 216 et seq.
Lee, General Robert E., 249
Le Roy, Commander William E., 229, 243 et seq.
Lexington, the, Union gunboat, 12, 18 et seq., 24, 28, 37 et seq., 50, 121, 178 et seq., 191, 193 et seq., 197 et seq., 206
Liddell, General, 197
Lincoln, President A., 94 (note)
Linden, the, 123, 171
Lioness, the, U. S. ram, 107, 119, 123, 143
Little Rebel, the, 47 ; taken into Union fleet, 49
Livingston, the, Confederate gunboat, 40
Lord, Lieutenant, 210
Loring, General, 145
Louisiana, the, Confederate vessel, 61, 69 et seq., 79 et seq., 85 et seq., 88
Louisville, the, Union gunboat, 14 ; injury sustained by, 27, 51, 103, 120 et seq., 147, 151, 155 et seq., 160, 191, 194, 207
Lovell, Colonel, 84 (note)
Lovell, General, 41 et seq. ; at New Orleans, 59 et seq., 81
Low, Lieutenant-Commander W. W., 247

McCann, Lieutenant-Commander William P., 229
McClernand, General, 20, 116 ; at Vicksburg, 120 et seq.
McCloskey, Captain, 129
McCulloch, General, 176
McGunnegle, Lieutenant, 46 (note), 48, 50
McIntosh, Captain, 88
McKean, Flag-Officer W. W., succeeds Mervine, 5 ; commands an indecisive affair in Pensacola Bay, 8 ; at Ship Island, 52
McKinstry, Captain J. P., 134, 137
Macomb, Commander William H., 134
McRae, Fort, see Fort McRae.
McRae, the, Confederate gunboat, 40, 61, 83 et seq.
Maitland, pilot, 201 et seq.
Manassas, the, Confederate ram, 61, 75, 78, 83, 84 (note), 100
Manhattan, the, 226 et seq., 229 232, 242 et seq., 245
Marchand, Captain John B., 229

Marmora, the, U. S. gunboat, 117, 123, 142, 178
Maurepas, the, Confederate gunboat, 40
Memphis, Tenn., 47 et seq.; surrender of, 49
Mervine, Flag-Officer William, 4 et seq.
Metacomet, the, 229, 232 et seq., 238 et seq., 242 (note), 244 (note), 248
Mexico, Gulf of, 1 et seq.
Miami, the, U. S. gunboat, 55 et seq., 87, 95
Milwaukee, the, 247 et seq.
Mississippi, doubtful allegiance of, 9
Mississippi River, Government's object in entering, 3; Union humiliation in, 5 et seq.; description of, 9 et seq.; importance of controlling, 11 et seq.; successes on, 23 et seq.; encounter between gunboats on, 43; Confederate rams, 43 et seq.; Confederate fleet conquered, 49 et seq.; naval forces from Gulf and upper river meet in, 51; obstructions in, 64 et seq.; cleared by Caldwell, 68 et seq.; unhealthiness of, 104; controlled by Confederates from Vicksburg to Port Hudson, 106; change of commanders in, 110; successes and disasters in, 125 et seq.; open from Cairo to Gulf, 173
Mississippi, the, tonnage of, 54, 71, 73 et seq., 76, 83, 86, 134, 137 et seq.
Missouri, doubtful allegiance of, 9
Missouri, the, U. S. ship, 138
Mitchell, Commander, 61, 69 et seq., 88
Mitchell, Lieutenant-Commander J. G., 191
Mobile, Ala., 3, 218 et seq.
Monarch, Union ram, 48 et seq., 107, 122 et seq.
Monongahela, the, 134 et seq., 184, 188, 229, 237, 240 et seq., 244 (note)
Montgomery, Captain, 41 et seq., 47
Moose, the, 183
Morgan, General J. H., daring raid of, 182
Morgan, Lieutenant, 210
Morgan, the, Confederate gunboat, 220, 239
Morning Light, the, 108
Morris, Captain H. W., 54
Morton, Acting-Master Gilbert, 215
Mosher, the, Confederate tug, 61, 76
Mound City, the, Union gunboat, 14 et seq., 42, 44 et seq.; catastrophe to, 50, 107, 123, 147, 155 et seq., 160, 162, 168, 170, 191, 194, 207
Mullany, Commander J. R. M., 229, 238
Murphy, Lieutenant J. M., 147, 149, 155
Murphy, Lieutenant P. M., 220

Napoleon III., unfriendly attitude toward the United States, 185, 249
Natchez, surrender of, 90
Naumkeag, the, 212 et seq.
Naval, operations, extent of, 1
Nelson, General, 37 et seq.

Neosho, the, 191, 194 et seq., 200, 202 et seq., 206 et seq., 216
New Madrid, Mo., 29; taken by Pope, 30 et seq.
New Orleans, 2, 59 et seq.; bombardment of, 69 et seq.; surrender of, 86 et seq.
Niagara, the, 8
Nichols, Lieutenant Ed. T., 54
Nicholson, Commander J. W. A., 229
Nields, Ensign H. C., 233 et seq.

OCTORARA, the, U. S. steamer, 95, 97, 229, 244 (note), 247 et seq.
Oneida, the, U. S. corvette, 54, 73, 76, 81 et seq., 94, 96, 229, 234 et seq., 238, 244 (note)
Osage, the, 191 et seq., 194 et seq., 197, 199, 202, 206 et seq., 247
Ossipee, the, 229, 237, 240, 243 et seq.
Ouachita, the, 191, 193
Owasco, the, U. S. gunboat, 55, 95, 188
Owen, Lieutenant-Commander E. K., 121, 147, 155, 191
Ozark, the, 191, 194, 206 et seq.

PADUCAH, Ky., seized by Grant, 18, 21
Palmer, Captain James S., of the Iroquois, 95; of the Hartford, 134
Palmer, Commodore of the Hartford, 167; left in command, 246, 248
Parker, Commodore Foxhall A., 240 (note)
Paulding, Lieutenant, of the St. Louis, 21; before Donelson, 27
Pearce, Lieutenant John, 191, 200
Pendergrast, Flag-Officer G. J., commands Home Squadron, 4
Pennock, Captain Alexander M., 179, 211
Pensacola Navy Yard, 3, 5, 8, 52, 60, 90, 107, 227 et seq., 242 (note), 246
Pensacola, the, U. S. vessel, 52 et seq., 73, 75, et seq., 78, 85, 100 (note)
Perkins, Lieutenant-Commander George H., 229, 242 (note), 247
Petrel, the, U. S. steamer, 142 et seq., 171
Phelps, Lieutenant-Commanding S. L., of the Conestoga, 18, 21, 24 et seq., 28; of the Benton, 42; commands an expedition from Helena, 107, 179, 182; at Grand Ecore, 195, 198, 200 et seq.
Pickens, Fort, see Fort Pickens.
Pierce, Captain, 129
Pillow, Fort, see Fort Pillow.
Pinola, the, U. S. gunboat, 54, 66 et seq., 71, 77 et seq., 80 et seq., 95
Pittsburg Landing, 36 et seq.
Pittsburg, the, Union gunboat, 15, 27, 34, 42, 44, 117, 123, 147, 155, 157, 160 et seq., 166, 191, 194, 207
Point of Rocks, 158, 161
Polk, the, Confederate gunboat, 40
Ponchartrain, the, Confederate gunboat, 40, 50
Pope, General, at New Madrid, 30 et seq., 34, 36; at Fort Pillow, 39 et seq.
Porter, Admiral David D., 53, 79, 85, 87, 88, 90 et seq., 94; ordered to Hampton Roads,

97; relieves Captain Davis, 110; his orders to Walke, 116; Colonel Dunnington surrenders to, 122 et seq.; success and disasters in Mississippi, 126 et seq.; hopes frustrated, 132, 139 et seq.; undertakes to reach the Yazoo, 147 et seq.; before Vicksburg, 154, 158, 161; at Grand Gulf, 163, 165 et seq.; assumes command of river; 174; inaugurates raids, 177, 179, 189 et seq.; in the Red River, 194 et seq.; 200 et seq., 204; at Red River Dam, 206; relieved by Pennock, 211
Porter, Commander William D., 15, 21, 23, 103 et seq.
Port Hudson, 11, 173
Port Royal, the, 229
Portsmouth, the, U. S. sloop, 80, 87
Preble Lieutenant George H., 54
Preble, the, sailing sloop, 5, 7
Prentiss, General, 176
Princess Royal, the, 183
Pritchett, Lieutenant-Commander, 175 et seq.

QUEEN City, the, 212 et seq.
Queen of the West, Union ram, 48, et seq., 84 (note); "lives to fight another day," 99 et seq., 103 et seq., 117, 123 et seq., 140, 151, 165

RAMSAY, Lieutenant-Commander F. M., 163, 172
Ransom, Lieutenant George M., 54
Rattler, the, 121 et seq., 142 et seq., 145
Read, Abner, 184
Reed, Acting-Master J. F., 172
Reynolds, Master, 44
Richmond, steam sloop, 5 et seq.; 54, 77, 90, 94 et seq.; 134 et seq., 138, 153, 167, 217, 227 et seq., 232 et seq., 237, 244 (note)
River Defence Fleet, 42 et seq., 47, 49, 60 et seq., 81, 84 et seq.
Roberts, Colonel, 32
Rob Roy, the, 197
Rodgers, Commander John, 12; relieved by Captain Foote, 16
Rodolph, the, 248
Roe, Lieutenant, 75
Royal Yacht, Confederate schooner, 8
Romeo, the, 123, 142 et seq.
Russell, Lieutenant J. H., 5, 54

SABINE Pass, 106
Sachem, the, U. S. schooner, 87, 187
St. Charles, 50 et seq.
St. Clair, the, 181
St. Louis, the, Union gunboat, 15, 21; injury sustained by, 27, 42, 45, 48, 50 et seq., 118, 177. See the DeKalb.
St. Philip, Fort, see Fort St. Philip.
Samson, the, U. S. ram, 107, 114
Santee, U. S. frigate, 7 et seq., 42
Schofield, General, 215
Sciota, the, U. S. gunboat, 54, 77 et seq., 95, 249
Selfridge, Lieutenant-Commanding, 117, 173, 177 et seq., 191, 197 et seq.

Selma, the, Confederate gunboat, 220, 239
Seminole, the, 229
Shepperd, Lieutenant, F. E. 145
Sherman, General W. T., at Haines's Bluff, 119; directed to support Porter, 148, 150 et seq., 163, 168, 170, 173; confers with Banks, 189 et seq., at Alexandria, 203, 225
Sherman, of the tug Mosher, 77
Shirk, Lieutenant J. W., of the Lexington, 21; gallant service at Pittsburg Landing, 37 et seq.; at Memphis, 50, 155, 213 et seq.
Ship Island, 52
Signal, the, U. S. gunboat, 117, 123, 142, 171, 207, 210
Silver Wave, the, U. S. transport, 155
Smith, Colonel Giles A., 150
Smith, Commander Melancton, 54, 134, 138
Smith, General A. J., 190, 193 et seq., 211
Smith, General M. L., 69
Smith, General T. Kilby, 194, 196 et seq.
Smithland, Ky., seized by Grant, 18
Smith, Lieutenant Albert N., 54
Smith, Lieutenant-Commander Watson, 121, 143
Sproston, Lieutenant, 5
Squadron, Atlantic, 4, 249
Squadron, East Gulf, 8, 249
Squadron, Home, 4, 249
Squadron, Mississippi, 55, 107, 211, 216 et seq.
Squadron, Western Gulf Blockading, 8, 52, 187, 249
Squadron, West India, 4
Squires, Captain, 60
Star of the West, the, 144
Steele, General, 168, 189 et seq., 212, 246
Stembel, Commander, of the Lexington, 18 et seq., 21; of the Cincinnati, 42; dangerously shot, 44
Stephenson, Captain, 61
Stevens, Commander Thomas H., 229, 232, 238
Stevens, Lieutenant, 105
Stevenson, General, 132
Stonewall Jackson, the, Confederate vessel, 81 et seq.
Stringham, Flag-Officer, commands Atlantic Squadron, 4
Strong, Captain James H., 188, 229, 237
Sumter, Fort, see Fort Sumter.
Switzerland, the, Union ram, 49, 123, 140, 151 et seq., 166 et seq.

TALLAHASSEE, Fla., 3
Tawah, the, 214
Taylor, General Richard, 129, 164, 167; engages a negro brigade, 176 et seq., 249
Tecumseh, the, 226 et seq., 244 (note)
Tennessee, the, Confederate ram, 220 et seq., 231, 236 et seq., 240 et seq.
Terry, Lieutenant-Commander Edward, 167
Thatcher, Master Charles, 191
Thatcher, Rear-Admiral H. K., 246, 248 et seq.
Theron, Monsieur, French Consul in Texas, 185 et seq.
Thomas, General, 216

Thomas, Lieutenant-Commander N. W., 137
Thompson, Lieutenant E., of the Pittsburg, 27, 42
Tilghman, General, surrenders Fort Henry to Union fleet, 23
Tinclads, description of, 110
Tiptonville, Tenn., 29 et seq., 35
Todd, Captain, 94 (note)
Torpedoes, 117, 224
Townsend, Captain, 41
Townsend, Commander Robert, 190
Tuscumbia, the, U.S. vessel, 111 et seq., 155, 157, 160 et seq., 168
Tyler, the, Union gunboat, 12, 19 et seq., 24, 27 et seq., 37 et seq., 99 et seq., 123, 175, 212 et seq.

UNDINE, the, 214
United States Navy, anomalous position of, 17, 20 et seq.; seventeen vessels in, and their tonnage, 54; six gunboats, 55 et seq.; tinclads, 110 et seq.

VARUNA, U. S. corvette, 54 et seq., 73, 81 et seq.
Velocity, the, 108
Vicksburg, Miss., 11, 51, 90 et seq.; description, 93 et seq.; surrender of, 173
Vicksburg, the, 125, 151
Vincennes, the, sailing-sloop, 5 et seq.
Virginia, the, 188
Virginius, the, Confederate steamer, 50

WADE, Colonel, 163
Wainwright, Commander Richard, 54
Wainwright, Lieutenant Jonathan M., of the Harriet Lane, 56
Walke, Commander Henry, of the Tyler, 19 et seq.; commands the Carondelet, 26; his gallant passage down the river, 32 et seq., 42; in the Yazoo, 99 et seq.; at Helena, 110; in the Yazoo, 116 et seq., 139, 155; at Alexandria, 166 et seq.
Walker, General, 192
Walker, Lieutenant-Commander John G., 118, 121 et seq., 142, 169, 171; sent to Yazoo City, 177
Warley, Lieutenant A. F., commands the Enoch Train, 5, 61, 84 (note)
Warner, the, 209 et seq.
Water Witch, the, steamer, 5, 7
Watson, captain, 201
Watters, Lieutenant-Commander John, 134, 183
Weaver, Lieutenant-Commander, 183
Webb, the, Confederate gunboat, 128 et seq., 217
Welles, Secretary of Navy, 88
Wells, Lieutenant-Commander Clark H., 229
Westfield, the, U. S. gunboat, 55 et seq., 95, 108
Wharton, General, 181
Wharton, Lieutenant, 231
Wheeler, General, 181
Williams, General, at Baton Rouge 104 et seq.
Wilson, Charles, 33
Wilson, Lieutenant Byron, of the Mound City, 147, 155, 191
Wilson, Lieutenant-Colonel James H., 142 et seq.

Winona, the, U. S. gunboat, 54, 77, 80, 95, 183
Winnebago, the, 226 et seq., 229, 232, 234, 238, 242 et seq., 247
Winslow, Lieutenant Francis, holds his ground in Water Witch, 7
Wisconsin, regiment of: Fourth, 204
Wissahickon, the, U. S. gunboat, 54, 73, 76, 85, 90, 95
Woods, Colonel, 107
Woodworth, Lieutenant Selim E., 56, 155 et seq.
Woolsey, Commander, 183

YANKEE, the, Confederate gunboat, 18
Yazoo Valley, description of, 115 et seq., 141 et seq.

For EU product safety concerns, contact us at Calle de José Abascal, 56–1°,
28003 Madrid, Spain or eugpsr@cambridge.org.

www.ingramcontent.com/pod-product-compliance
Ingram Content Group UK Ltd.
Pitfield, Milton Keynes, MK11 3LW, UK
UKHW010347140625
459647UK00010B/898

* 9 7 8 1 1 0 8 0 2 6 2 2 2 *